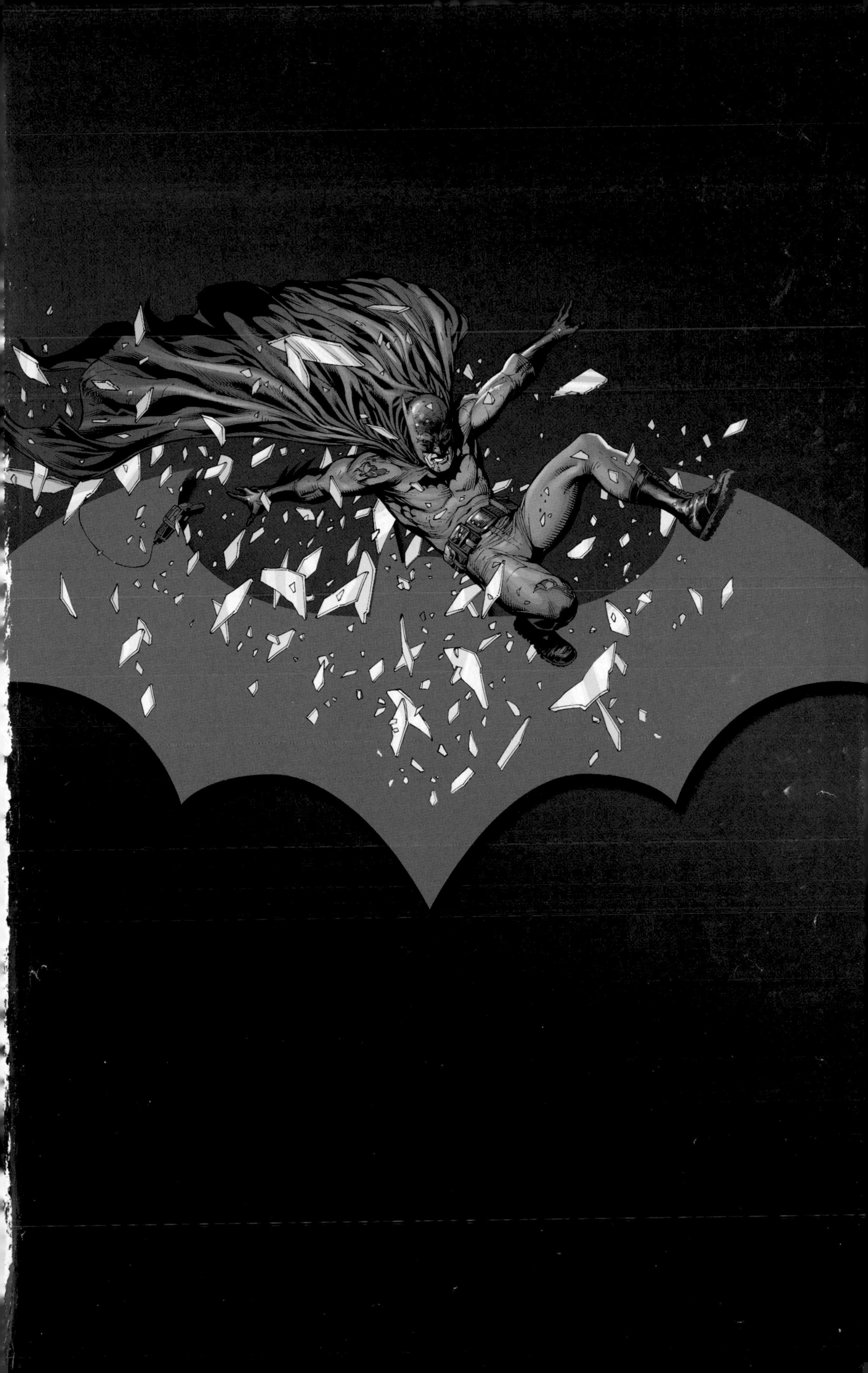

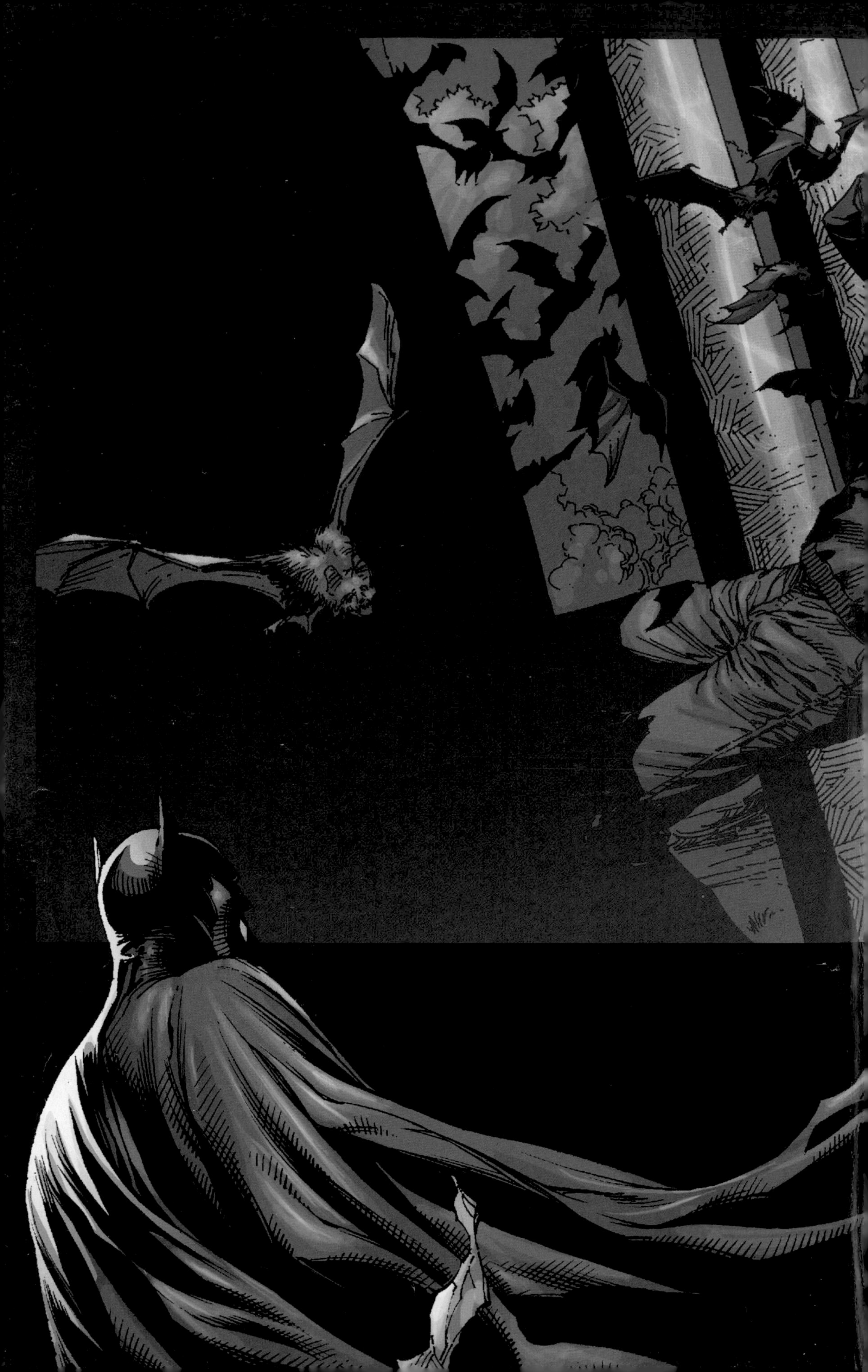

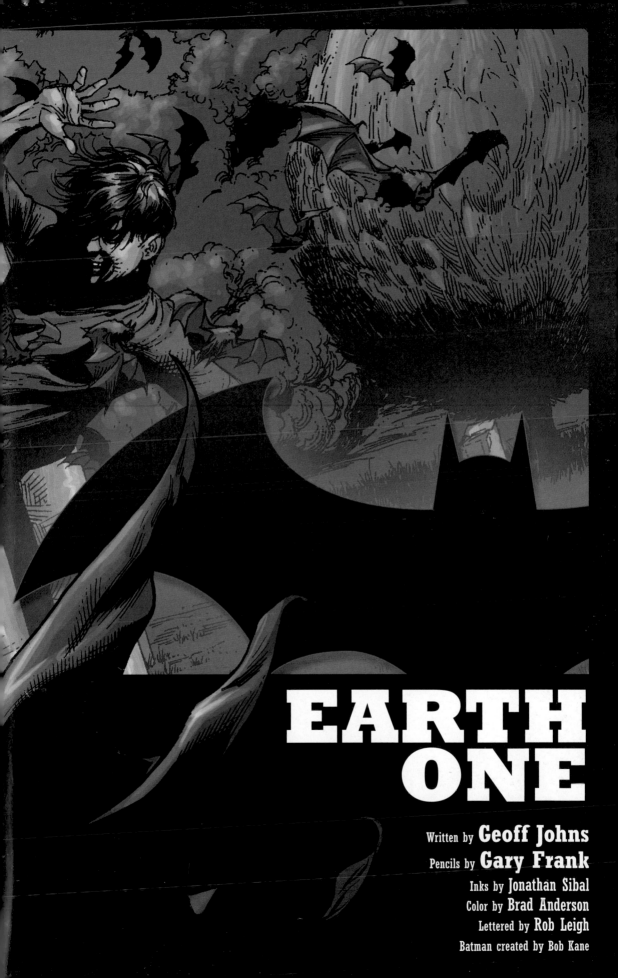

EARTH ONE

Written by **Geoff Johns**
Pencils by **Gary Frank**

Inks by **Jonathan Sibal**
Color by **Brad Anderson**
Lettered by **Rob Leigh**
Batman created by Bob Kane

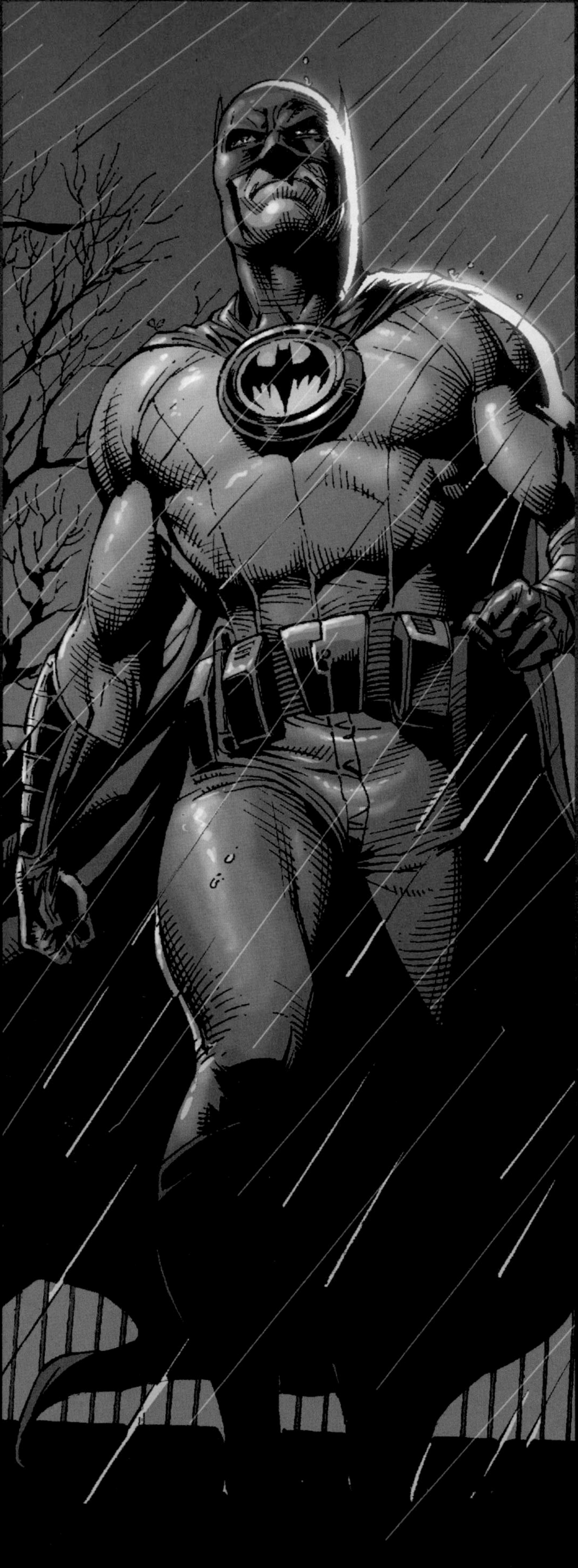

DEDICATIONS

For his shining gentle spirit and the light it cast all around him. This book is dedicated to the memory of our beloved archivist Roger Bonas. He was the guardian of DC's past and he will forever be part of its legacy.

— Geoff Johns

For Ian Meek.
A great friend, an inspiration to many and walking proof that adversity can lead some men to become heroes.

— Gary Frank

Eddie Berganza Editor
Darren Shan Assistant Editor
Robbin Brosterman Design Director – Books
Curtis King Jr. Publication Design

Bob Harras VP – Editor-in-Chief

Diane Nelson President
Dan DiDio and **Jim Lee** Co-Publishers
Geoff Johns Chief Creative Officer
John Rood Executive VP – Sales, Marketing and Business Development
Amy Genkins Senior VP – Business and Legal Affairs
Nairi Gardiner Senior VP – Finance
Jeff Boison VP – Publishing Operations
Mark Chiarello VP – Art Direction and Design
John Cunningham VP – Marketing
Terri Cunningham VP – Talent Relations and Services
Alison Gill Senior VP – Manufacturing and Operations
David Hyde VP – Publicity
Hank Kanalz Senior VP – Digital
Jay Kogan VP – Business and Legal Affairs, Publishing
Jack Mahan VP – Business Affairs, Talent
Nick Napolitano VP – Manufacturing Administration
Sue Pohja VP – Book Sales
Courtney Simmons Senior VP – Publicity
Bob Wayne Senior VP – Sales

BATMAN: EARTH ONE

Published by DC Comics, 1700 Broadway, New York, NY 10019.

DC Comics, 1700 Broadway, New York, NY 10019.
A Warner Bros. Entertainment Company
Printed by RR Donnelley, Salem, VA, USA. 5/18/12. First Printing.
HC ISBN: 978-1-4012-3208-5
SC ISBN: 978-1-4012-3209-2

SUSTAINABLE FORESTRY INITIATIVE Certified Chain of Custody
At Least 25% Certified Forest Content
www.sfiprogram.org
SFI-01042
APPLIES TO TEXT STOCK ONLY

Library of Congress Cataloging-in-Publication Data

Johns, Geoff, 1973-
Batman : earth one / Geoff Johns, Gary Frank.
p. cm.
ISBN 978-1-4012-3208-5 -- ISBN 978-1-4012-3209-2
1. Graphic novels. I. Frank, Gary, 1969- II. Title.
PN6728.B36J64 2012
741.5'973--dc23

2012000608

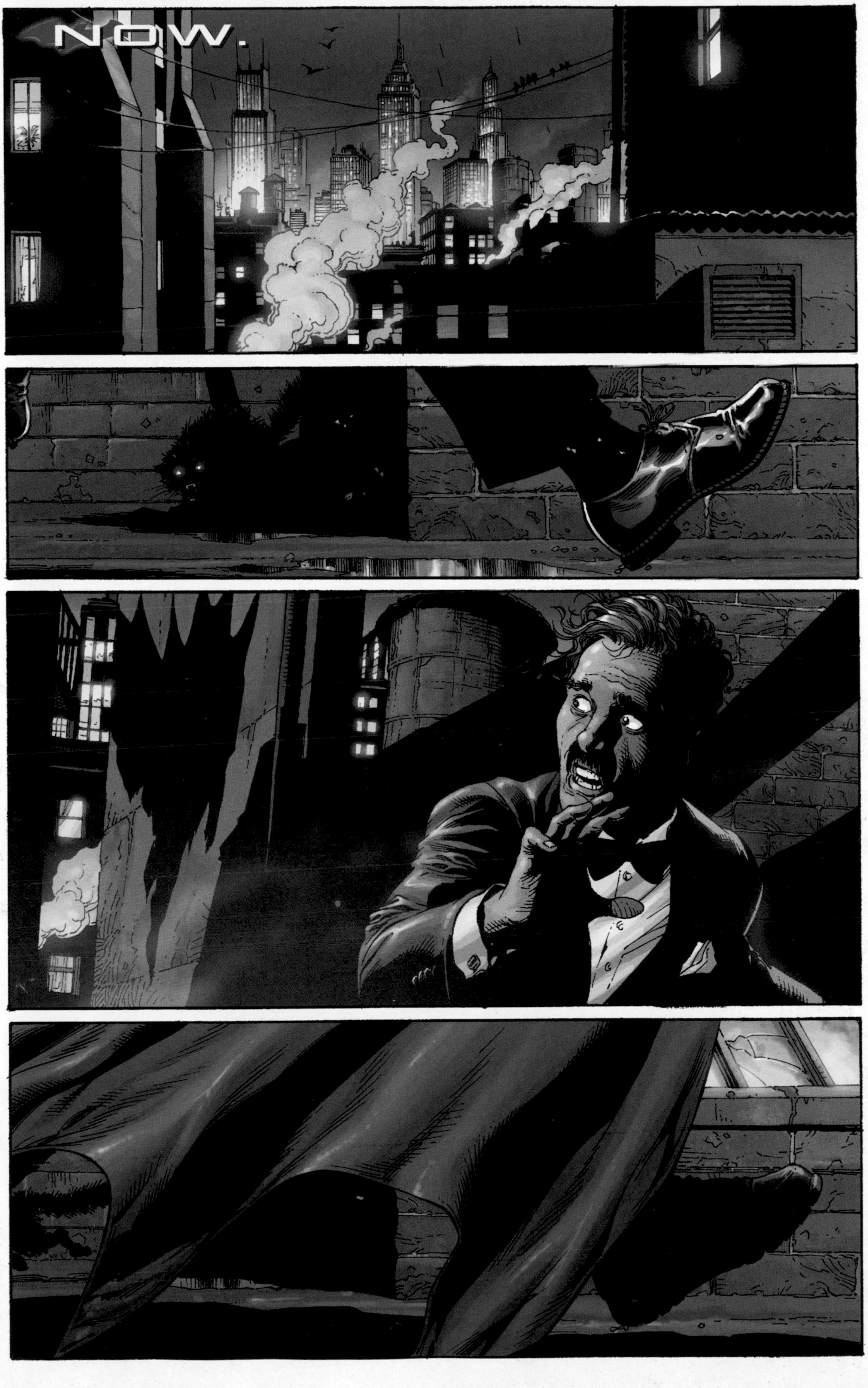
NOW.

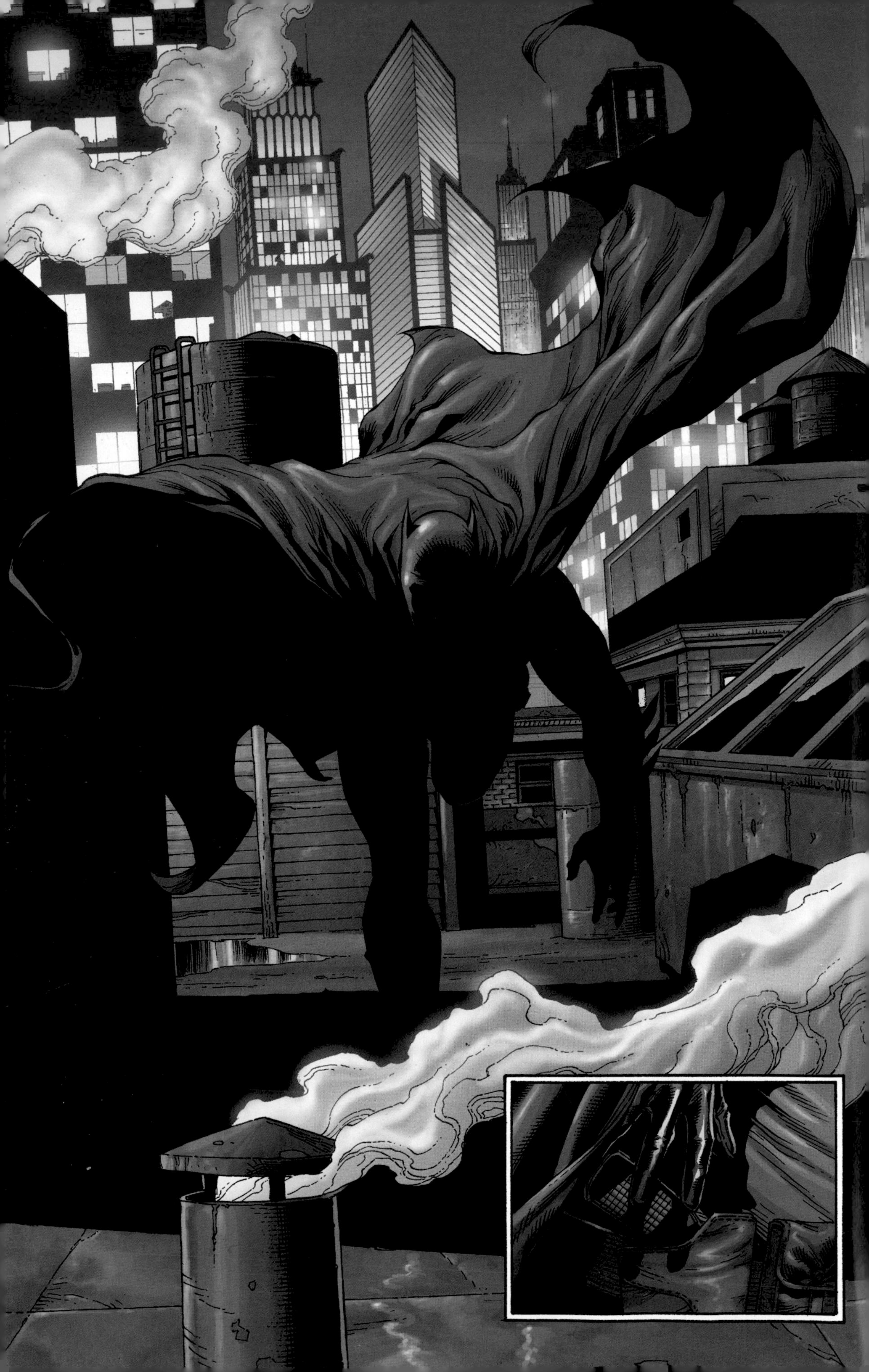

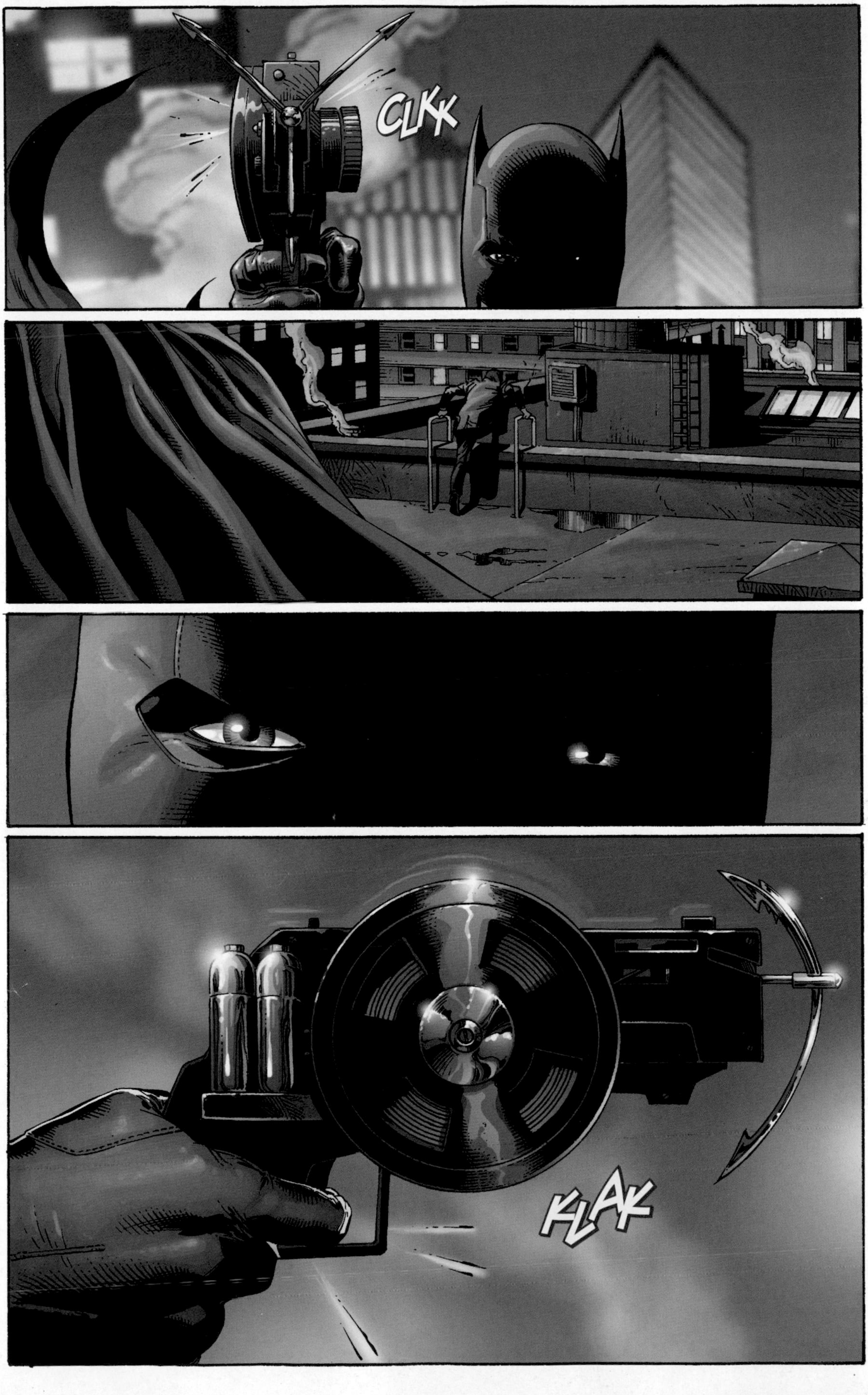
CLKK
KLAK

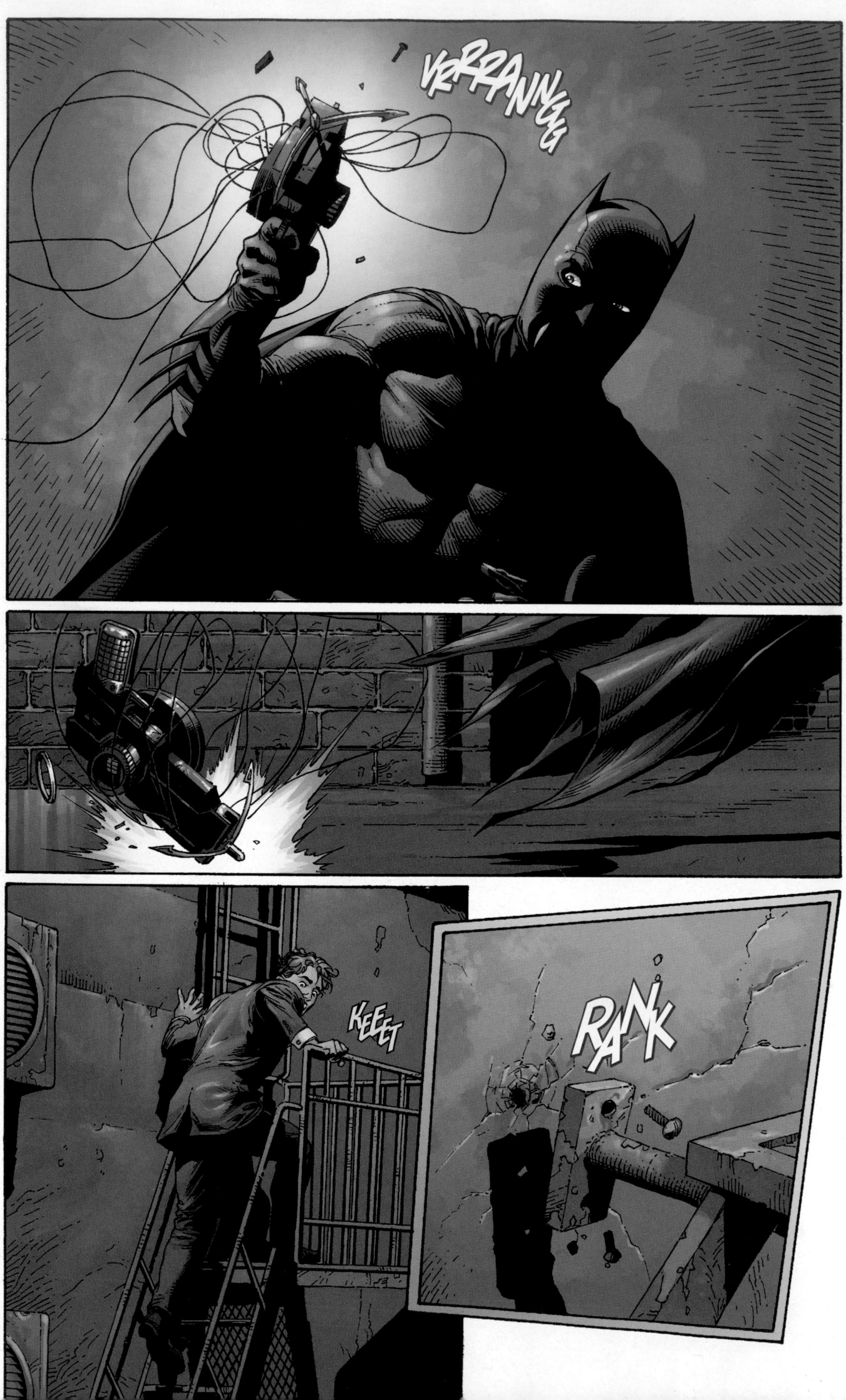
VRRRANNGG
KEEET
RANK

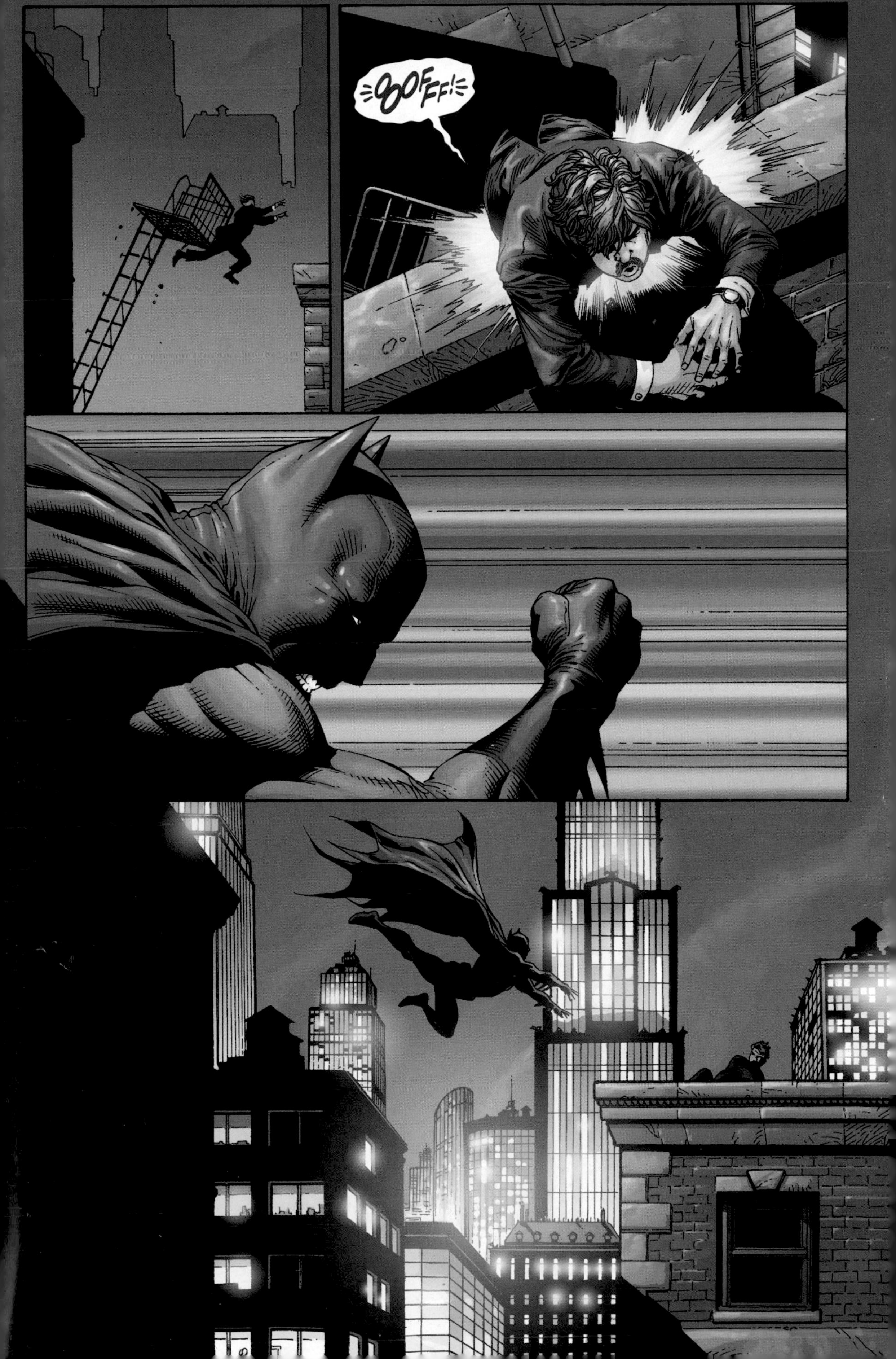
OOFFF!

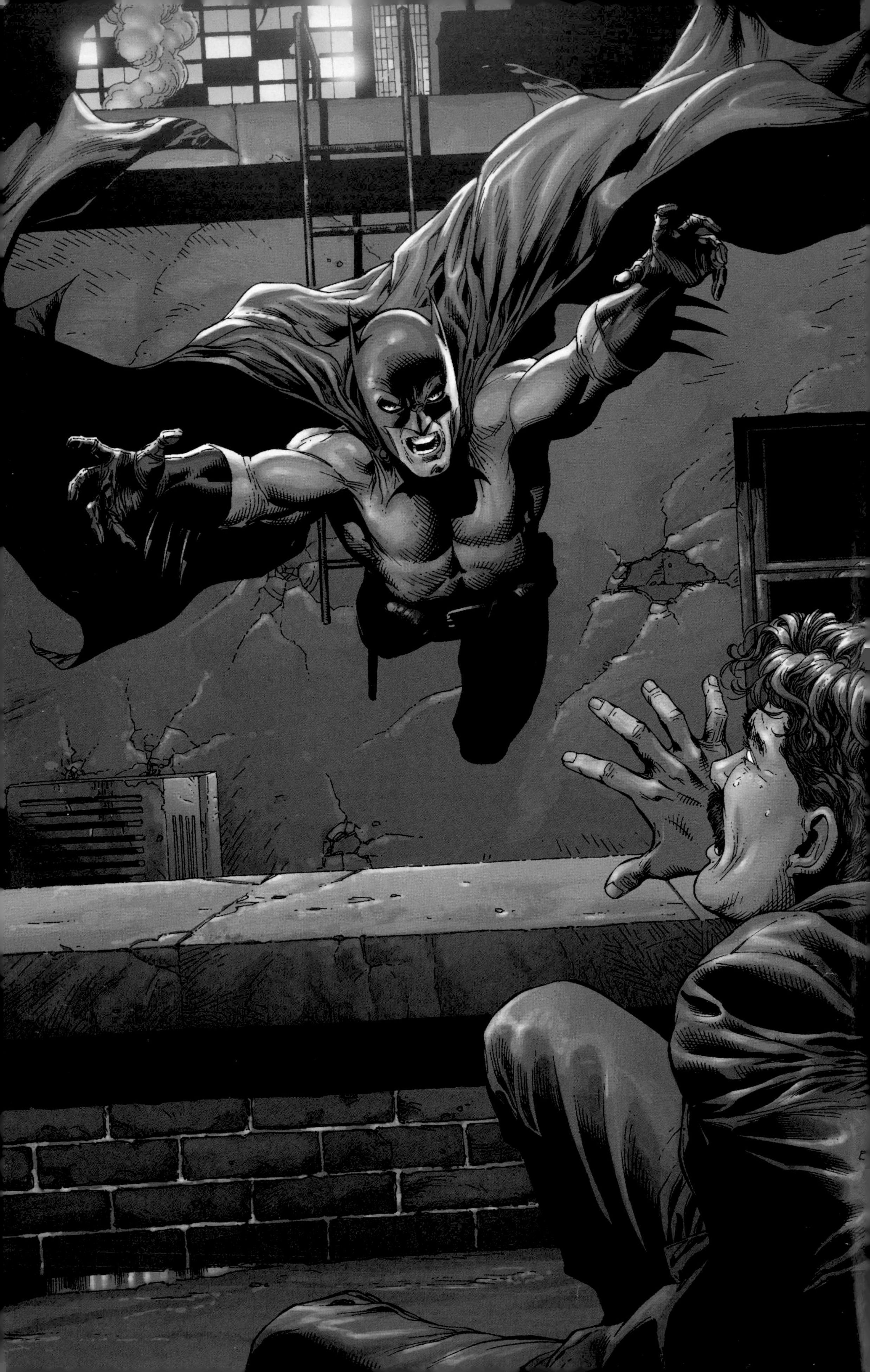

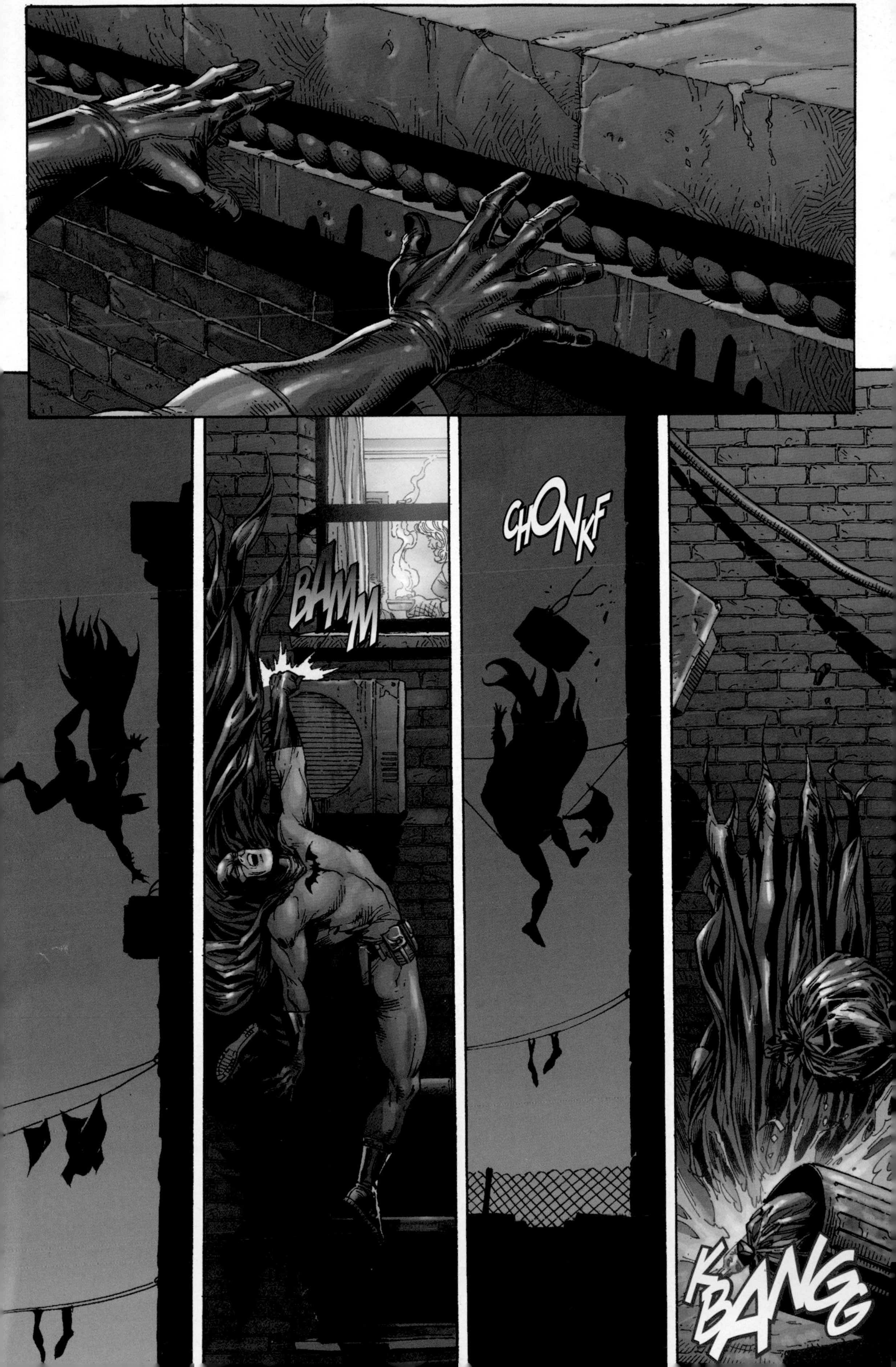
BAMMM
CHONKF
KBANGG

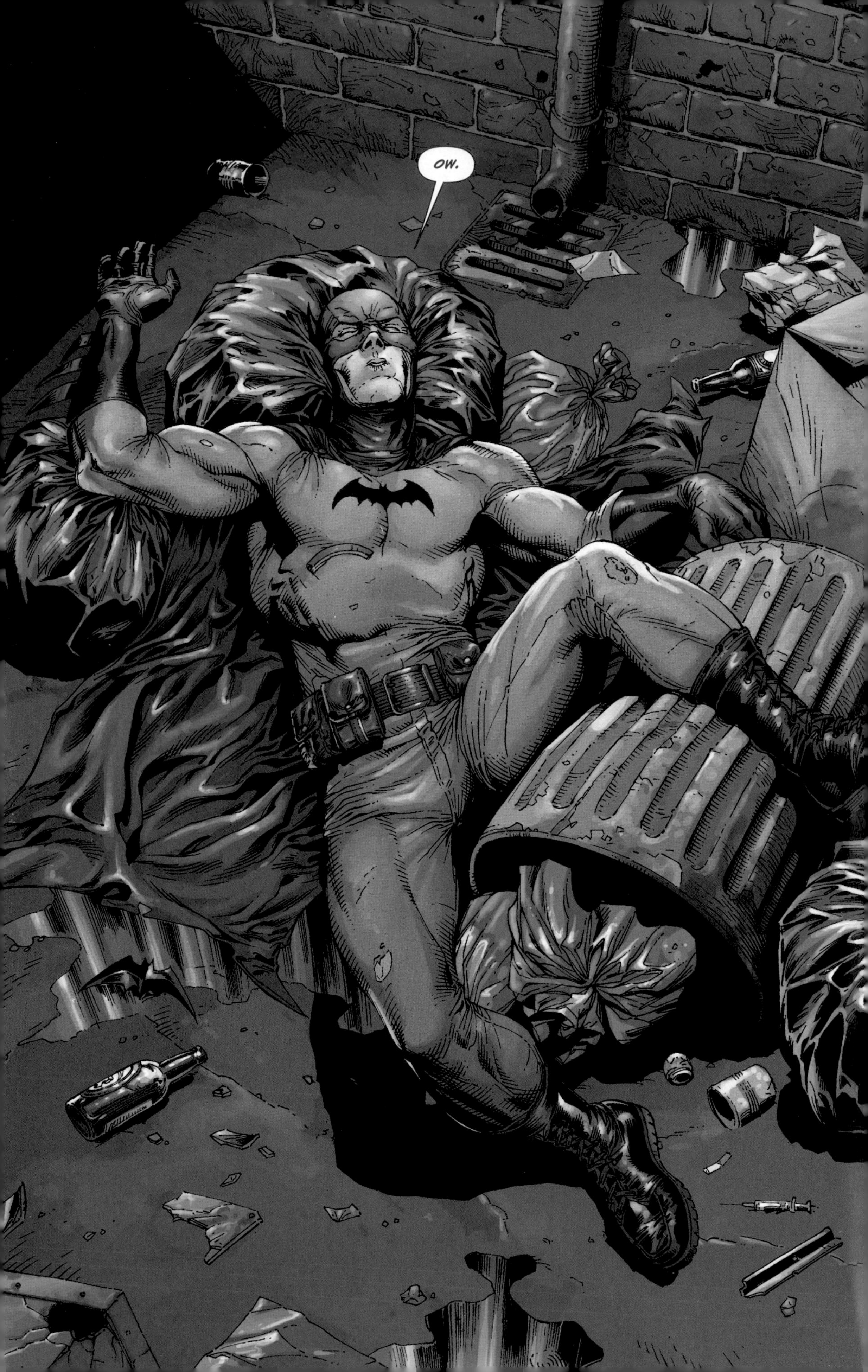
OW.

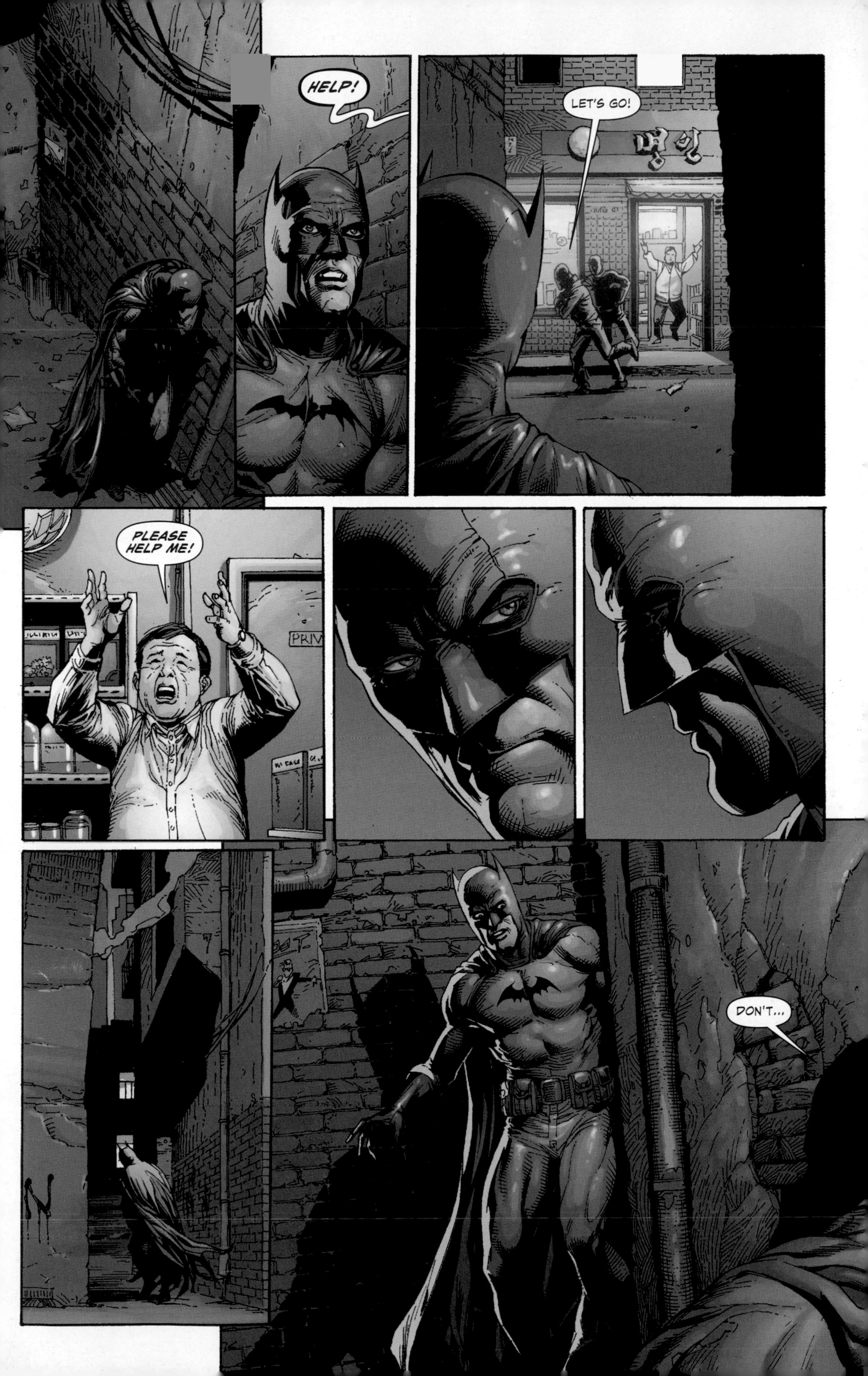
HELP!
LET'S GO!
PLEASE HELP ME!
DON'T...

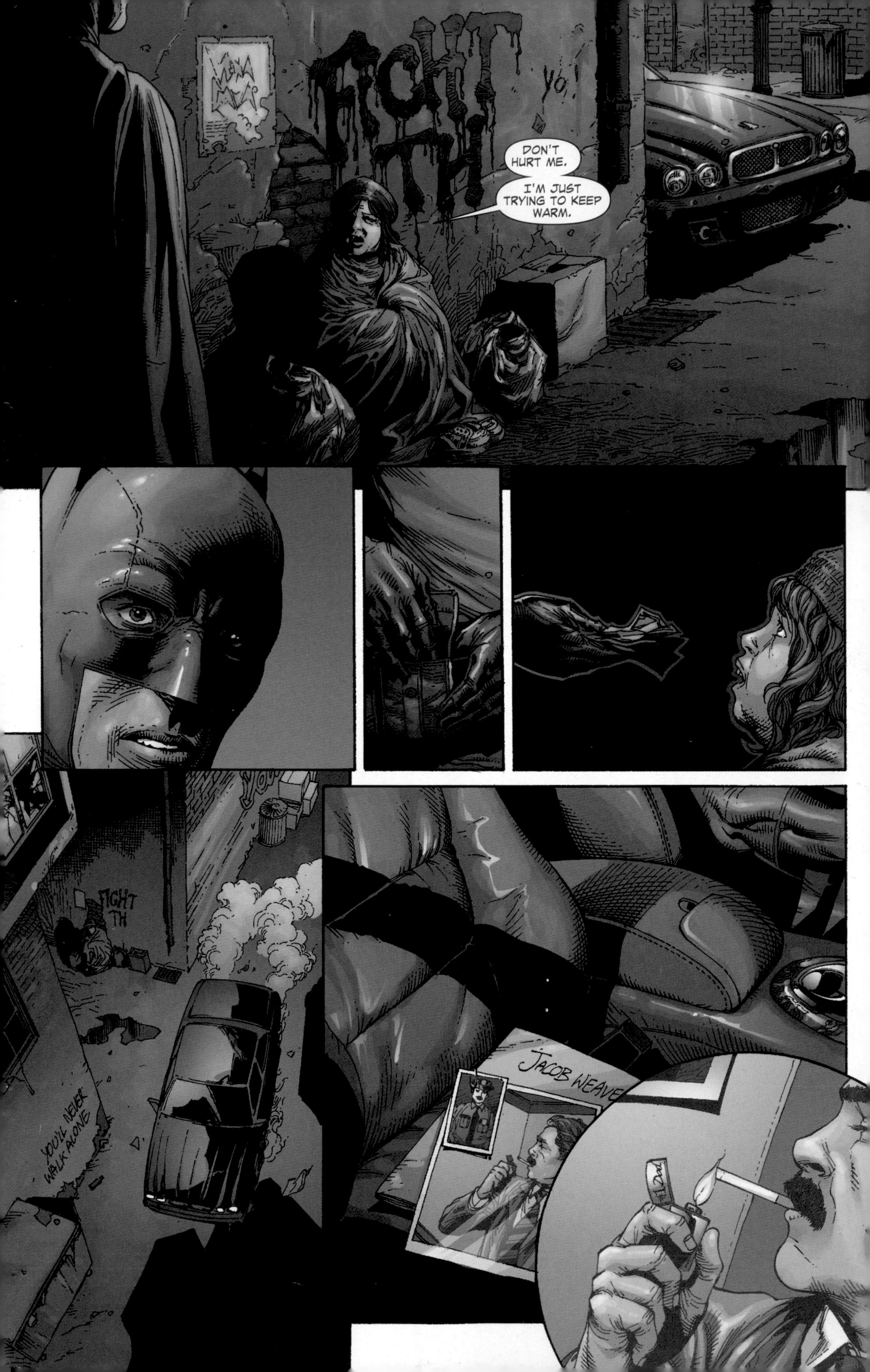
FIGHT TH
YO
DON'T HURT ME.
I'M JUST TRYING TO KEEP WARM.
FIGHT TH
YOU'LL NEVER WALK ALONE
JACOB WEAVE

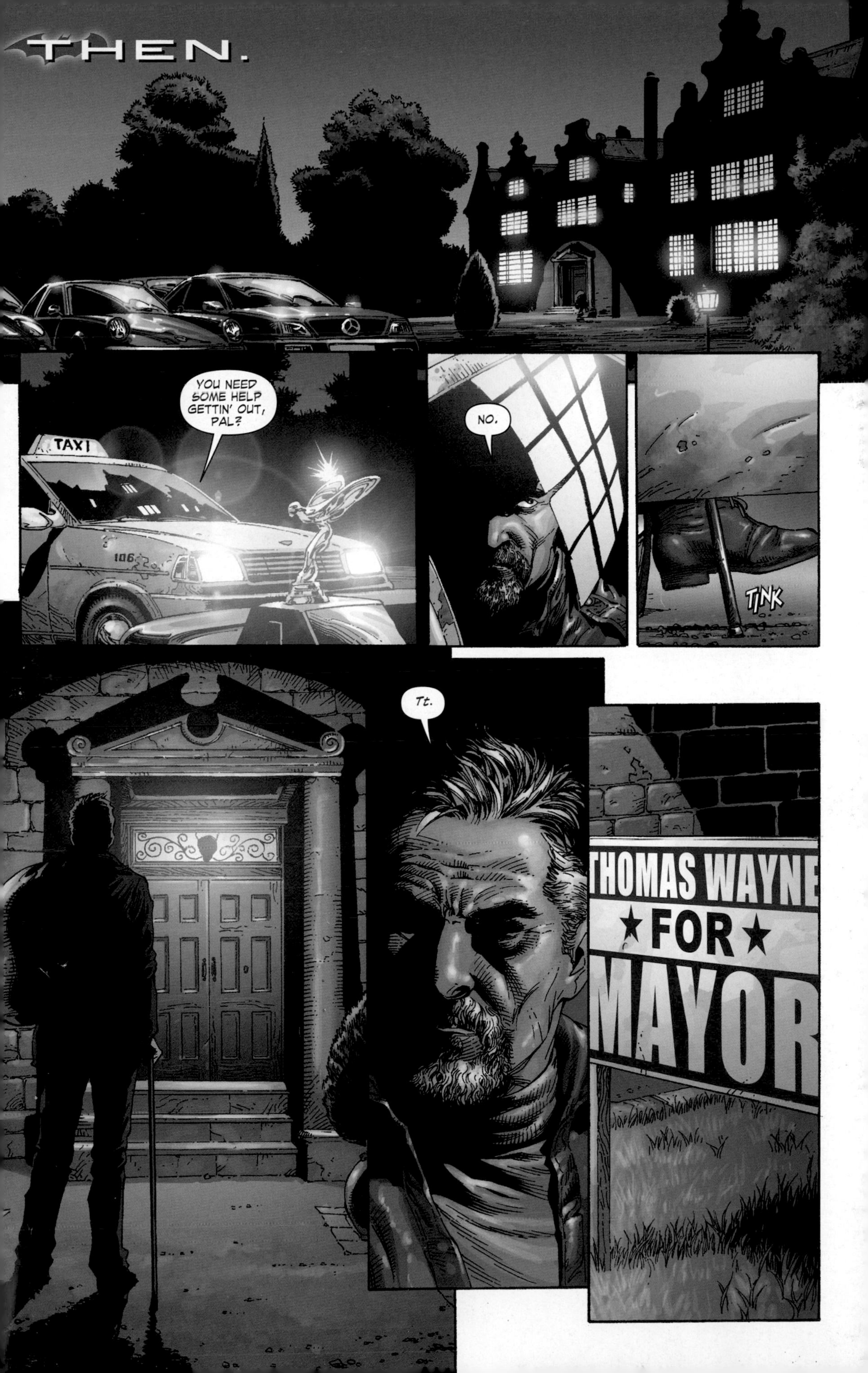
THEN.
YOU NEED SOME HELP GETTIN' OUT, PAL?
TAXI
106
NO.
TINK
Tt.
THOMAS WAYNE
FOR
MAYOR

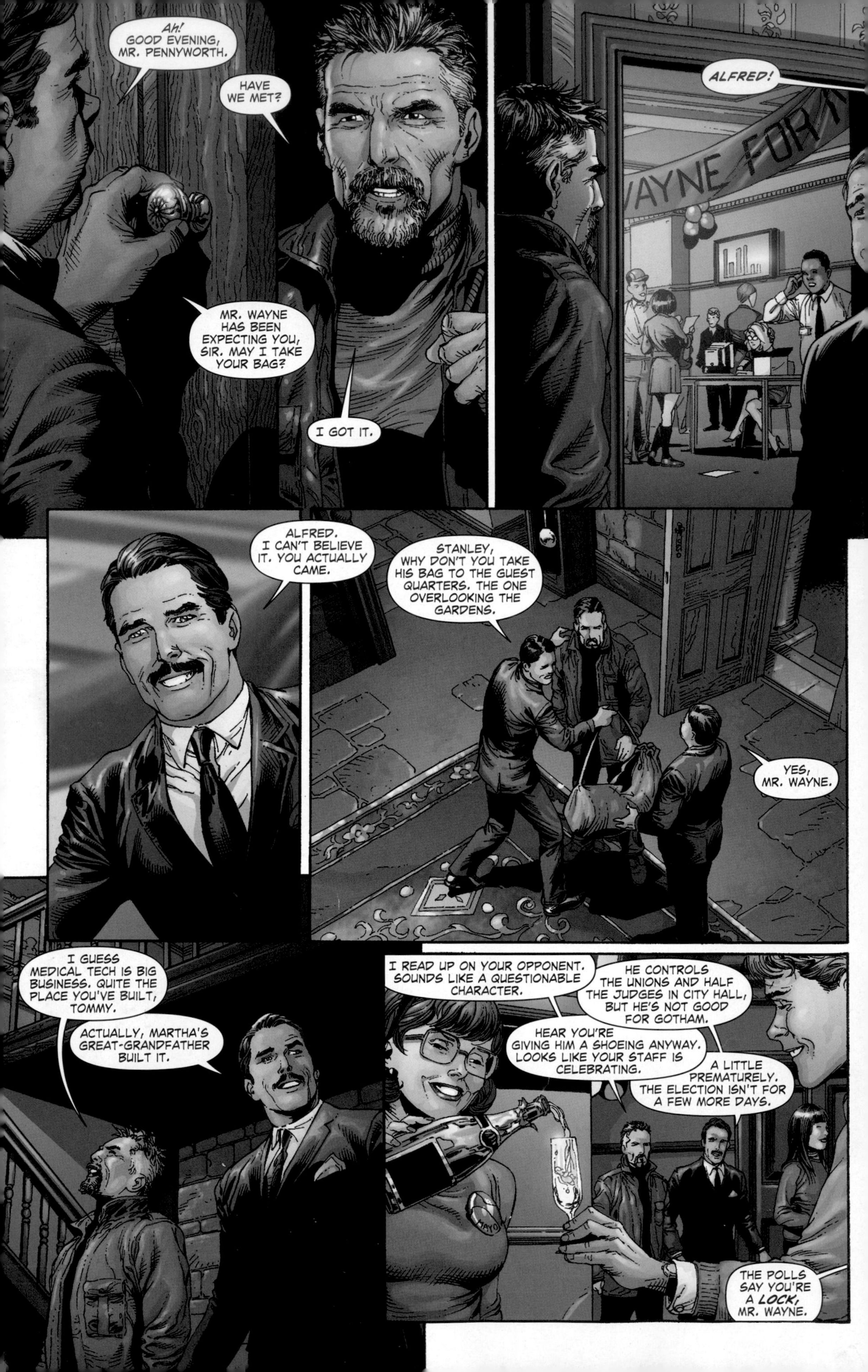
Ah! GOOD EVENING, MR. PENNYWORTH.
HAVE WE MET?
MR. WAYNE HAS BEEN EXPECTING YOU, SIR. MAY I TAKE YOUR BAG?
I GOT IT.
ALFRED!
WAYNE FOR
ALFRED. I CAN'T BELIEVE IT. YOU ACTUALLY CAME.
STANLEY, WHY DON'T YOU TAKE HIS BAG TO THE GUEST QUARTERS. THE ONE OVERLOOKING THE GARDENS.
YES, MR. WAYNE.
I GUESS MEDICAL TECH IS BIG BUSINESS. QUITE THE PLACE YOU'VE BUILT, TOMMY.
ACTUALLY, MARTHA'S GREAT-GRANDFATHER BUILT IT.
I READ UP ON YOUR OPPONENT. SOUNDS LIKE A QUESTIONABLE CHARACTER.
HE CONTROLS THE UNIONS AND HALF THE JUDGES IN CITY HALL, BUT HE'S NOT GOOD FOR GOTHAM.
HEAR YOU'RE GIVING HIM A SHOEING ANYWAY. LOOKS LIKE YOUR STAFF IS CELEBRATING.
A LITTLE PREMATURELY. THE ELECTION ISN'T FOR A FEW MORE DAYS.
THE POLLS SAY YOU'RE A LOCK, MR. WAYNE.

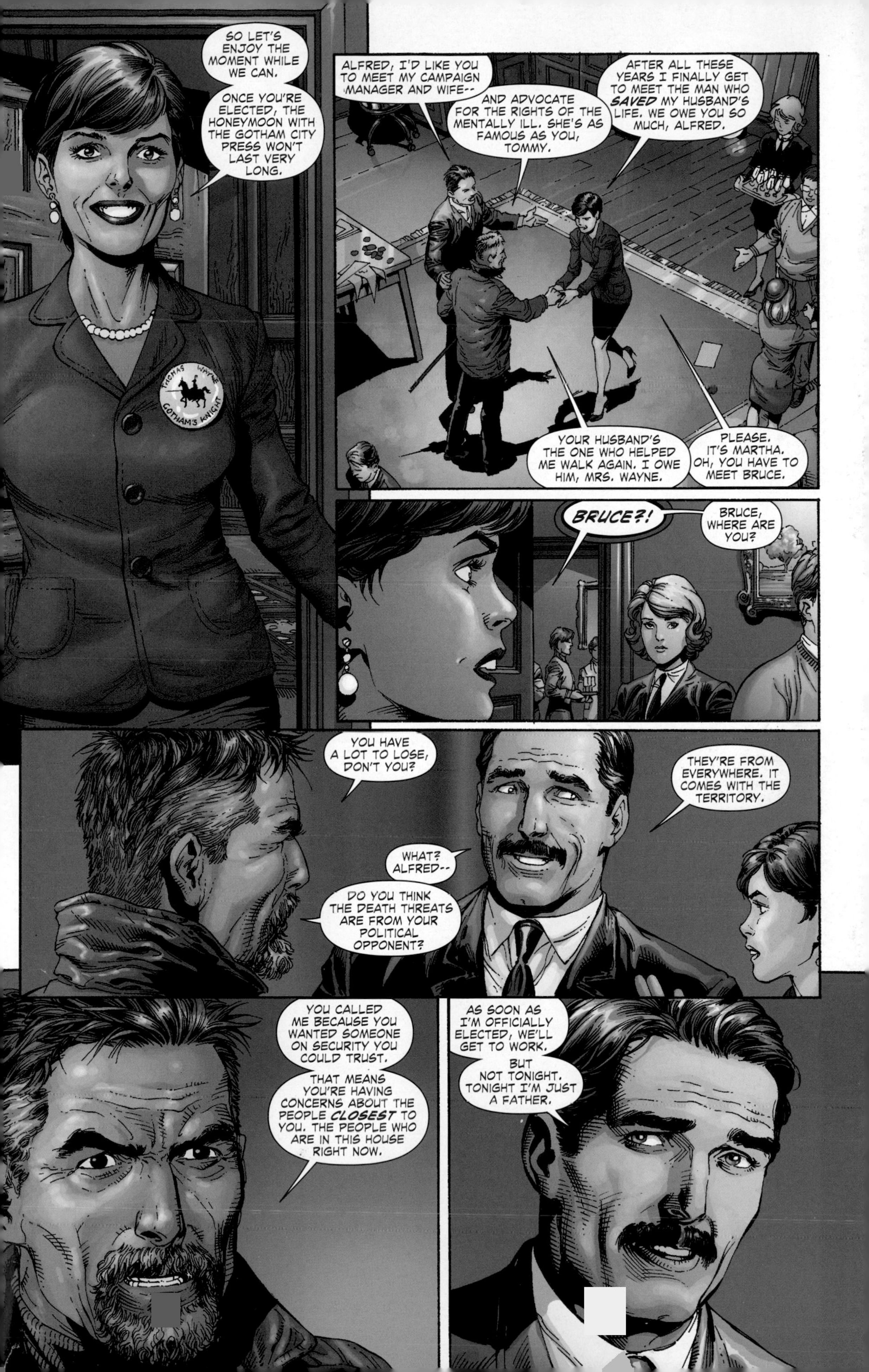
SO LET'S ENJOY THE MOMENT WHILE WE CAN.
ONCE YOU'RE ELECTED, THE HONEYMOON WITH THE GOTHAM CITY PRESS WON'T LAST VERY LONG.
THOMAS WAYNE GOTHAM'S KNIGHT
ALFRED, I'D LIKE YOU TO MEET MY CAMPAIGN MANAGER AND WIFE--
AND ADVOCATE FOR THE RIGHTS OF THE MENTALLY ILL. SHE'S AS FAMOUS AS YOU, TOMMY.
AFTER ALL THESE YEARS I FINALLY GET TO MEET THE MAN WHO SAVED MY HUSBAND'S LIFE. WE OWE YOU SO MUCH, ALFRED.
YOUR HUSBAND'S THE ONE WHO HELPED ME WALK AGAIN. I OWE HIM, MRS. WAYNE.
PLEASE. IT'S MARTHA. OH, YOU HAVE TO MEET BRUCE.
BRUCE?!
BRUCE, WHERE ARE YOU?
YOU HAVE A LOT TO LOSE, DON'T YOU?
THEY'RE FROM EVERYWHERE. IT COMES WITH THE TERRITORY.
WHAT? ALFRED--
DO YOU THINK THE DEATH THREATS ARE FROM YOUR POLITICAL OPPONENT?
YOU CALLED ME BECAUSE YOU WANTED SOMEONE ON SECURITY YOU COULD TRUST.
THAT MEANS YOU'RE HAVING CONCERNS ABOUT THE PEOPLE CLOSEST TO YOU. THE PEOPLE WHO ARE IN THIS HOUSE RIGHT NOW.
AS SOON AS I'M OFFICIALLY ELECTED, WE'LL GET TO WORK.
BUT NOT TONIGHT. TONIGHT I'M JUST A FATHER.

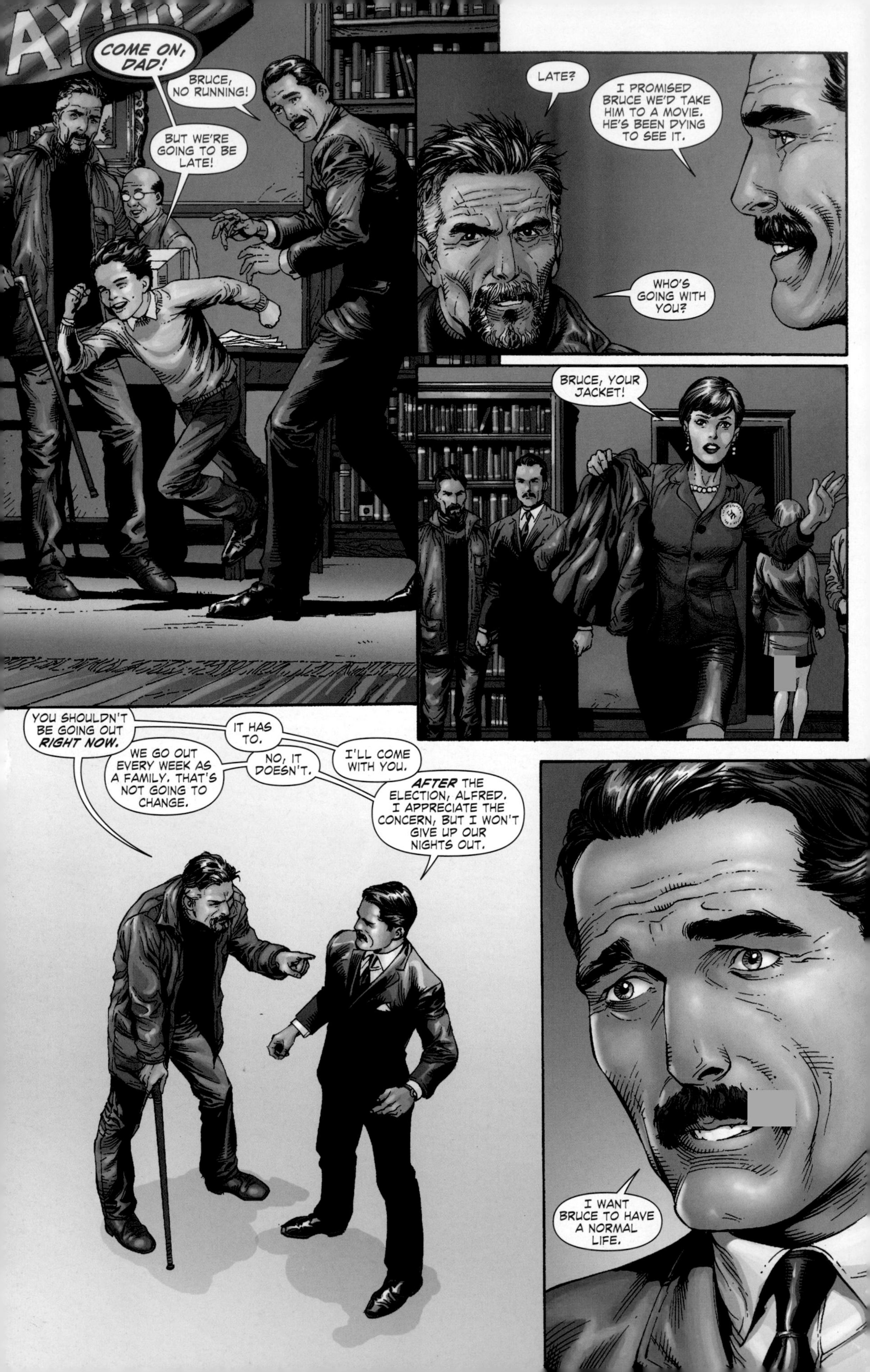
COME ON, DAD!
BRUCE, NO RUNNING!
BUT WE'RE GOING TO BE LATE!
LATE?
I PROMISED BRUCE WE'D TAKE HIM TO A MOVIE. HE'S BEEN DYING TO SEE IT.
WHO'S GOING WITH YOU?
BRUCE, YOUR JACKET!
YOU SHOULDN'T BE GOING OUT RIGHT NOW.
IT HAS TO.
WE GO OUT EVERY WEEK AS A FAMILY. THAT'S NOT GOING TO CHANGE.
NO, IT DOESN'T.
I'LL COME WITH YOU.
AFTER THE ELECTION, ALFRED. I APPRECIATE THE CONCERN, BUT I WON'T GIVE UP OUR NIGHTS OUT.
I WANT BRUCE TO HAVE A NORMAL LIFE.

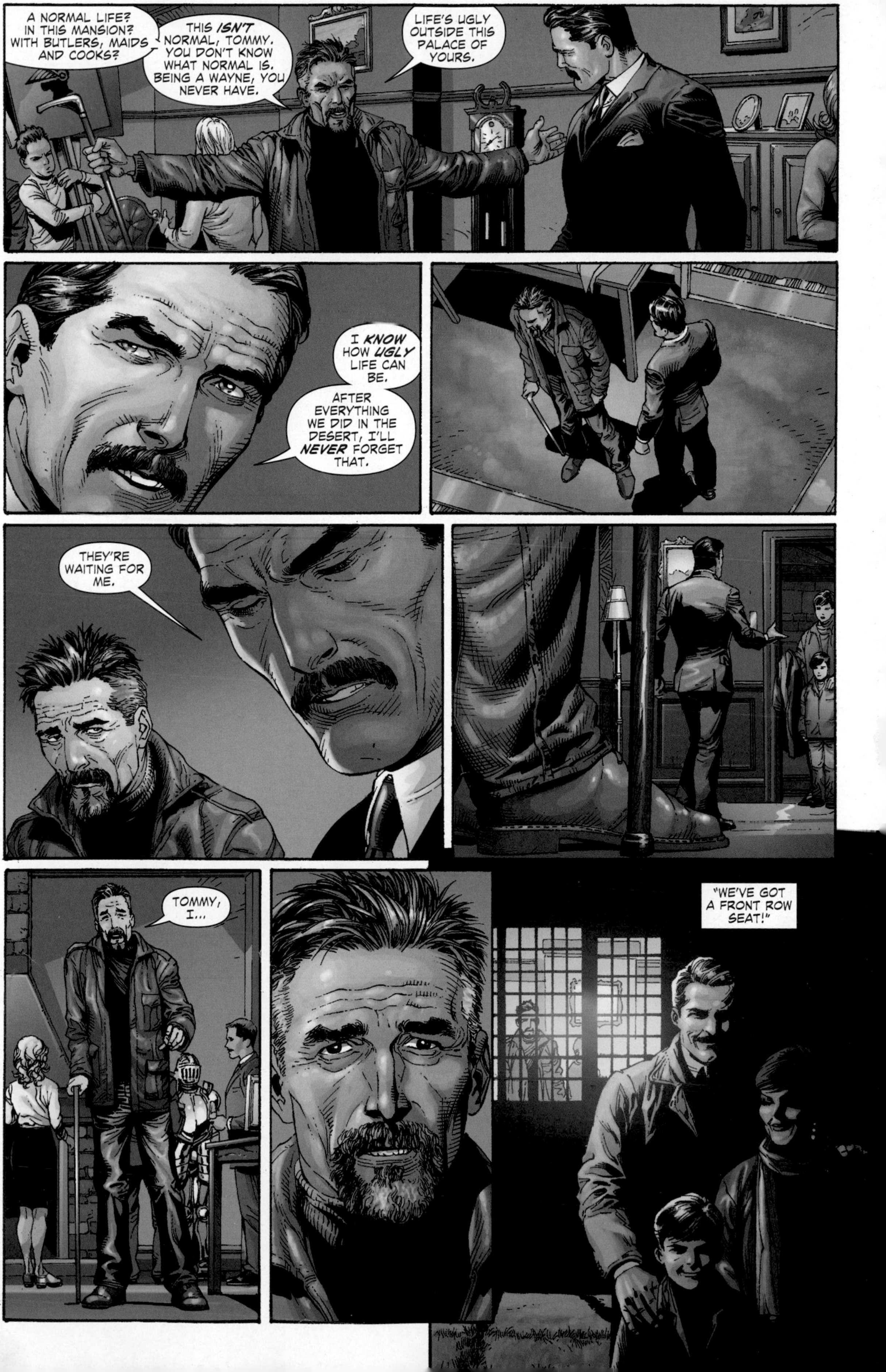

A NORMAL LIFE? IN THIS MANSION? WITH BUTLERS, MAIDS AND COOKS?
THIS *ISN'T* NORMAL, TOMMY. YOU DON'T KNOW WHAT NORMAL IS. BEING A WAYNE, YOU NEVER HAVE.
LIFE'S UGLY OUTSIDE THIS PALACE OF YOURS.
I *KNOW* HOW *UGLY* LIFE CAN BE.
AFTER EVERYTHING WE DID IN THE DESERT, I'LL *NEVER* FORGET THAT.
THEY'RE WAITING FOR ME.
TOMMY, I...
"WE'VE GOT A FRONT ROW SEAT!"

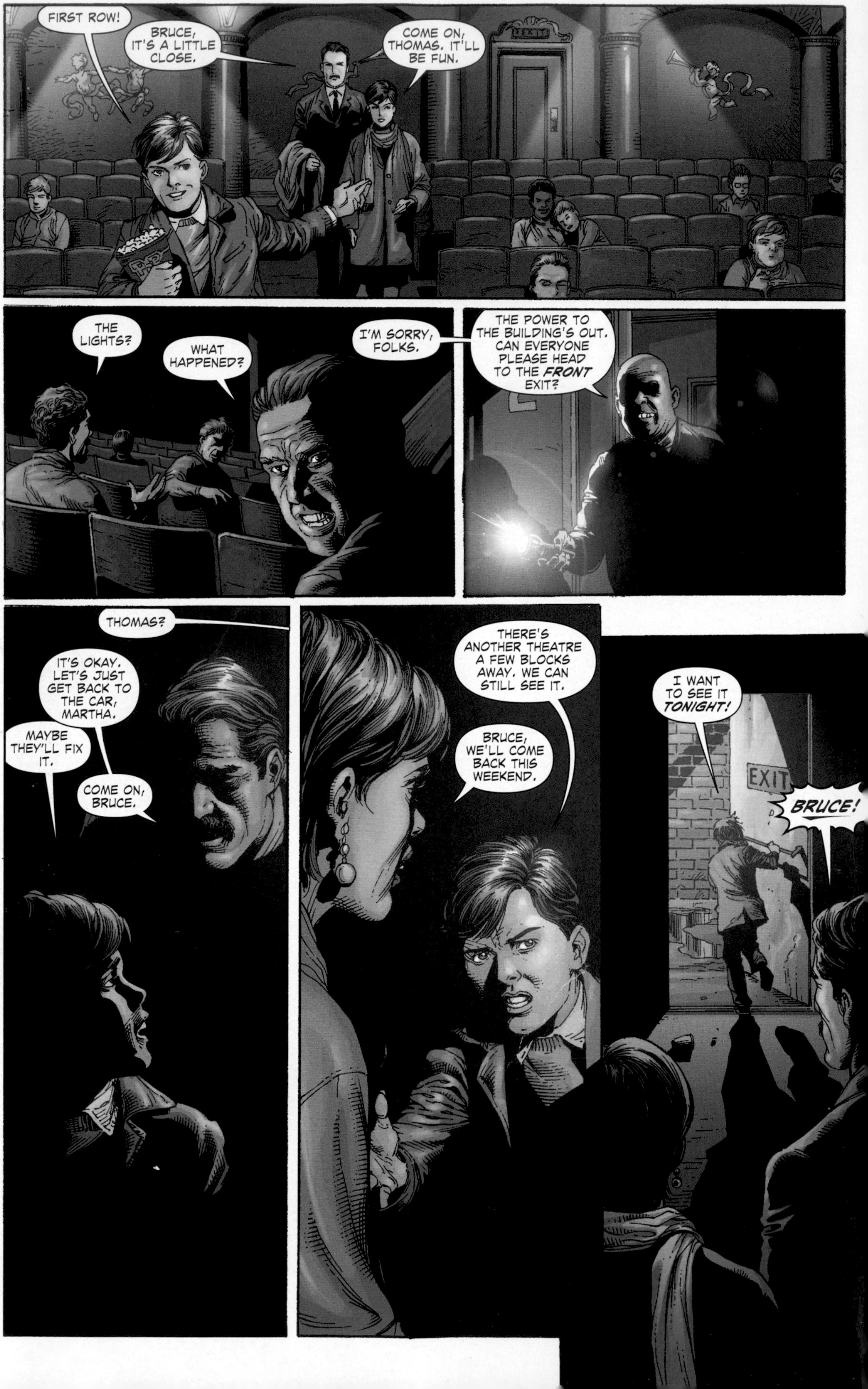
FIRST ROW!
BRUCE, IT'S A LITTLE CLOSE.
COME ON, THOMAS. IT'LL BE FUN.
THE LIGHTS?
WHAT HAPPENED?
I'M SORRY, FOLKS.
THE POWER TO THE BUILDING'S OUT. CAN EVERYONE PLEASE HEAD TO THE *FRONT* EXIT?
THOMAS?
IT'S OKAY. LET'S JUST GET BACK TO THE CAR, MARTHA.
MAYBE THEY'LL FIX IT.
COME ON, BRUCE.
THERE'S ANOTHER THEATRE A FEW BLOCKS AWAY. WE CAN STILL SEE IT.
BRUCE, WE'LL COME BACK THIS WEEKEND.
I WANT TO SEE IT *TONIGHT!*
EXIT
BRUCE!

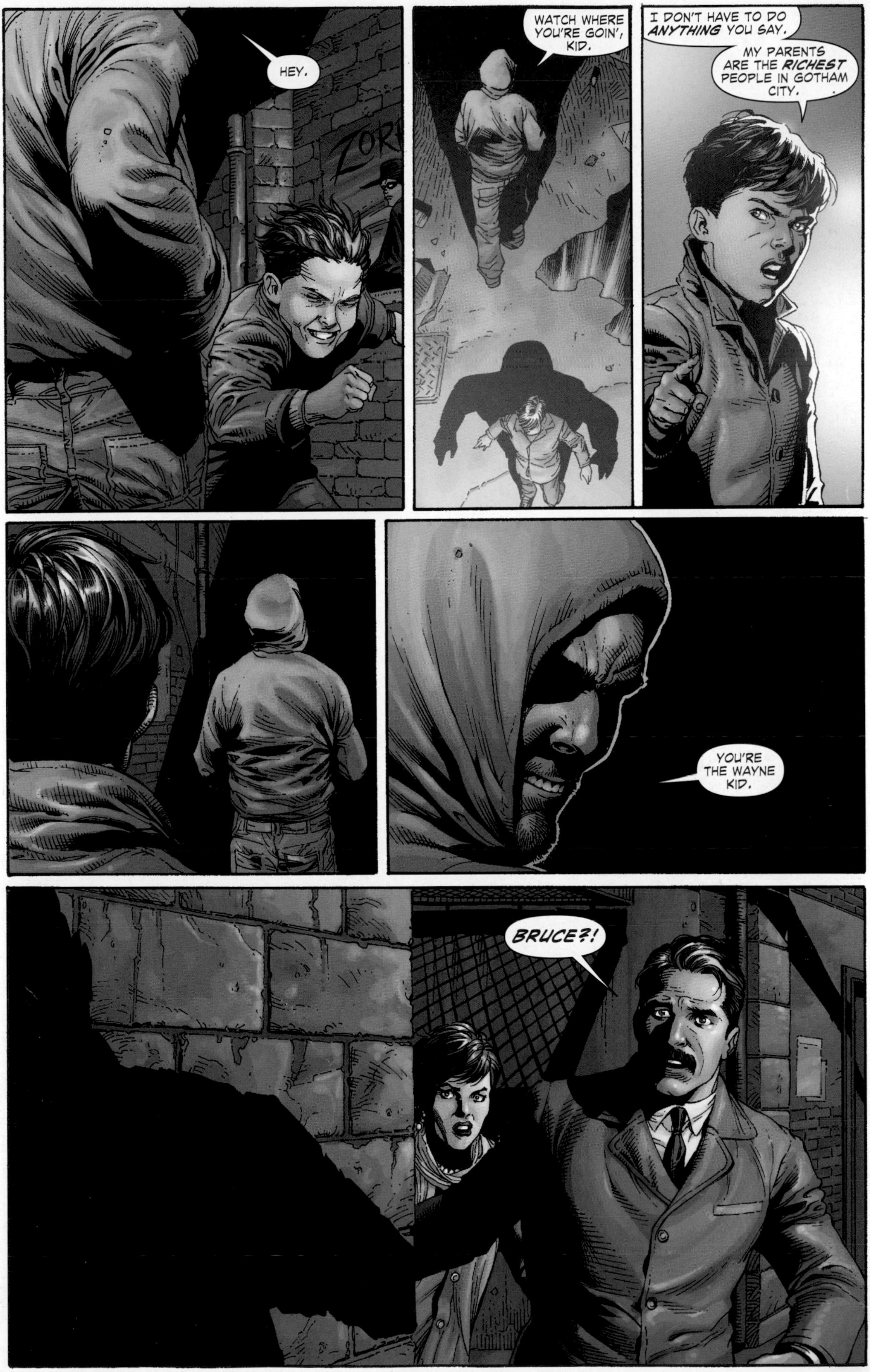
HEY.
WATCH WHERE YOU'RE GOIN', KID.
I DON'T HAVE TO DO ANYTHING YOU SAY.
MY PARENTS ARE THE RICHEST PEOPLE IN GOTHAM CITY.
YOU'RE THE WAYNE KID.
BRUCE?!

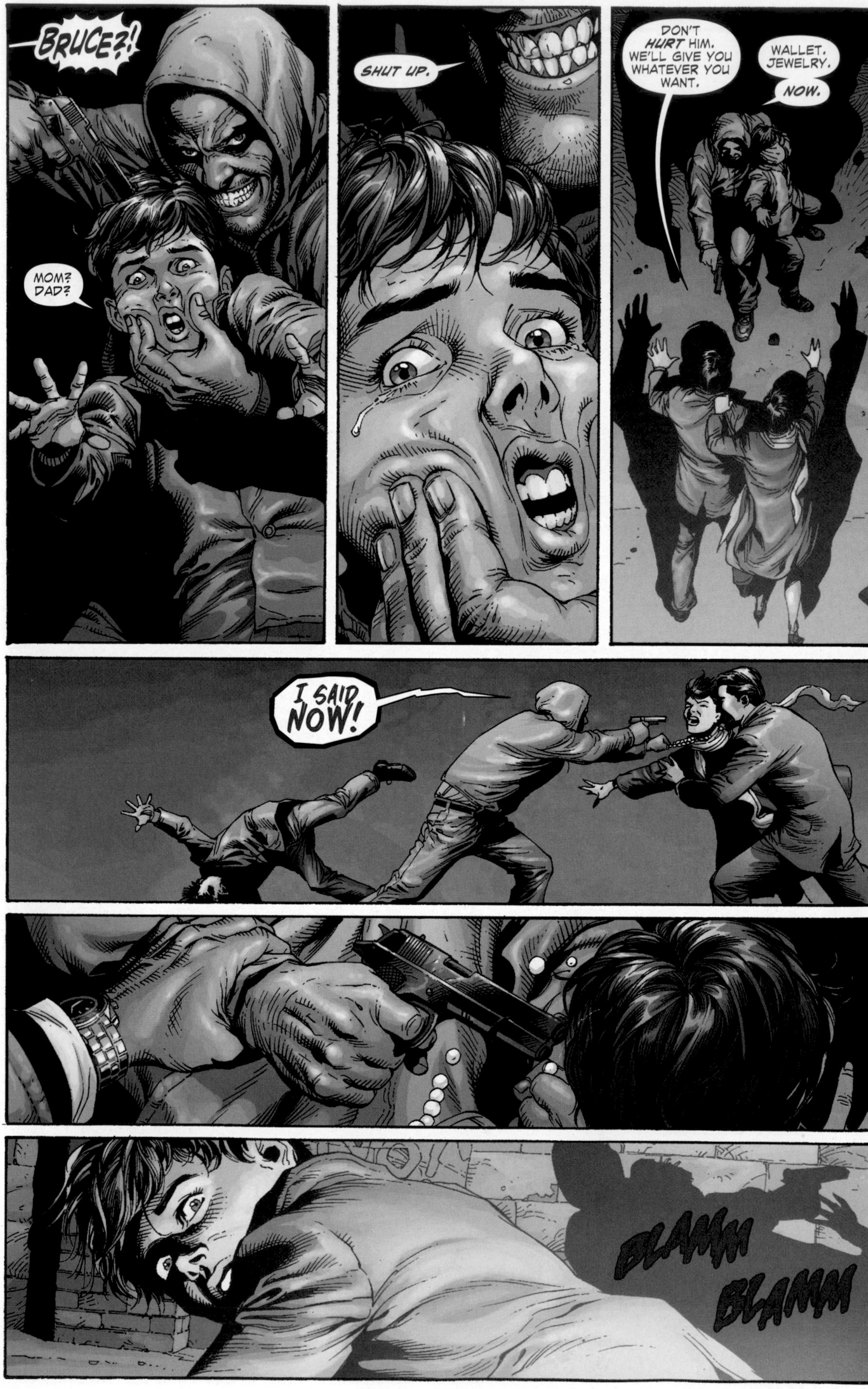
BRUCE?!
MOM? DAD?
SHUT UP.
DON'T HURT HIM. WE'LL GIVE YOU WHATEVER YOU WANT.
WALLET. JEWELRY.
NOW.
I SAID NOW!
BLAMM
BLAMM

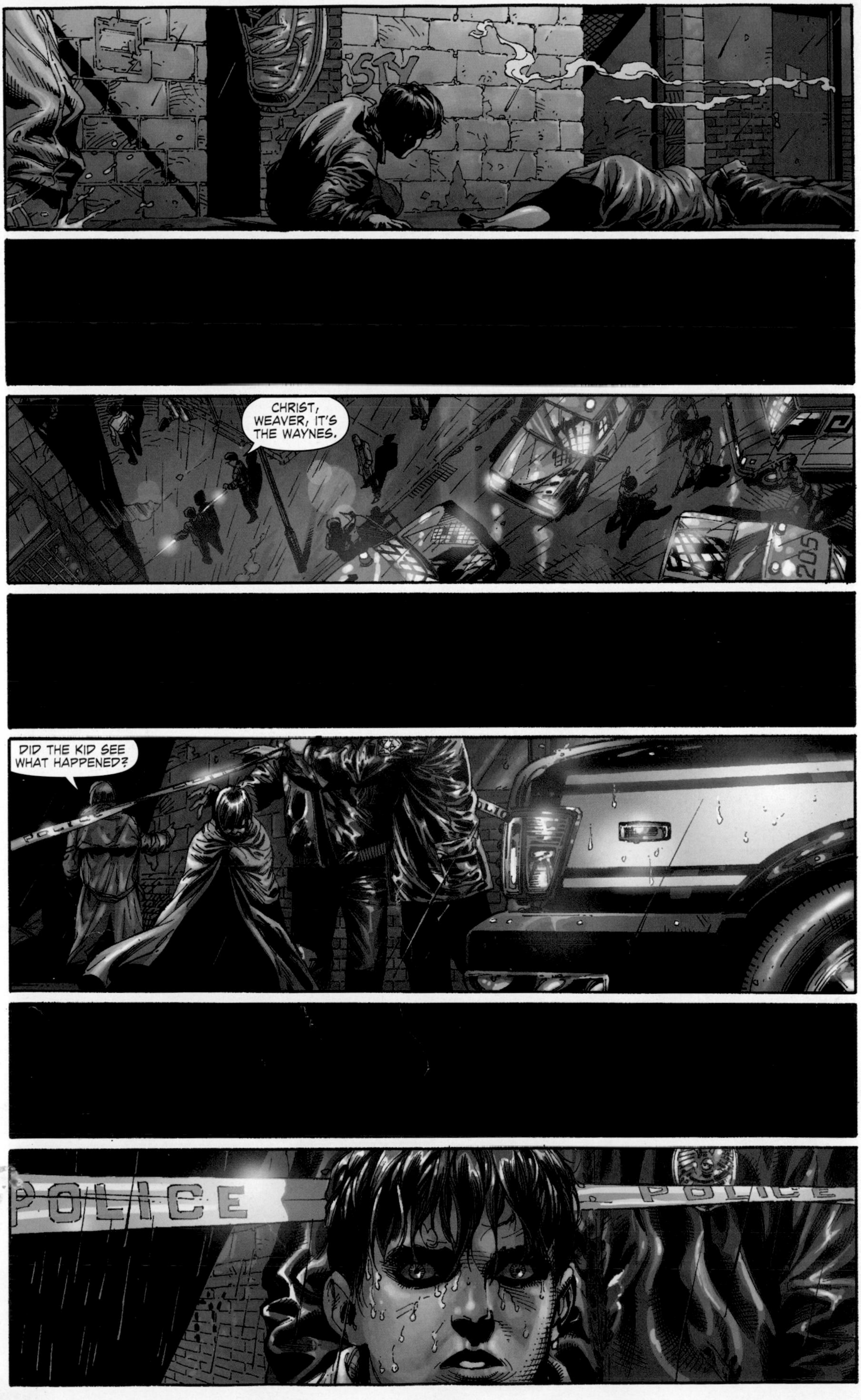
CHRIST, WEAVER, IT'S THE WAYNES.
205
DID THE KID SEE WHAT HAPPENED?
POLICE
POLICE

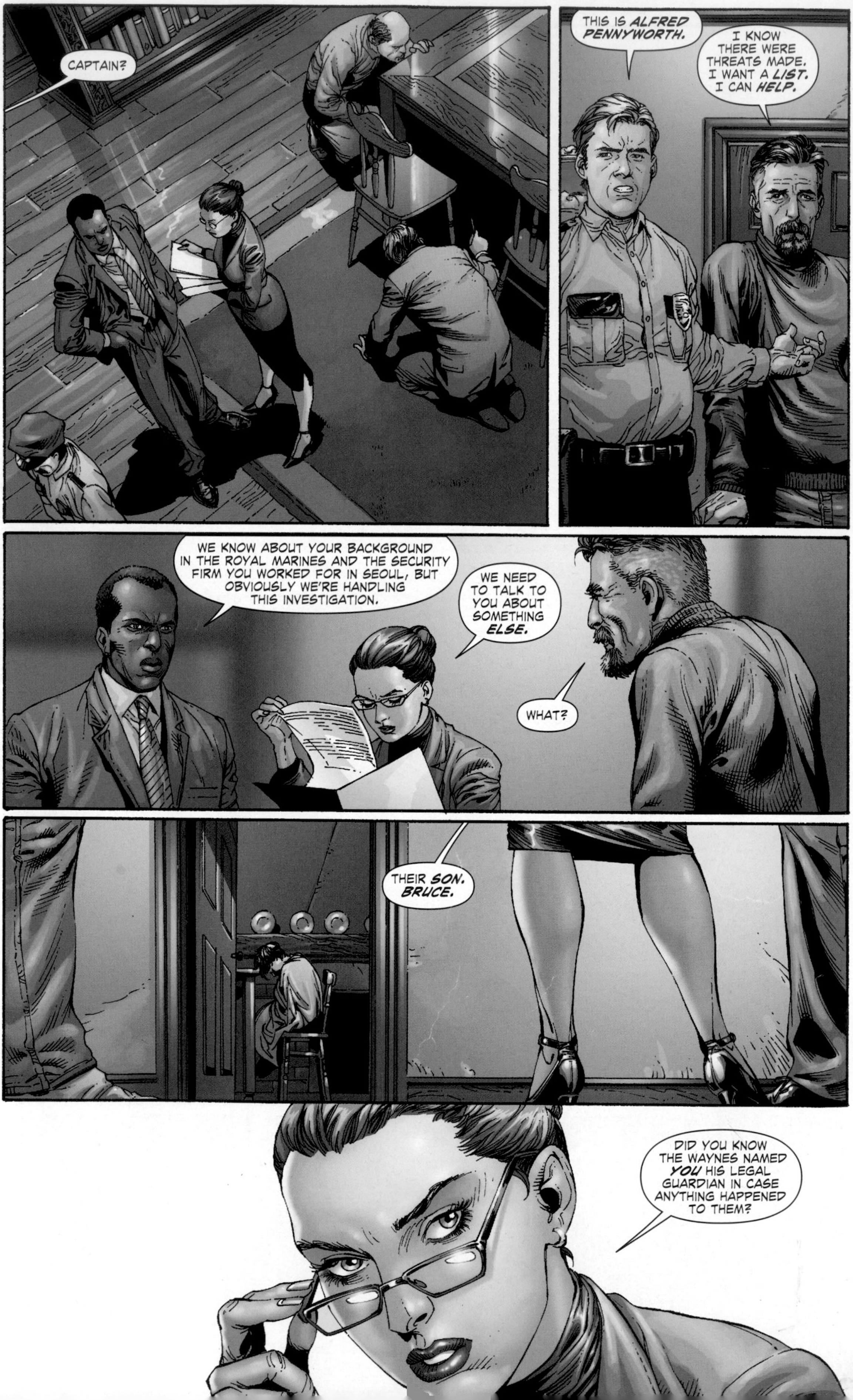
CAPTAIN?
THIS IS ALFRED PENNYWORTH.
I KNOW THERE WERE THREATS MADE. I WANT A LIST. I CAN HELP.
WE KNOW ABOUT YOUR BACKGROUND IN THE ROYAL MARINES AND THE SECURITY FIRM YOU WORKED FOR IN SEOUL, BUT OBVIOUSLY WE'RE HANDLING THIS INVESTIGATION.
WE NEED TO TALK TO YOU ABOUT SOMETHING ELSE.
WHAT?
THEIR SON. BRUCE.
DID YOU KNOW THE WAYNES NAMED YOU HIS LEGAL GUARDIAN IN CASE ANYTHING HAPPENED TO THEM?

LEGAL GUARDIAN?

I'M NOT A PARENT.

ACCORDING TO THIS, YOU HAVE A DAUGHTER.

SHE LIVES WITH HER MOTHER.

IN SEOUL?

THAT'S NOT WHAT I MEANT WHEN I SAID I'M NOT A PARENT. I MEANT I'M NOT INTERESTED IN BEING ANYONE'S GUARDIAN.

I JUST WANT TO KNOW WHO KILLED THE WAYNES.

THAT'S THE POLICE'S JOB, MR. PENNYWORTH. MY JOB IS TO SORT OUT WHAT HAPPENS TO THIS POOR BOY.

HE WON'T TALK TO ANYONE. HE HASN'T EATEN ANYTHING.

THERE HAS TO BE SOMEONE ELSE WHO CAN WATCH OVER HIM.

THOMAS AND MARTHA WERE THE LAST OF THEIR RESPECTIVE FAMILIES. THE LAST OF THE WAYNES AND THE ARKHAMS.

WHAT HAPPENS IF I SAY "NO"?

HE GOES TO CHILD SERVICES.

AND INTO FOSTER CARE.

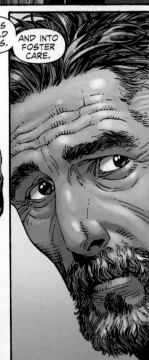

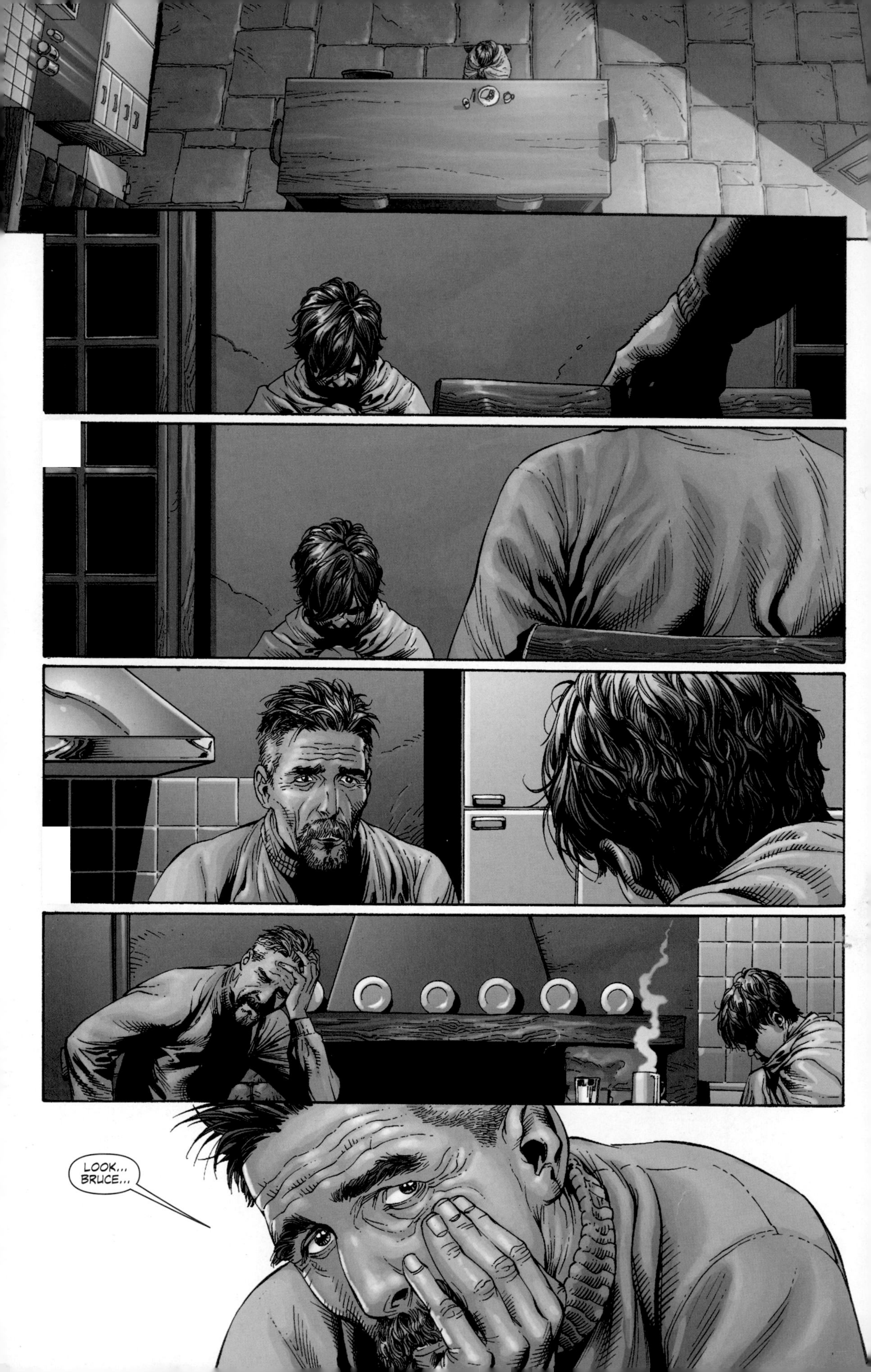
LOOK... BRUCE...

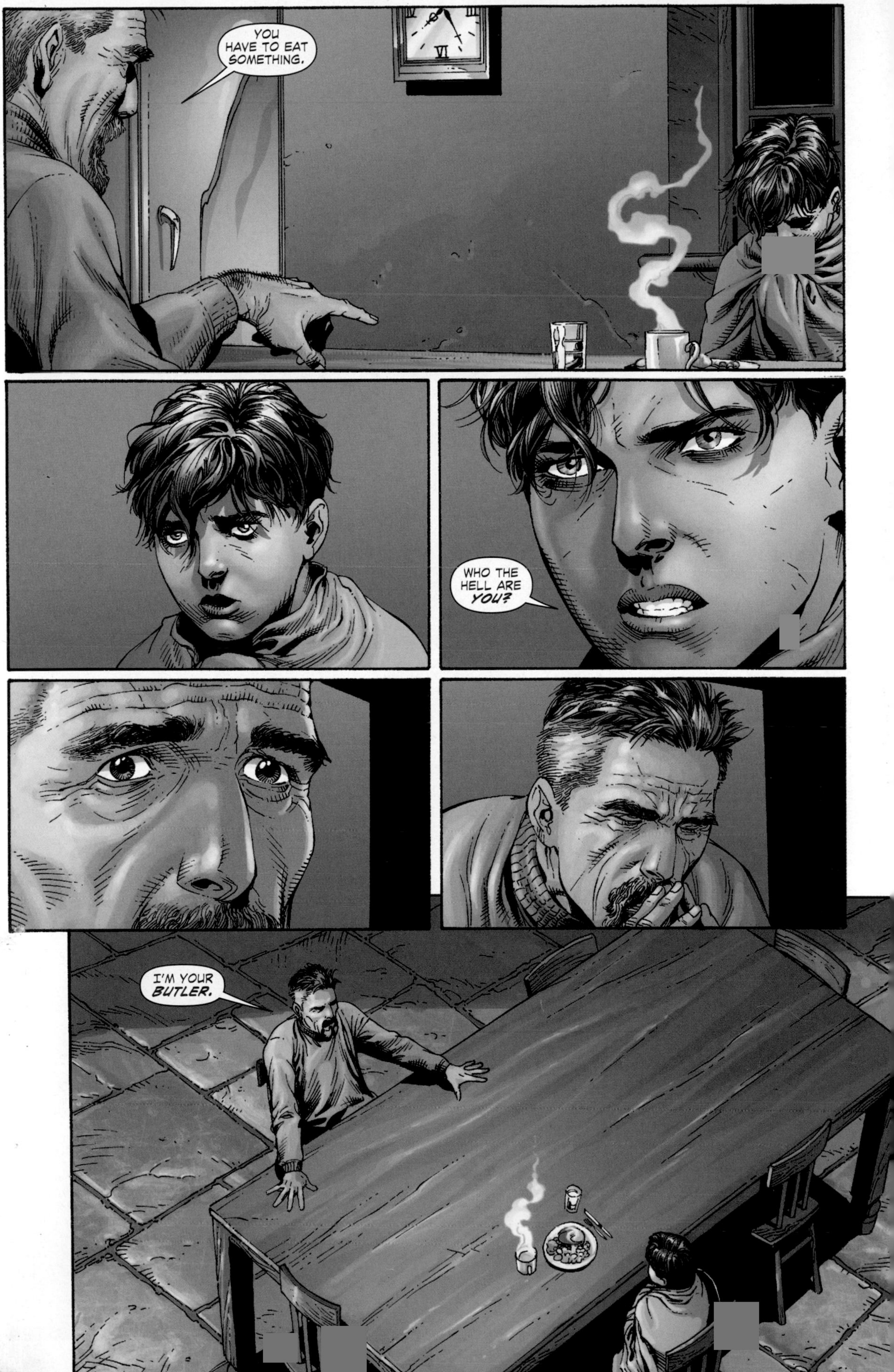
YOU HAVE TO EAT SOMETHING.
WHO THE HELL ARE *YOU?*
I'M YOUR *BUTLER.*

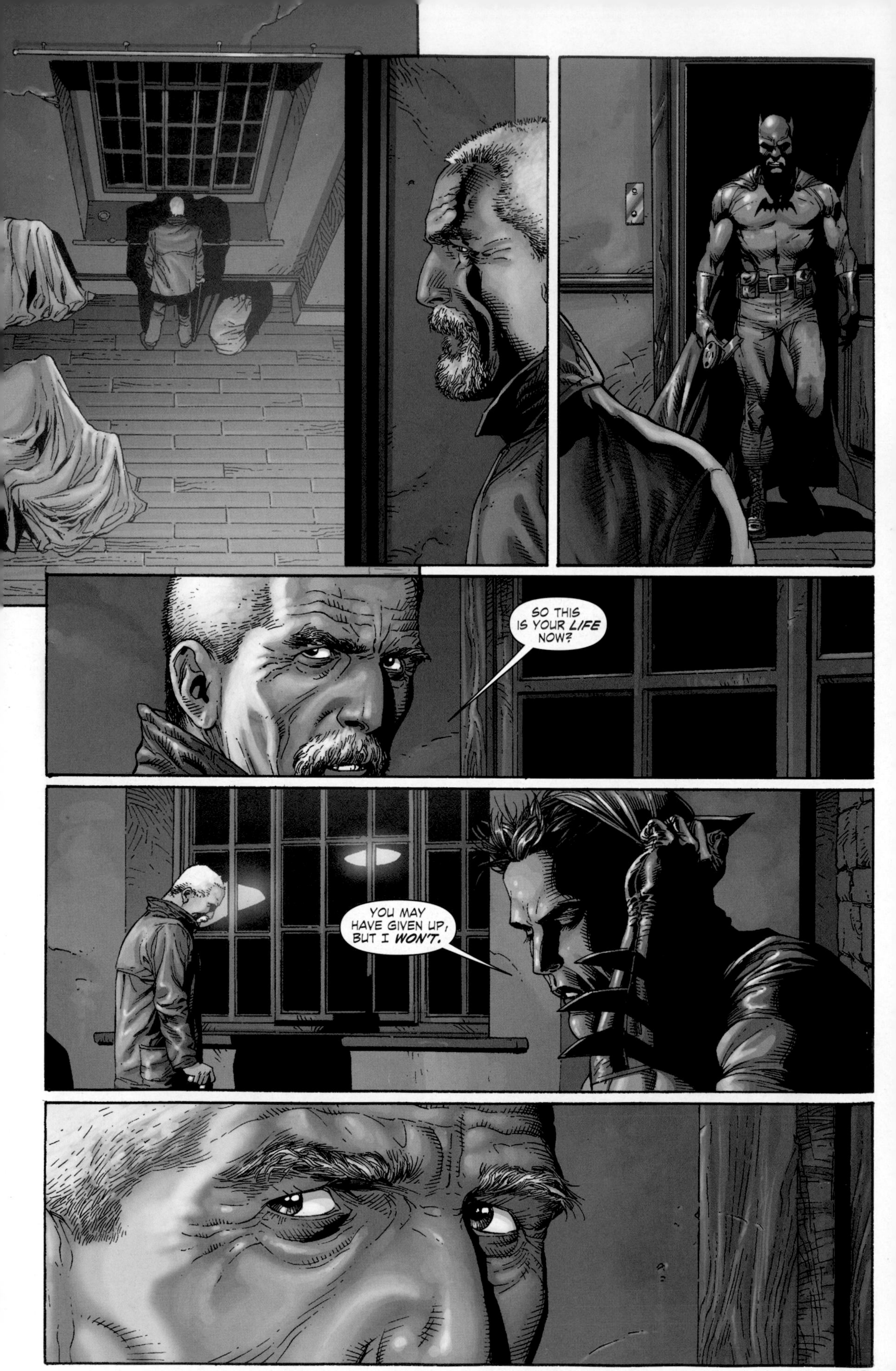
SO THIS IS YOUR LIFE NOW?
YOU MAY HAVE GIVEN UP, BUT I WON'T.

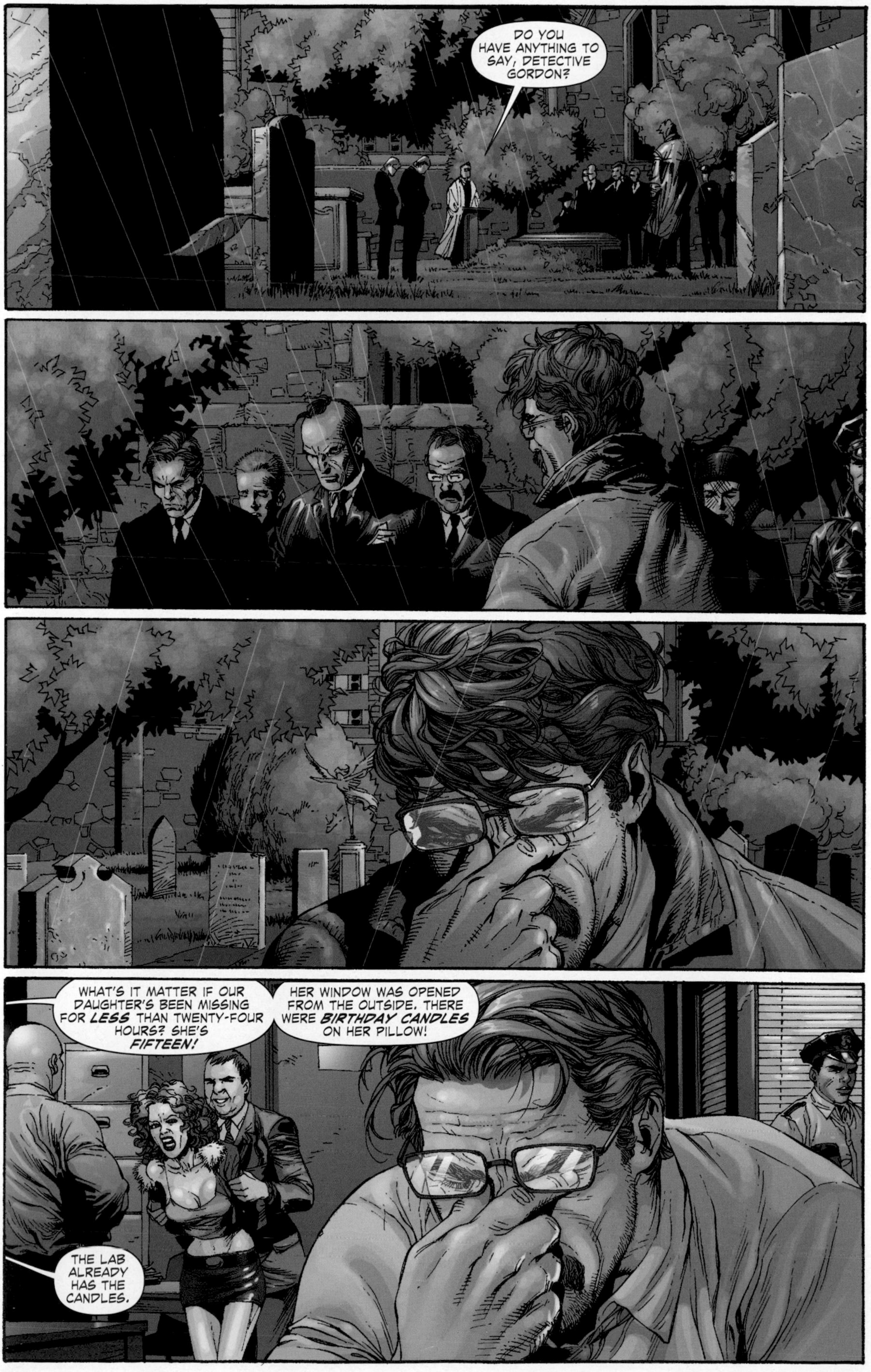
DO YOU HAVE ANYTHING TO SAY, DETECTIVE GORDON?
WHAT'S IT MATTER IF OUR DAUGHTER'S BEEN MISSING FOR LESS THAN TWENTY-FOUR HOURS? SHE'S FIFTEEN!
HER WINDOW WAS OPENED FROM THE OUTSIDE. THERE WERE BIRTHDAY CANDLES ON HER PILLOW!
THE LAB ALREADY HAS THE CANDLES.

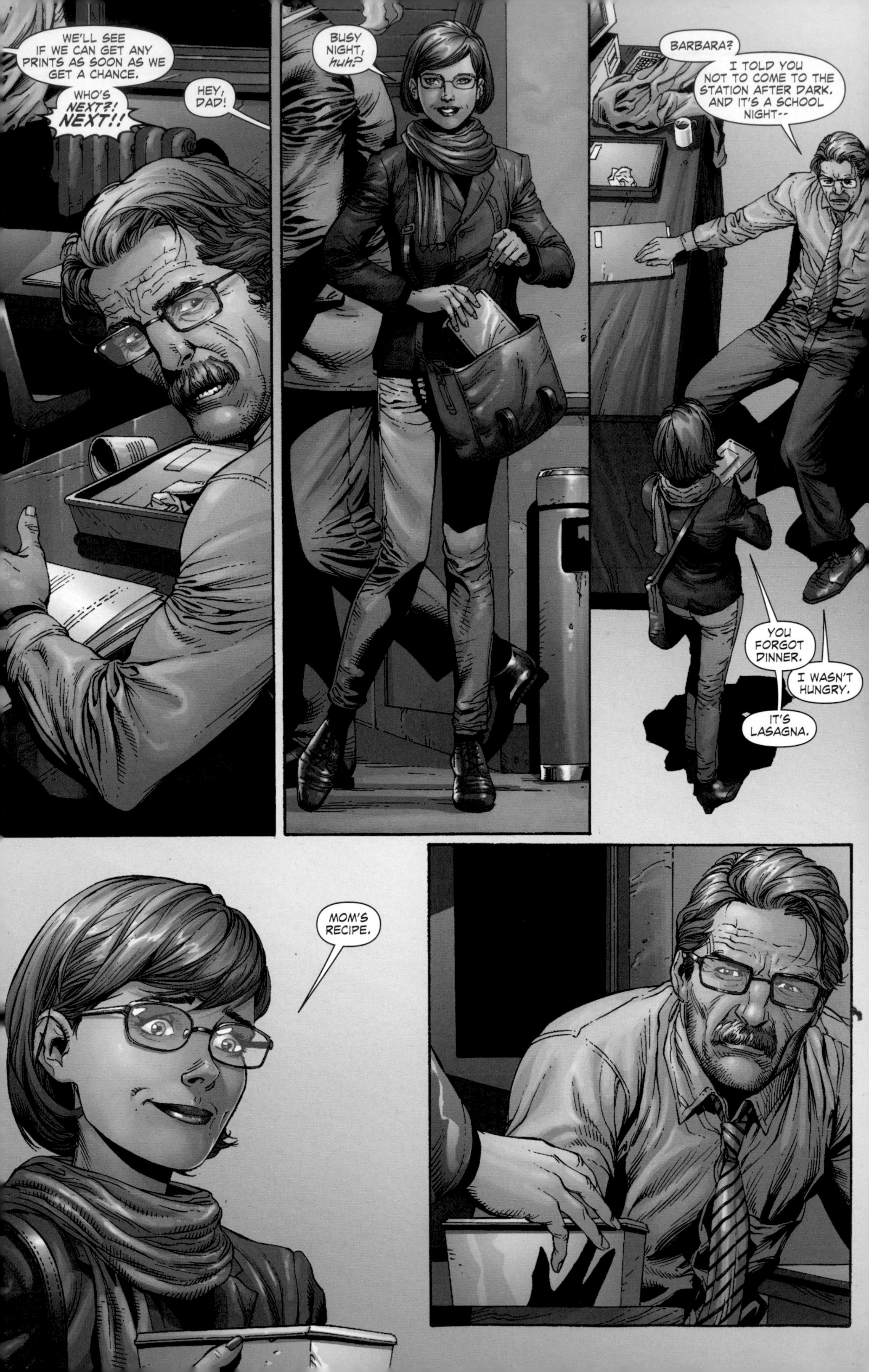
WE'LL SEE IF WE CAN GET ANY PRINTS AS SOON AS WE GET A CHANCE.
WHO'S *NEXT?!* NEXT!!
HEY, DAD!
BUSY NIGHT, *huh?*
BARBARA?
I TOLD YOU NOT TO COME TO THE STATION AFTER DARK. AND IT'S A SCHOOL NIGHT--
YOU FORGOT DINNER.
I WASN'T HUNGRY.
IT'S LASAGNA.
MOM'S RECIPE.

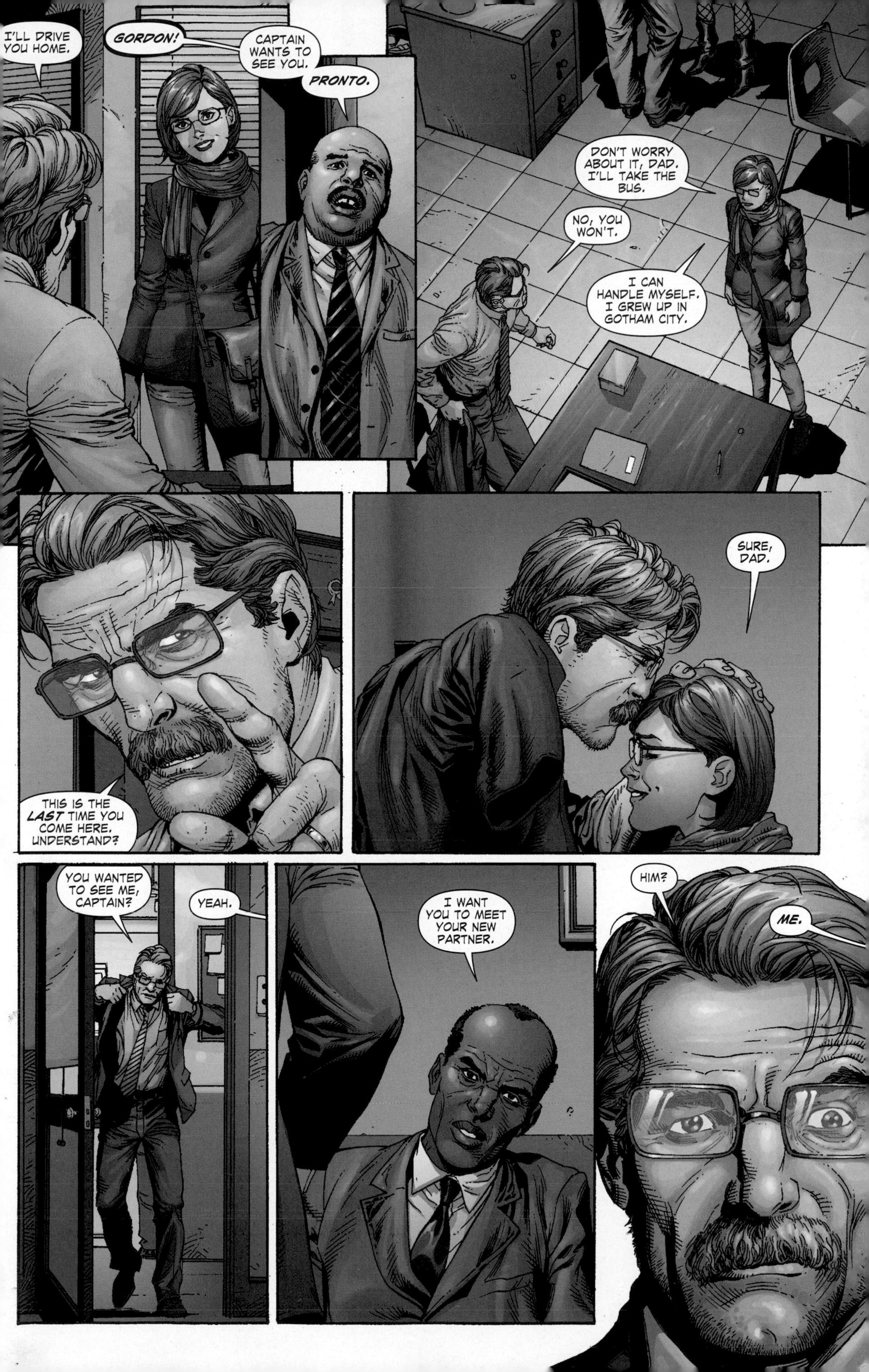
I'LL DRIVE YOU HOME.
GORDON!
CAPTAIN WANTS TO SEE YOU.
PRONTO.
DON'T WORRY ABOUT IT, DAD. I'LL TAKE THE BUS.
NO, YOU WON'T.
I CAN HANDLE MYSELF. I GREW UP IN GOTHAM CITY.
THIS IS THE LAST TIME YOU COME HERE. UNDERSTAND?
SURE, DAD.
YOU WANTED TO SEE ME, CAPTAIN?
YEAH.
I WANT YOU TO MEET YOUR NEW PARTNER.
HIM?
ME.

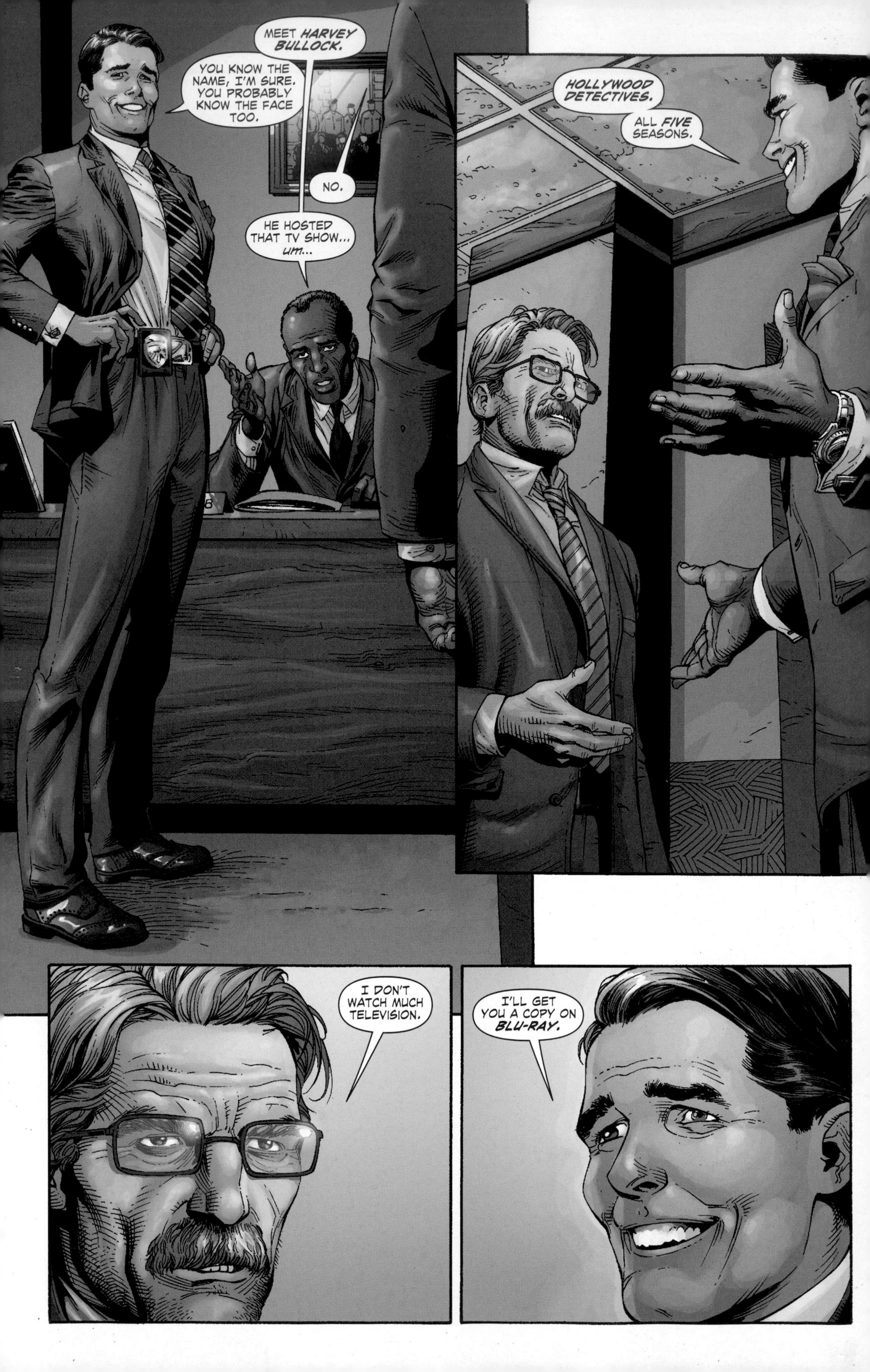

MEET HARVEY BULLOCK.
YOU KNOW THE NAME, I'M SURE. YOU PROBABLY KNOW THE FACE TOO.
NO.
HE HOSTED THAT TV SHOW... UM...
HOLLYWOOD DETECTIVES.
ALL FIVE SEASONS.
I DON'T WATCH MUCH TELEVISION.
I'LL GET YOU A COPY ON BLU-RAY.

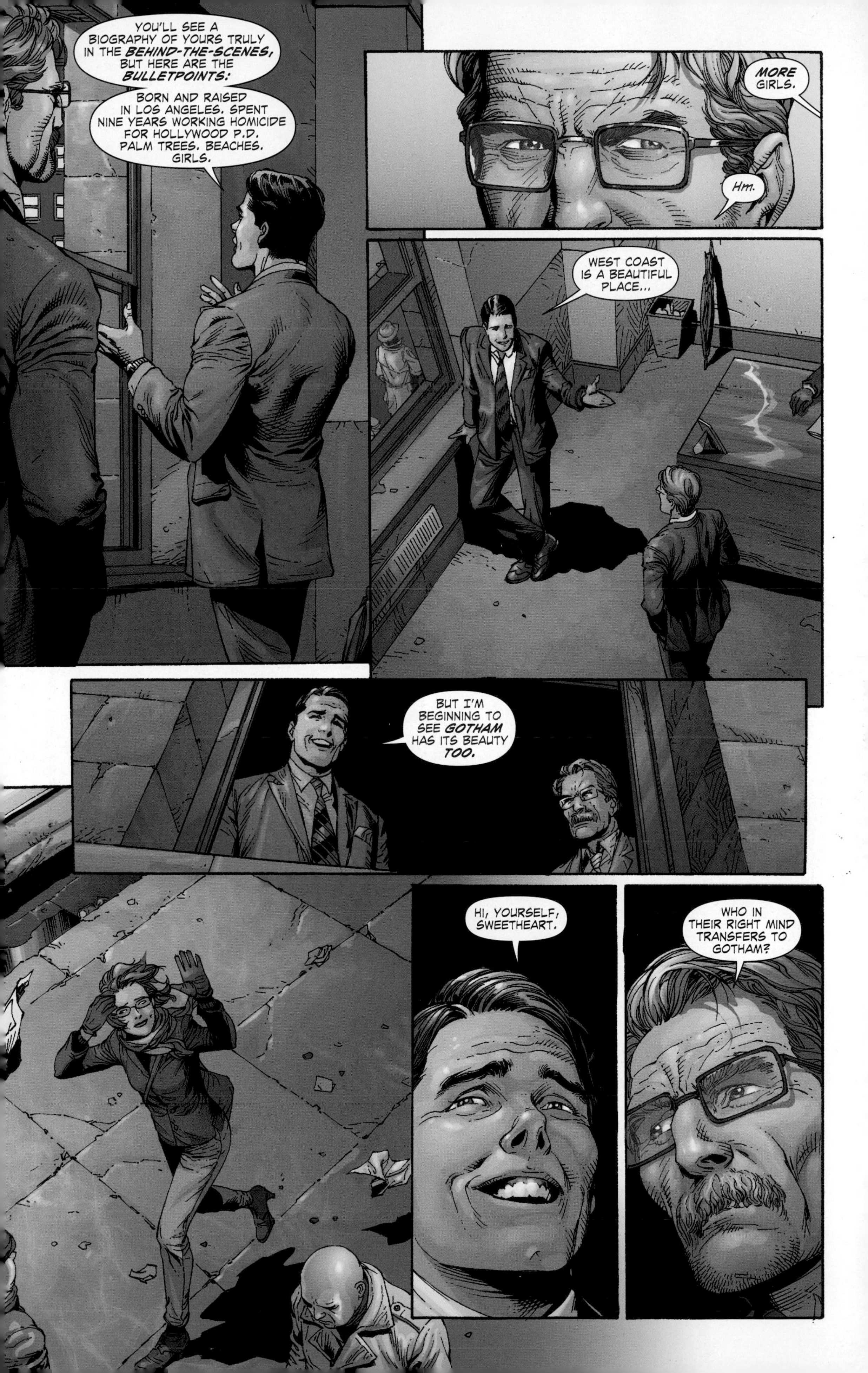
YOU'LL SEE A BIOGRAPHY OF YOURS TRULY IN THE *BEHIND-THE-SCENES,* BUT HERE ARE THE *BULLETPOINTS:*
BORN AND RAISED IN LOS ANGELES. SPENT NINE YEARS WORKING HOMICIDE FOR HOLLYWOOD P.D. PALM TREES. BEACHES. GIRLS.
MORE GIRLS.
Hm.
WEST COAST IS A BEAUTIFUL PLACE...
BUT I'M BEGINNING TO SEE *GOTHAM* HAS ITS BEAUTY *TOO.*
HI, YOURSELF, SWEETHEART.
WHO IN THEIR RIGHT MIND TRANSFERS TO GOTHAM?

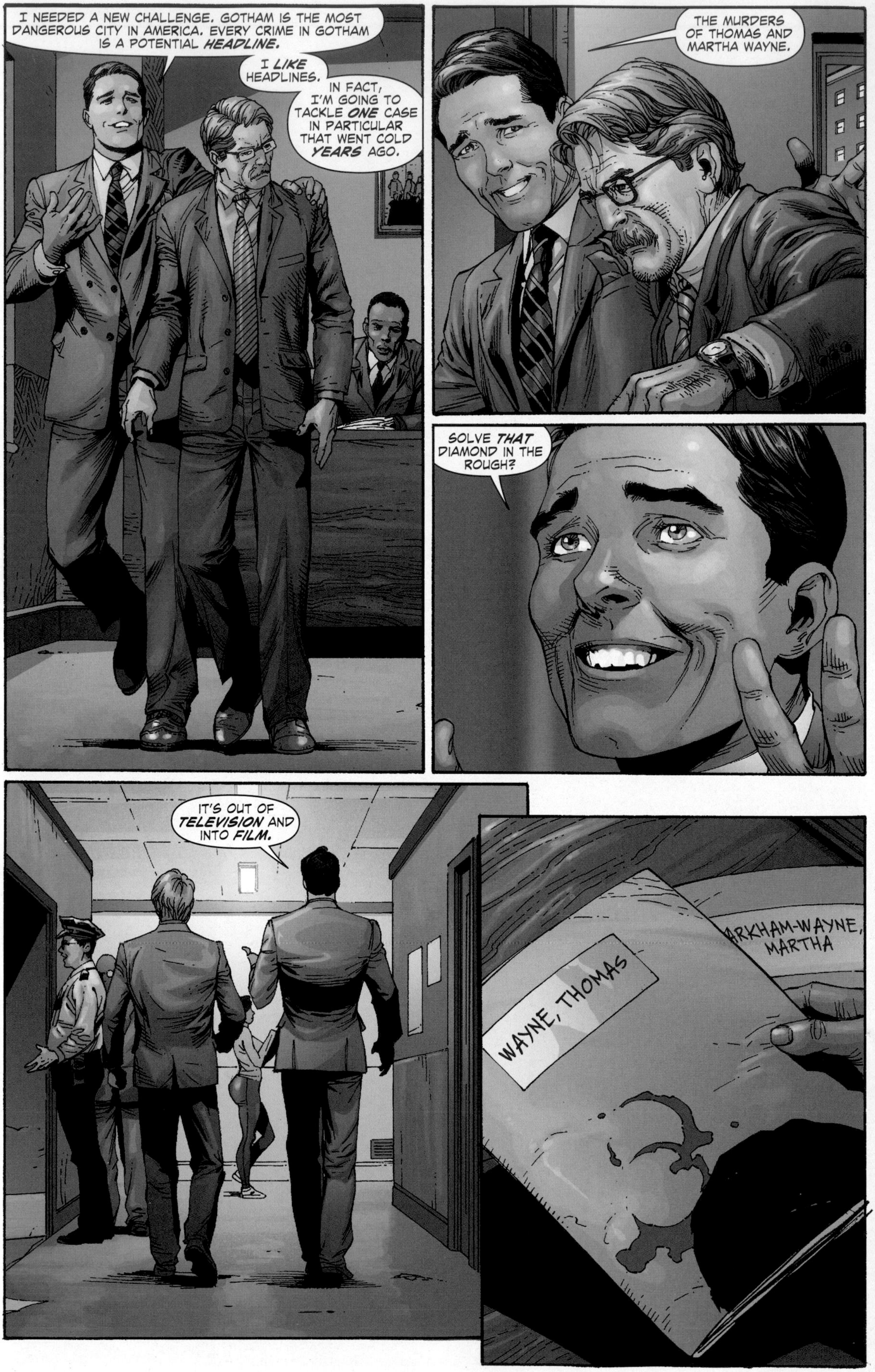
I NEEDED A NEW CHALLENGE. GOTHAM IS THE MOST DANGEROUS CITY IN AMERICA. EVERY CRIME IN GOTHAM IS A POTENTIAL HEADLINE.
I LIKE HEADLINES.
IN FACT, I'M GOING TO TACKLE ONE CASE IN PARTICULAR THAT WENT COLD YEARS AGO.
THE MURDERS OF THOMAS AND MARTHA WAYNE.
SOLVE THAT DIAMOND IN THE ROUGH?
IT'S OUT OF TELEVISION AND INTO FILM.
WAYNE, THOMAS
ARKHAM-WAYNE, MARTHA

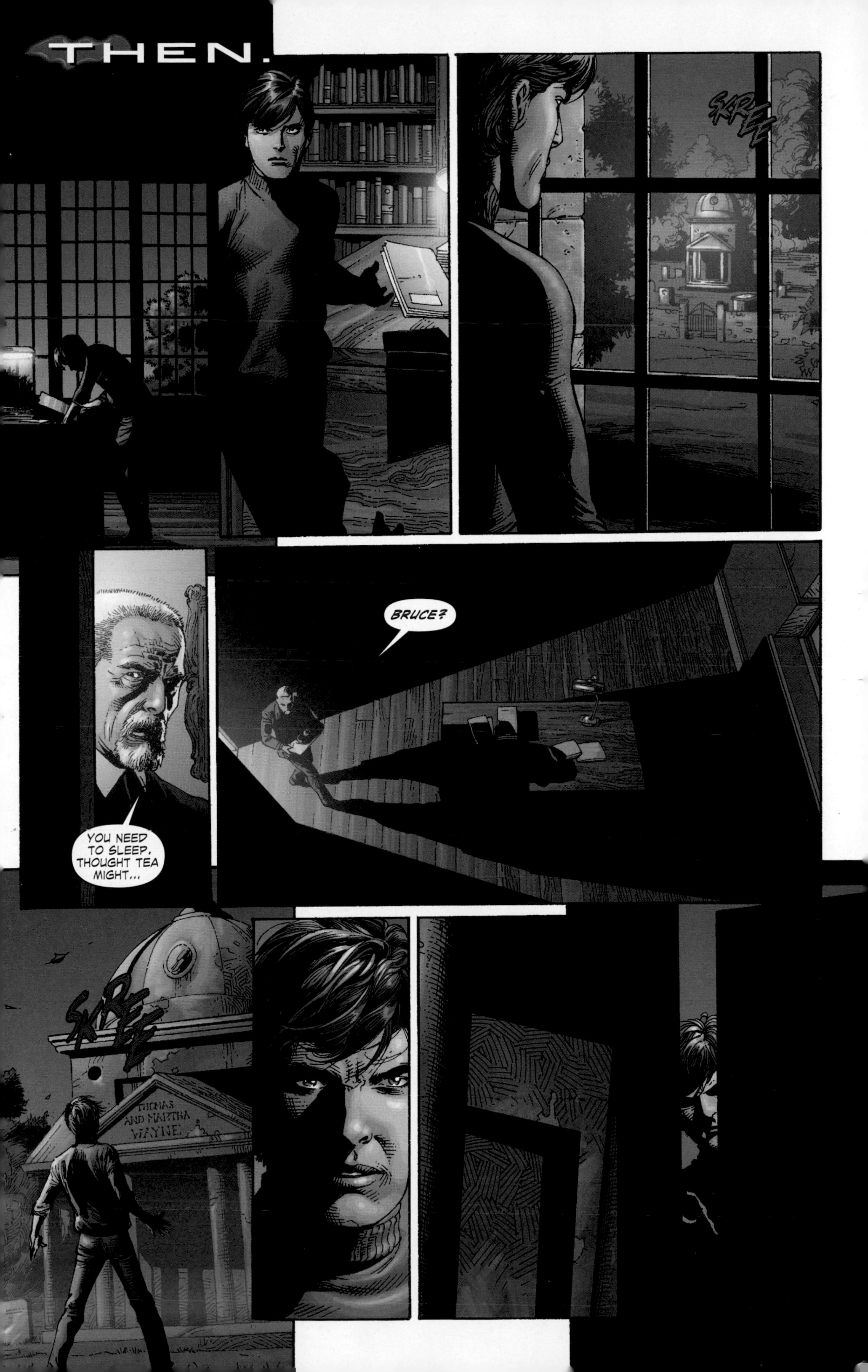
THEN.
SKREE
BRUCE?
YOU NEED TO SLEEP. THOUGHT TEA MIGHT...
SKREE
THOMAS AND MARTHA WAYNE

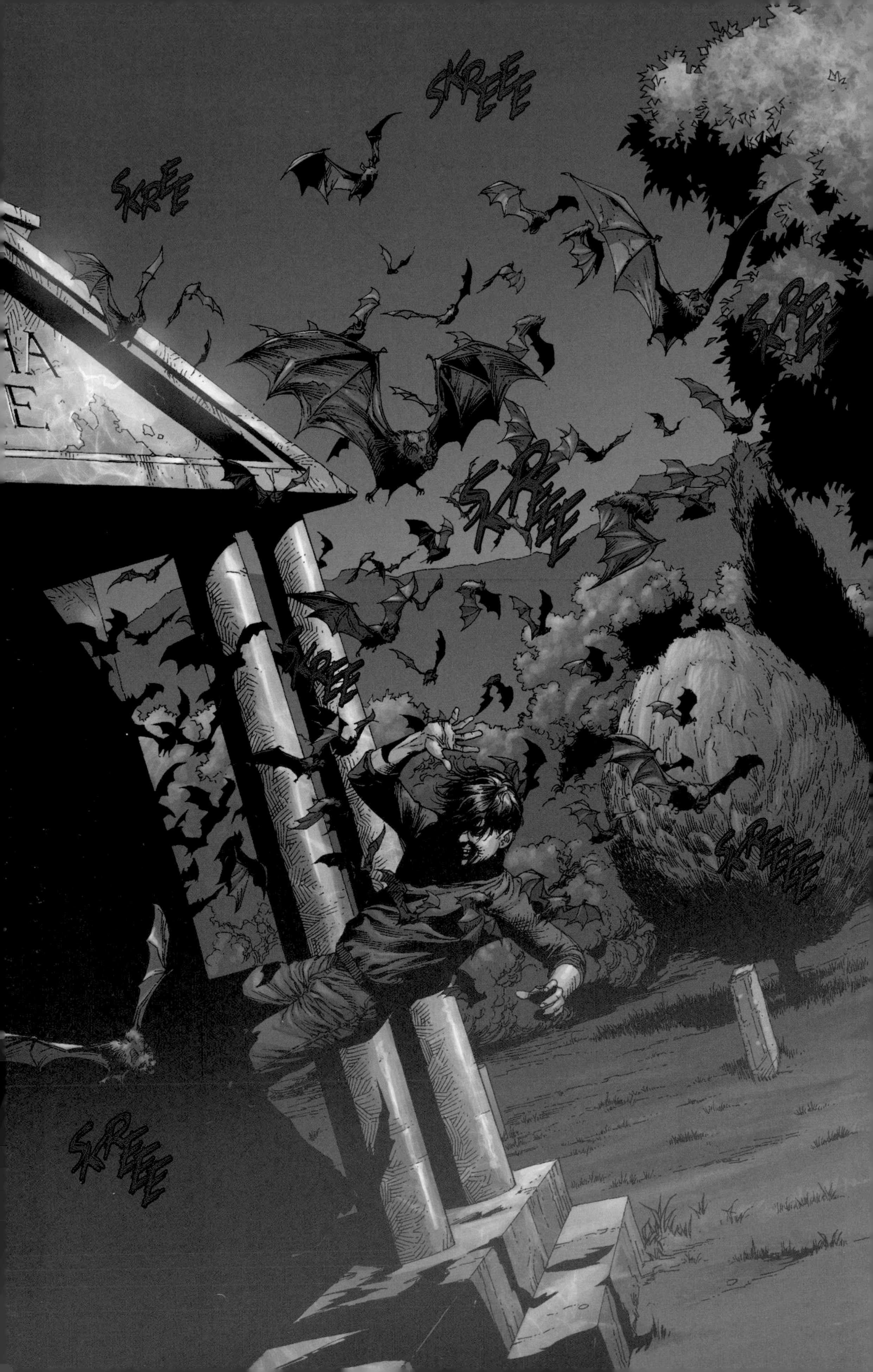

SKREEE
SKREE
SKREE
SKREEE
SKREEE
SKREEEE
SKREEE

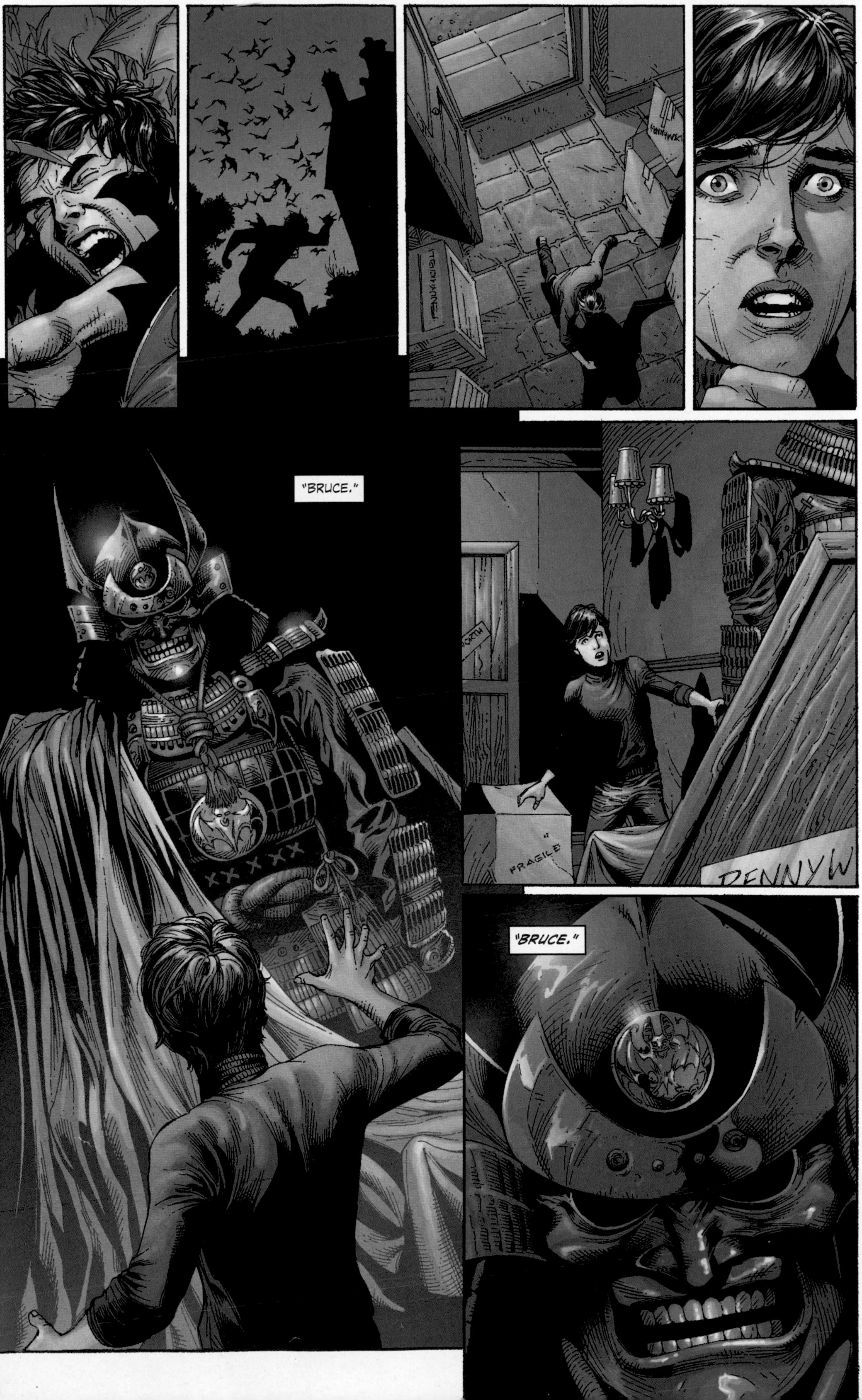
"BRUCE."
FRAGILE
PENNYW
"BRUCE."

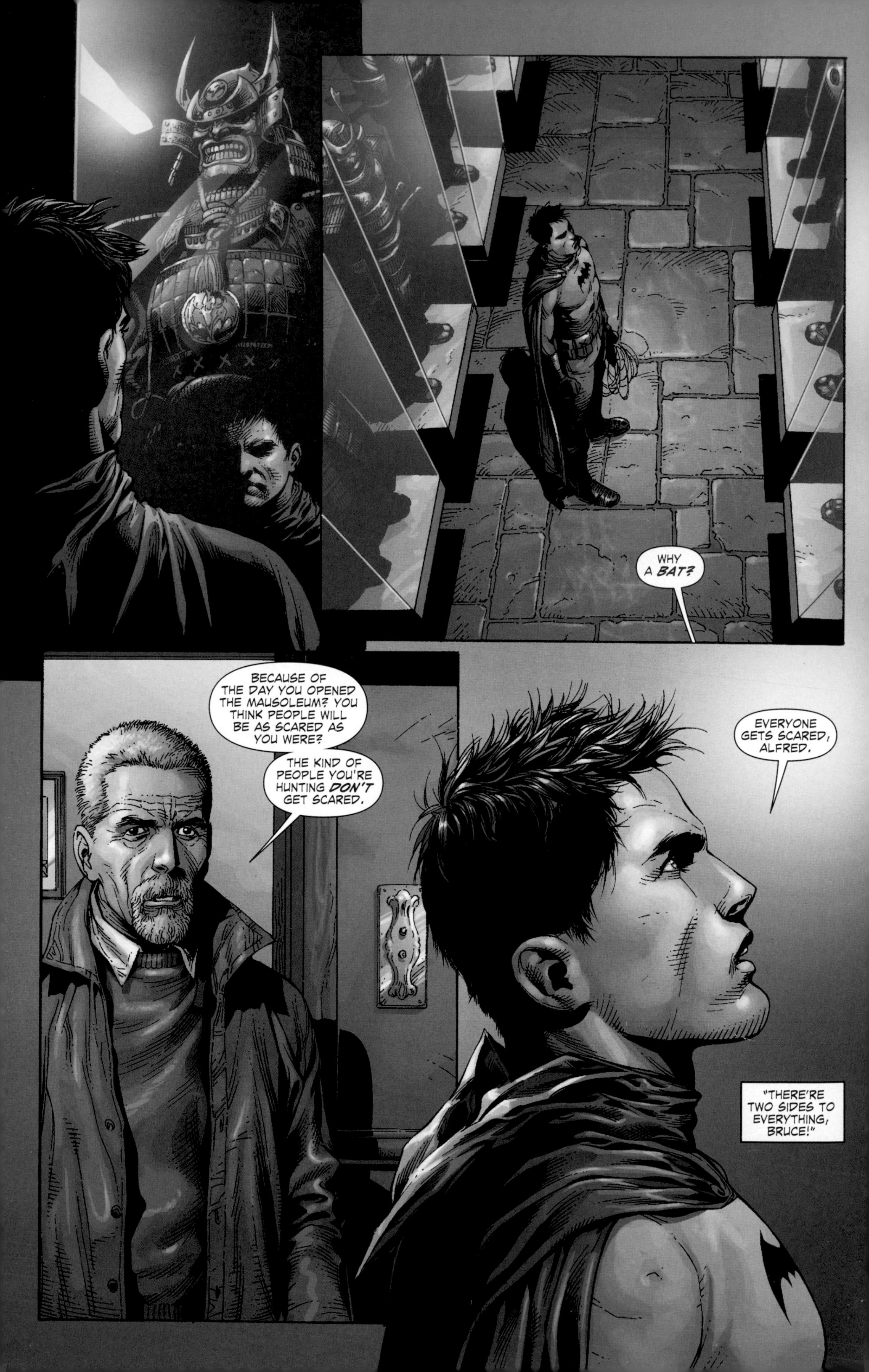
WHY A BAT?
BECAUSE OF THE DAY YOU OPENED THE MAUSOLEUM? YOU THINK PEOPLE WILL BE AS SCARED AS YOU WERE?
THE KIND OF PEOPLE YOU'RE HUNTING DON'T GET SCARED.
EVERYONE GETS SCARED, ALFRED.
"THERE'RE TWO SIDES TO EVERYTHING, BRUCE!"

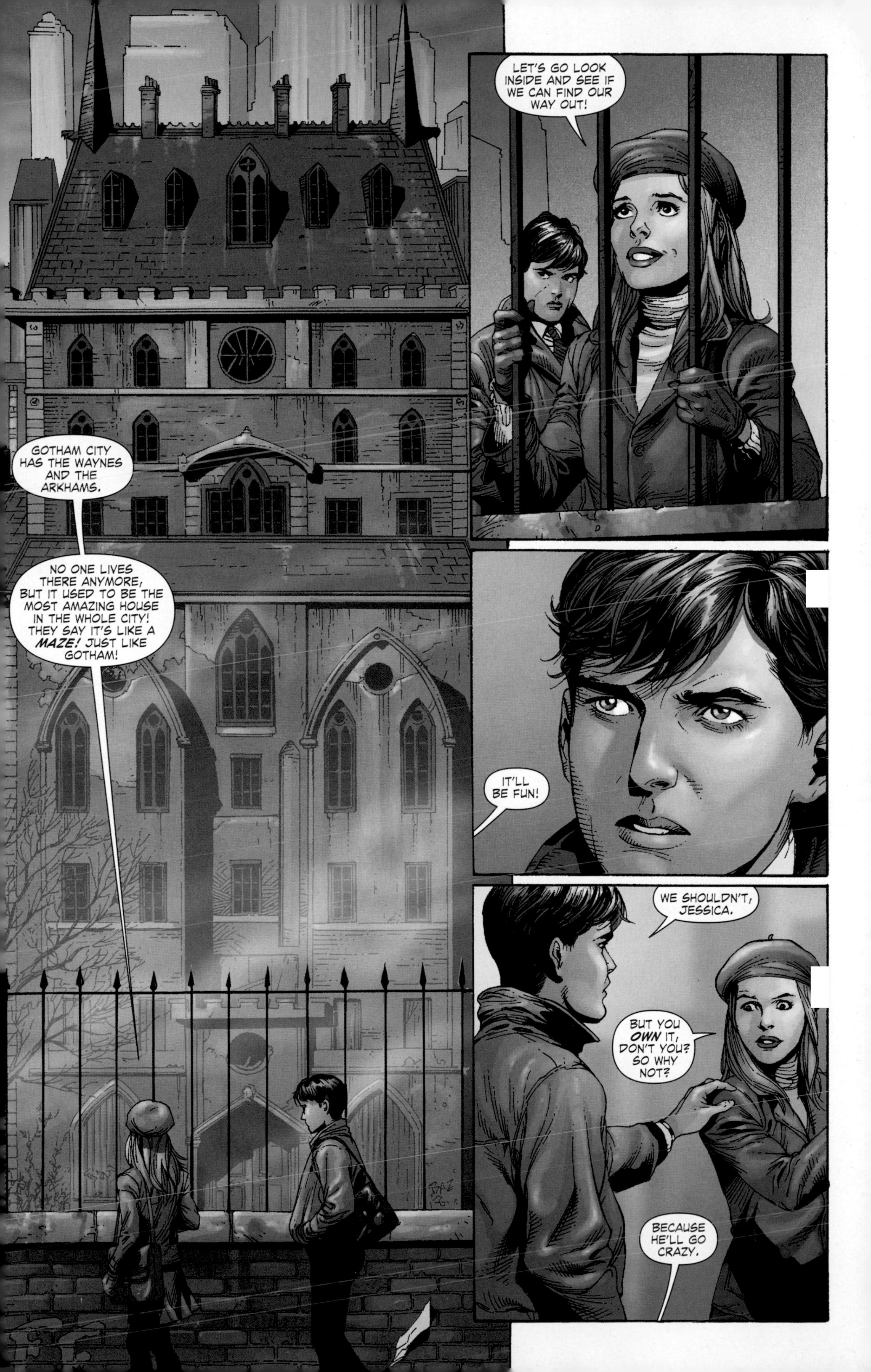
GOTHAM CITY HAS THE WAYNES AND THE ARKHAMS.
NO ONE LIVES THERE ANYMORE, BUT IT USED TO BE THE MOST AMAZING HOUSE IN THE WHOLE CITY! THEY SAY IT'S LIKE A *MAZE!* JUST LIKE GOTHAM!
LET'S GO LOOK INSIDE AND SEE IF WE CAN FIND OUR WAY OUT!
IT'LL BE FUN!
WE SHOULDN'T, JESSICA.
BUT YOU *OWN* IT, DON'T YOU? SO WHY NOT?
BECAUSE HE'LL GO CRAZY.

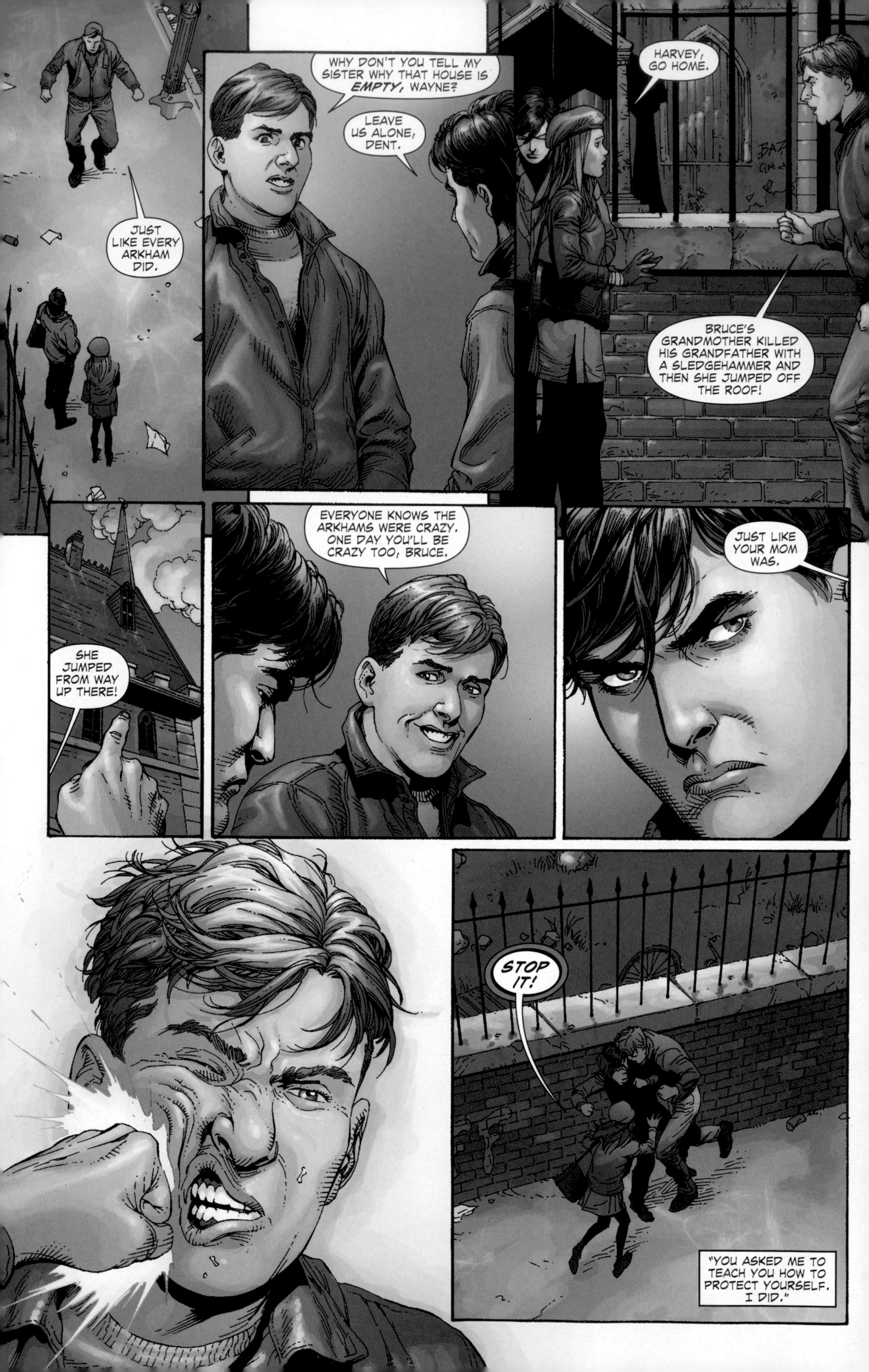
JUST LIKE EVERY ARKHAM DID.
WHY DON'T YOU TELL MY SISTER WHY THAT HOUSE IS EMPTY, WAYNE?
LEAVE US ALONE, DENT.
HARVEY, GO HOME.
BRUCE'S GRANDMOTHER KILLED HIS GRANDFATHER WITH A SLEDGEHAMMER AND THEN SHE JUMPED OFF THE ROOF!
SHE JUMPED FROM WAY UP THERE!
EVERYONE KNOWS THE ARKHAMS WERE CRAZY. ONE DAY YOU'LL BE CRAZY TOO, BRUCE.
JUST LIKE YOUR MOM WAS.
STOP IT!
"YOU ASKED ME TO TEACH YOU HOW TO PROTECT YOURSELF. I DID."

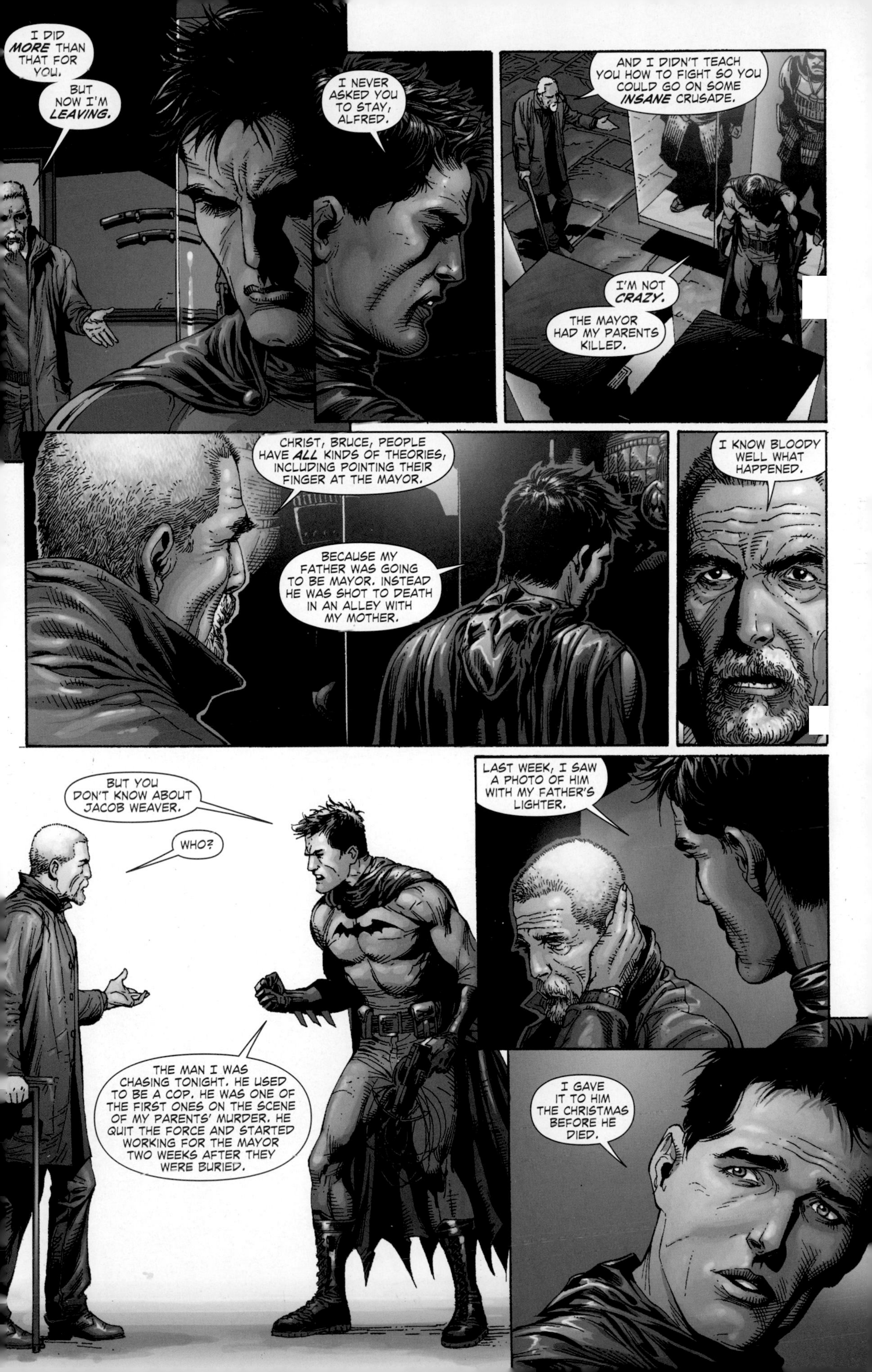
I DID MORE THAN THAT FOR YOU.
BUT NOW I'M LEAVING.
I NEVER ASKED YOU TO STAY, ALFRED.
AND I DIDN'T TEACH YOU HOW TO FIGHT SO YOU COULD GO ON SOME INSANE CRUSADE.
I'M NOT CRAZY.
THE MAYOR HAD MY PARENTS KILLED.
CHRIST, BRUCE, PEOPLE HAVE ALL KINDS OF THEORIES, INCLUDING POINTING THEIR FINGER AT THE MAYOR.
BECAUSE MY FATHER WAS GOING TO BE MAYOR. INSTEAD HE WAS SHOT TO DEATH IN AN ALLEY WITH MY MOTHER.
I KNOW BLOODY WELL WHAT HAPPENED.
BUT YOU DON'T KNOW ABOUT JACOB WEAVER.
WHO?
THE MAN I WAS CHASING TONIGHT. HE USED TO BE A COP. HE WAS ONE OF THE FIRST ONES ON THE SCENE OF MY PARENTS' MURDER. HE QUIT THE FORCE AND STARTED WORKING FOR THE MAYOR TWO WEEKS AFTER THEY WERE BURIED.
LAST WEEK, I SAW A PHOTO OF HIM WITH MY FATHER'S LIGHTER.
I GAVE IT TO HIM THE CHRISTMAS BEFORE HE DIED.

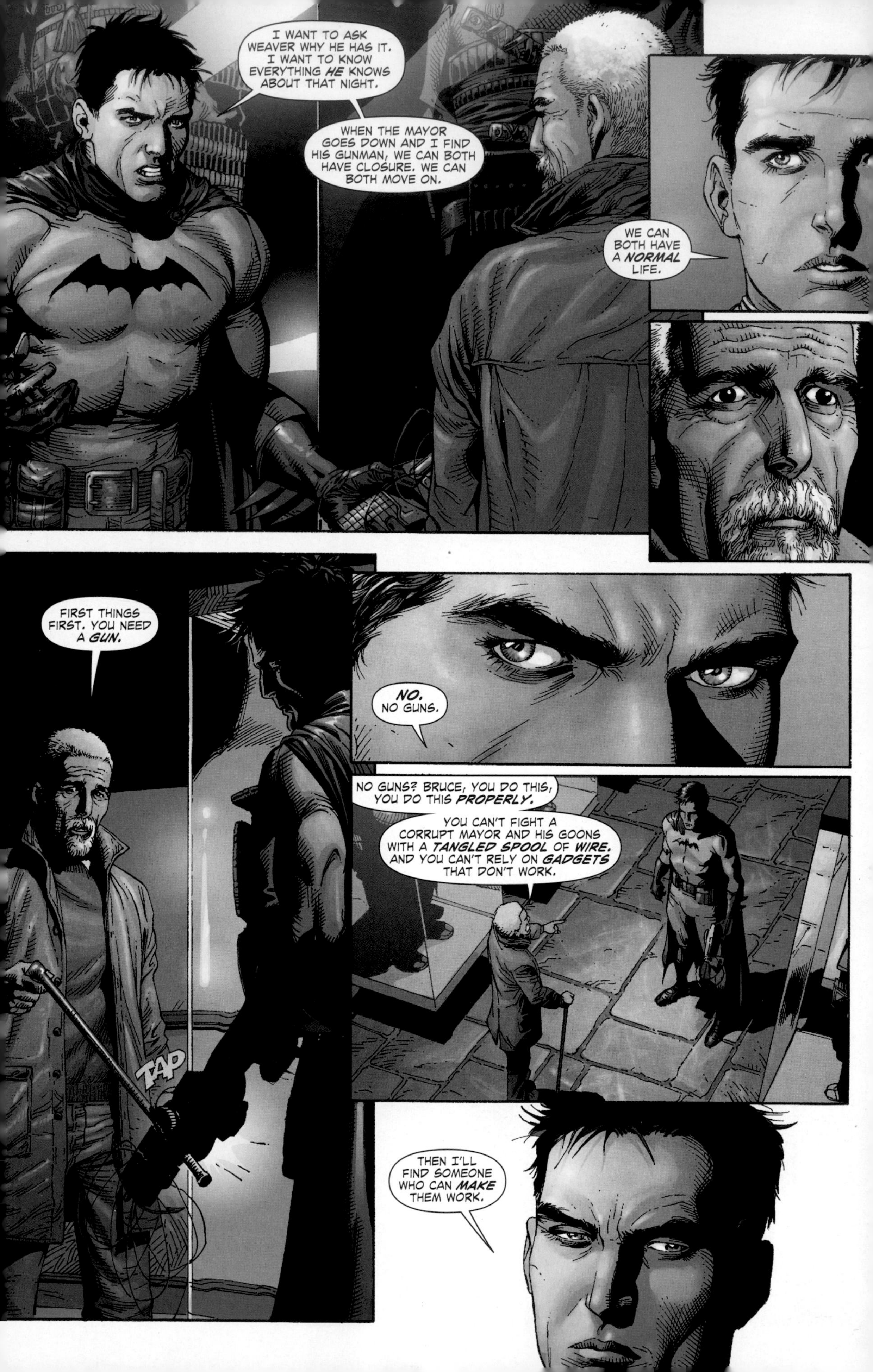
I WANT TO ASK WEAVER WHY HE HAS IT. I WANT TO KNOW EVERYTHING HE KNOWS ABOUT THAT NIGHT.
WHEN THE MAYOR GOES DOWN AND I FIND HIS GUNMAN, WE CAN BOTH HAVE CLOSURE. WE CAN BOTH MOVE ON.
WE CAN BOTH HAVE A NORMAL LIFE.
FIRST THINGS FIRST. YOU NEED A GUN.
TAP
NO. NO GUNS.
NO GUNS? BRUCE, YOU DO THIS, YOU DO THIS PROPERLY.
YOU CAN'T FIGHT A CORRUPT MAYOR AND HIS GOONS WITH A TANGLED SPOOL OF WIRE. AND YOU CAN'T RELY ON GADGETS THAT DON'T WORK.
THEN I'LL FIND SOMEONE WHO CAN MAKE THEM WORK.

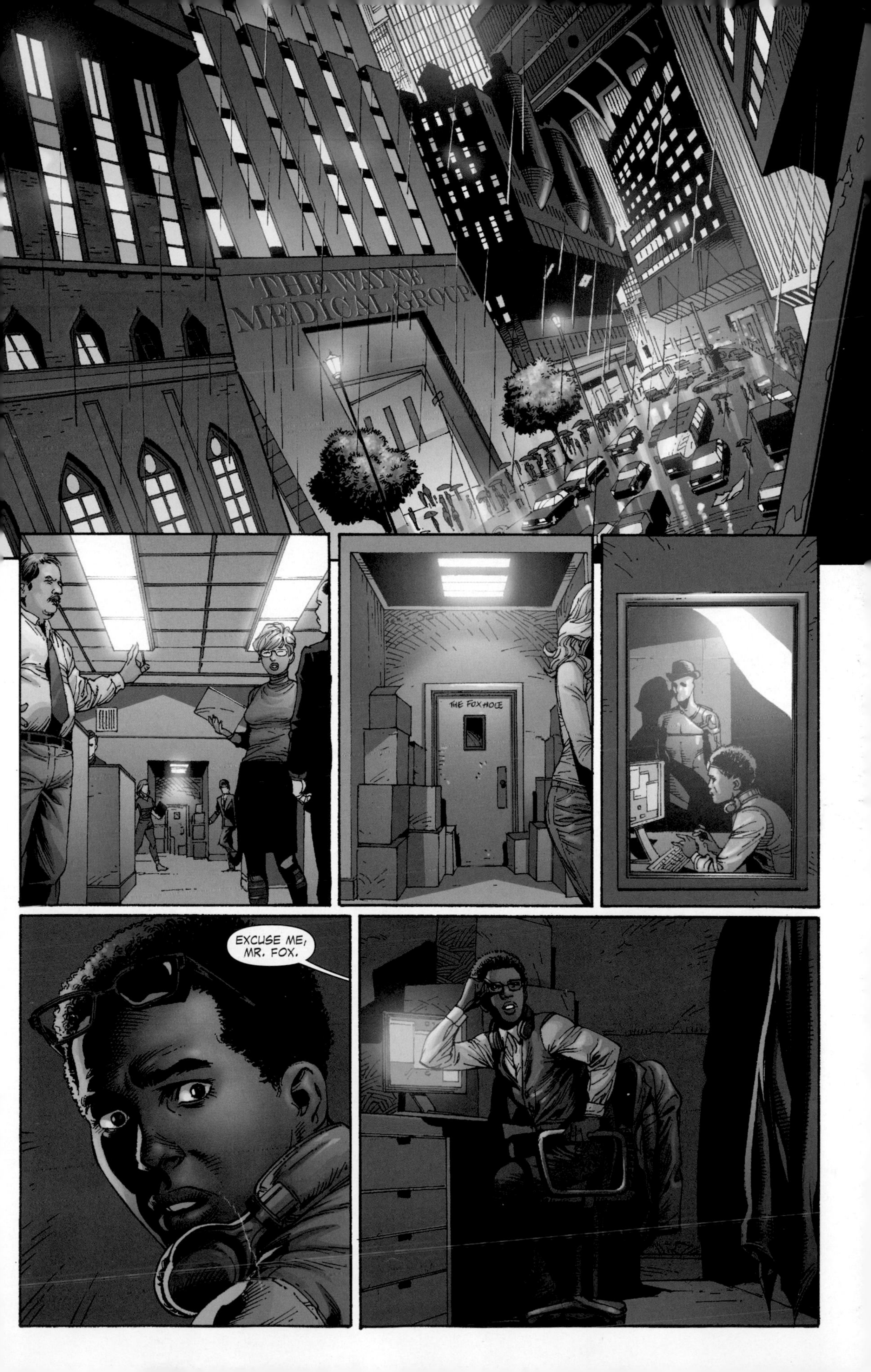
THE WAYNE MEDICAL GROUP
THE FOX HOLE
EXCUSE ME, MR. FOX.

YOU... YOU'RE BRUCE WAYNE.

YES.

ARE YOU LOOKING FOR THE WAYNE BOARDROOM? IT'S, *uh*, IT'S ON THE TOP FLOOR.

THIS IS DESIGN AND ENGINEERING.

I KNOW.

DID I DO SOMETHING WRONG? AM I FIRED? I SWEAR I DIDN'T THINK THE SPOT WAS *RESERVED*. YOU HAVEN'T EVER PARKED THERE, SO I THOUGHT--

I NEED YOU TO DO SOMETHING FOR ME.

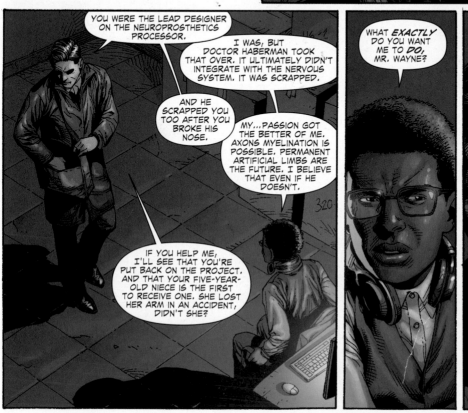

YOU WERE THE LEAD DESIGNER ON THE NEUROPROSTHETICS PROCESSOR.

I WAS, BUT DOCTOR HABERMAN TOOK THAT OVER. IT ULTIMATELY DIDN'T INTEGRATE WITH THE NERVOUS SYSTEM. IT WAS SCRAPPED.

AND HE SCRAPPED YOU TOO AFTER YOU BROKE HIS NOSE.

MY...PASSION GOT THE BETTER OF ME. AXONS MYELINATION IS POSSIBLE. PERMANENT ARTIFICIAL LIMBS ARE THE FUTURE. I BELIEVE THAT EVEN IF HE DOESN'T.

IF YOU HELP ME, I'LL SEE THAT YOU'RE PUT BACK ON THE PROJECT. AND THAT YOUR FIVE-YEAR-OLD NIECE IS THE FIRST TO RECEIVE ONE. SHE LOST HER ARM IN AN ACCIDENT, DIDN'T SHE?

WHAT *EXACTLY* DO YOU WANT ME TO *DO*, MR. WAYNE?

I WANT YOU TO KEEP THIS BETWEEN US.

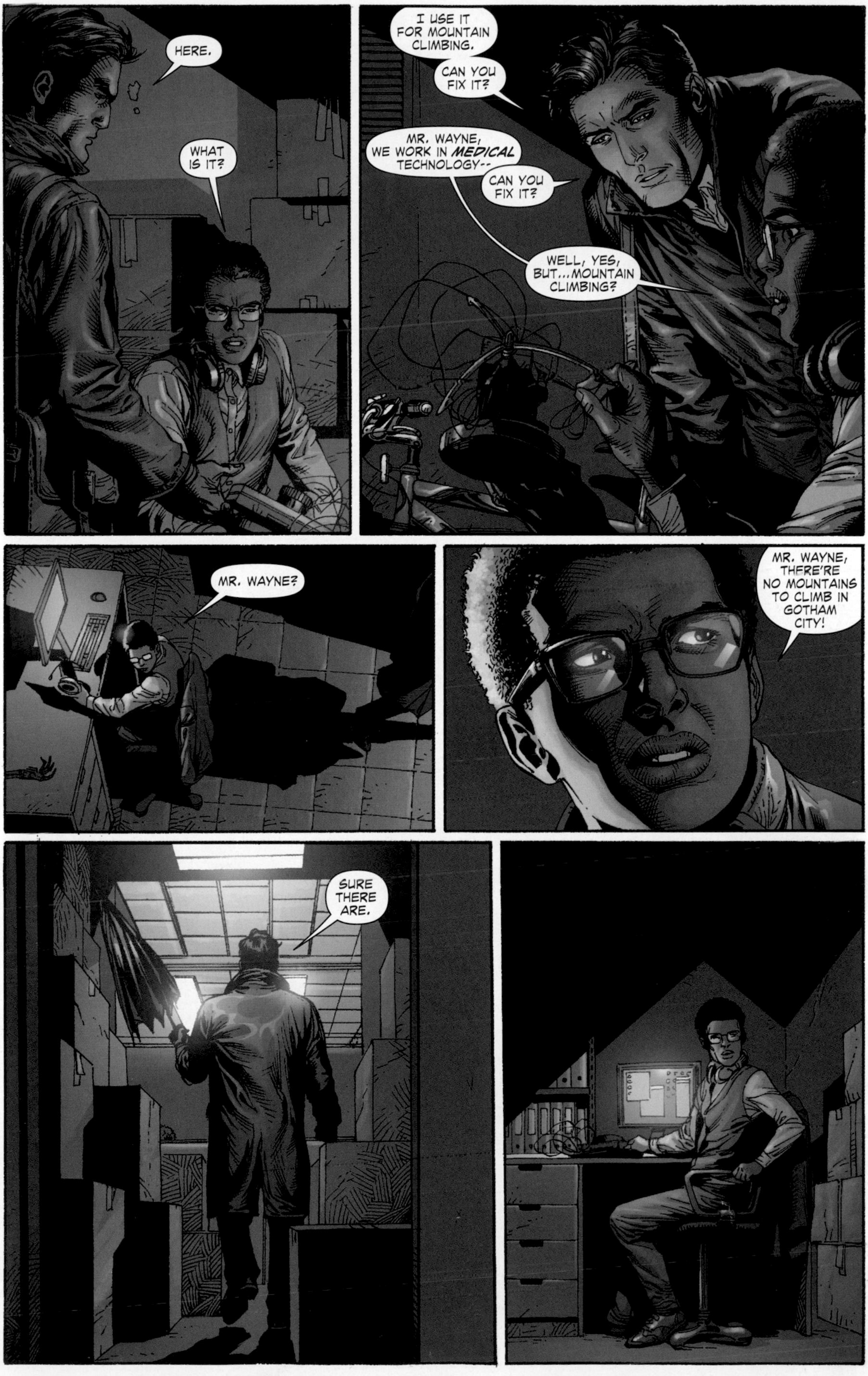
HERE.
WHAT IS IT?
I USE IT FOR MOUNTAIN CLIMBING.
CAN YOU FIX IT?
MR. WAYNE, WE WORK IN *MEDICAL* TECHNOLOGY--
CAN YOU FIX IT?
WELL, YES, BUT...MOUNTAIN CLIMBING?
MR. WAYNE?
MR. WAYNE, THERE'RE NO MOUNTAINS TO CLIMB IN GOTHAM CITY!
SURE THERE ARE.

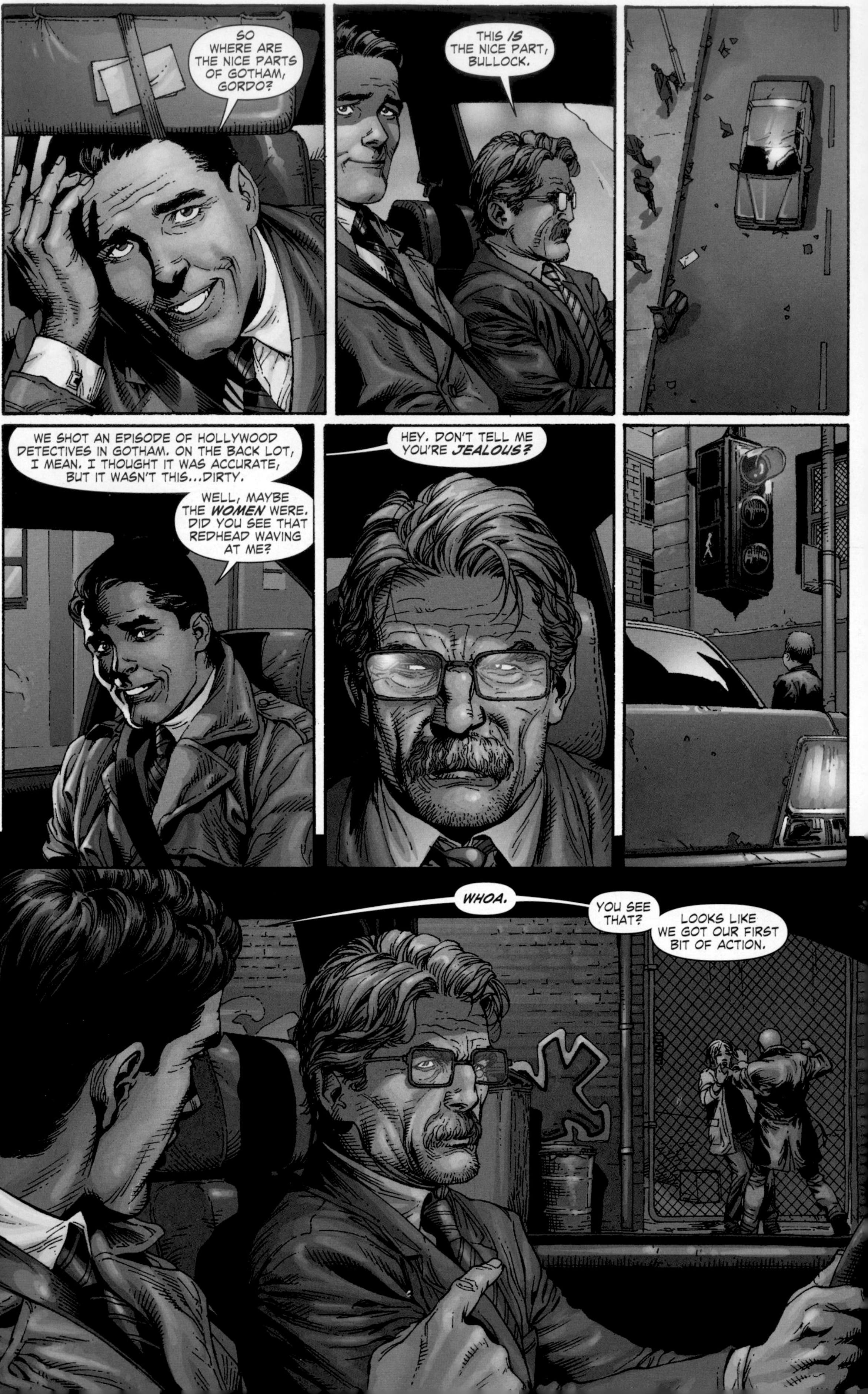
SO WHERE ARE THE NICE PARTS OF GOTHAM, GORDO?
THIS IS THE NICE PART, BULLOCK.
WE SHOT AN EPISODE OF HOLLYWOOD DETECTIVES IN GOTHAM. ON THE BACK LOT, I MEAN. I THOUGHT IT WAS ACCURATE, BUT IT WASN'T THIS...DIRTY.
WELL, MAYBE THE WOMEN WERE. DID YOU SEE THAT REDHEAD WAVING AT ME?
HEY. DON'T TELL ME YOU'RE JEALOUS?
WHOA.
YOU SEE THAT?
LOOKS LIKE WE GOT OUR FIRST BIT OF ACTION.

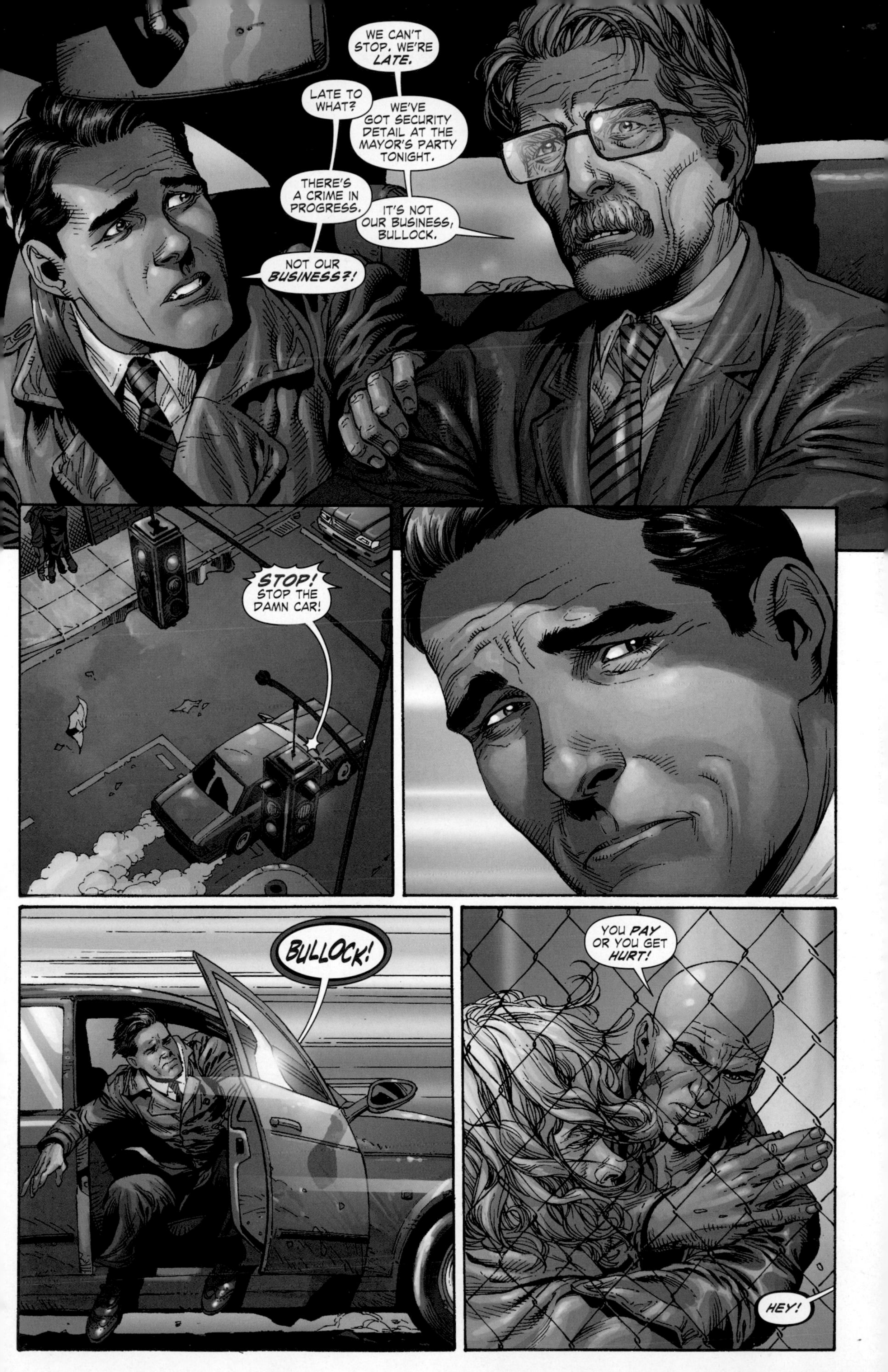
WE CAN'T STOP. WE'RE LATE.
LATE TO WHAT?
WE'VE GOT SECURITY DETAIL AT THE MAYOR'S PARTY TONIGHT.
THERE'S A CRIME IN PROGRESS.
IT'S NOT OUR BUSINESS, BULLOCK.
NOT OUR BUSINESS?!
STOP! STOP THE DAMN CAR!
BULLOCK!
YOU PAY OR YOU GET HURT!
HEY!

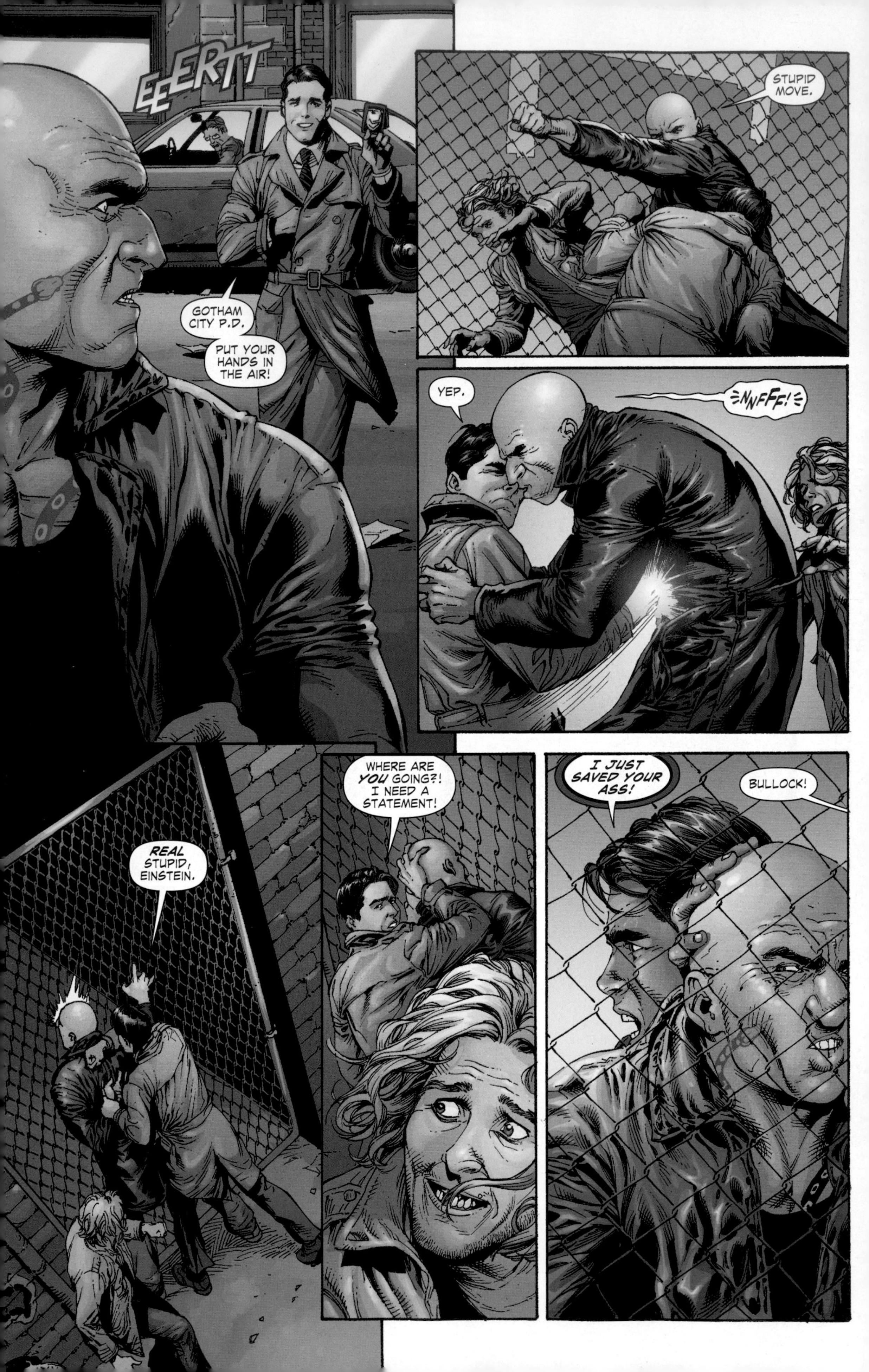
EEERTT
GOTHAM CITY P.D.
PUT YOUR HANDS IN THE AIR!
STUPID MOVE.
YEP.
NNFFF!
REAL STUPID, EINSTEIN.
WHERE ARE YOU GOING?! I NEED A STATEMENT!
I JUST SAVED YOUR ASS!
BULLOCK!

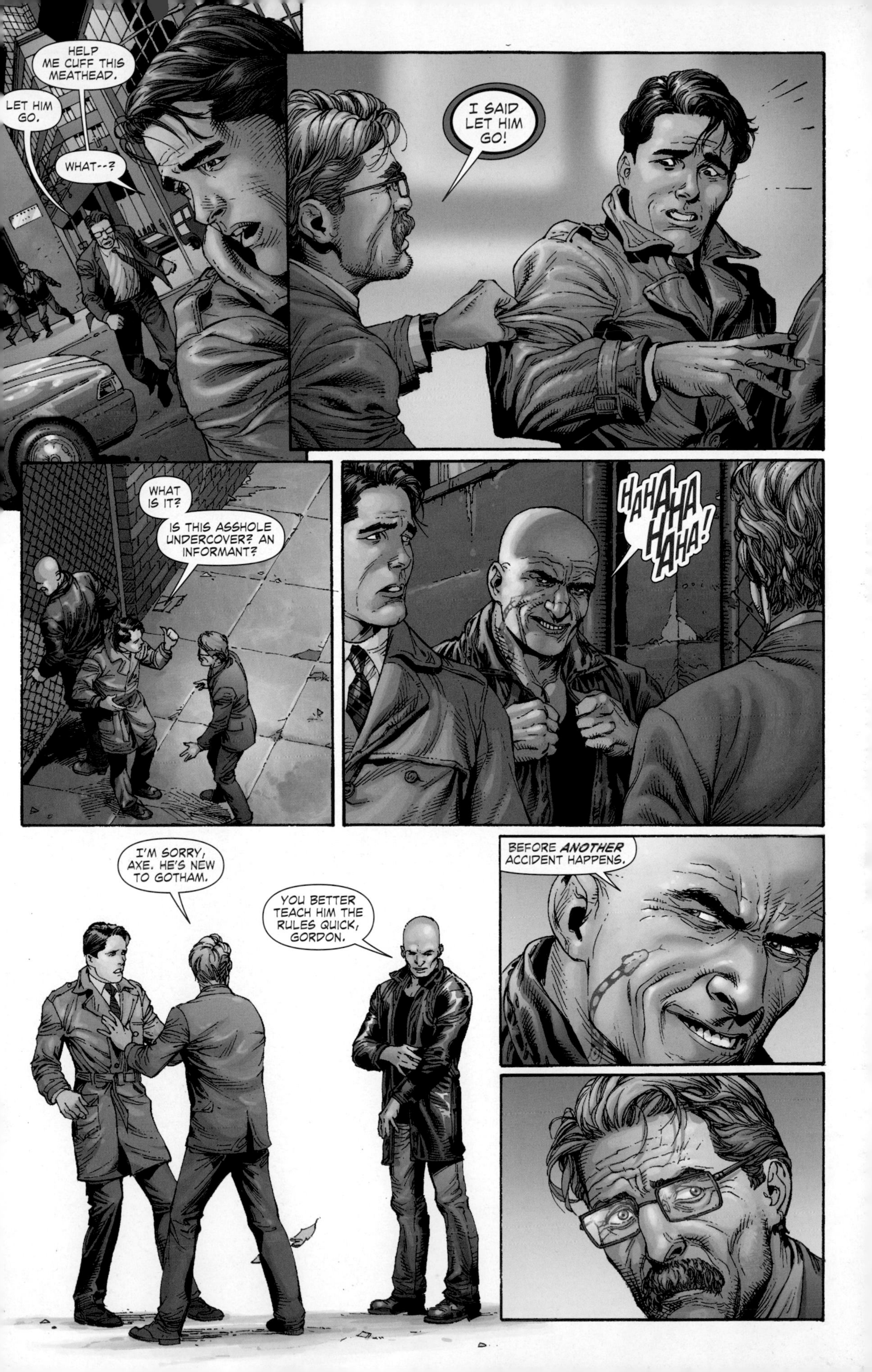
HELP ME CUFF THIS MEATHEAD.
LET HIM GO.
WHAT--?
I SAID LET HIM GO!
WHAT IS IT?
IS THIS ASSHOLE UNDERCOVER? AN INFORMANT?
HAHAHA HAHA HAHA!
I'M SORRY, AXE. HE'S NEW TO GOTHAM.
YOU BETTER TEACH HIM THE RULES QUICK, GORDON.
BEFORE ANOTHER ACCIDENT HAPPENS.

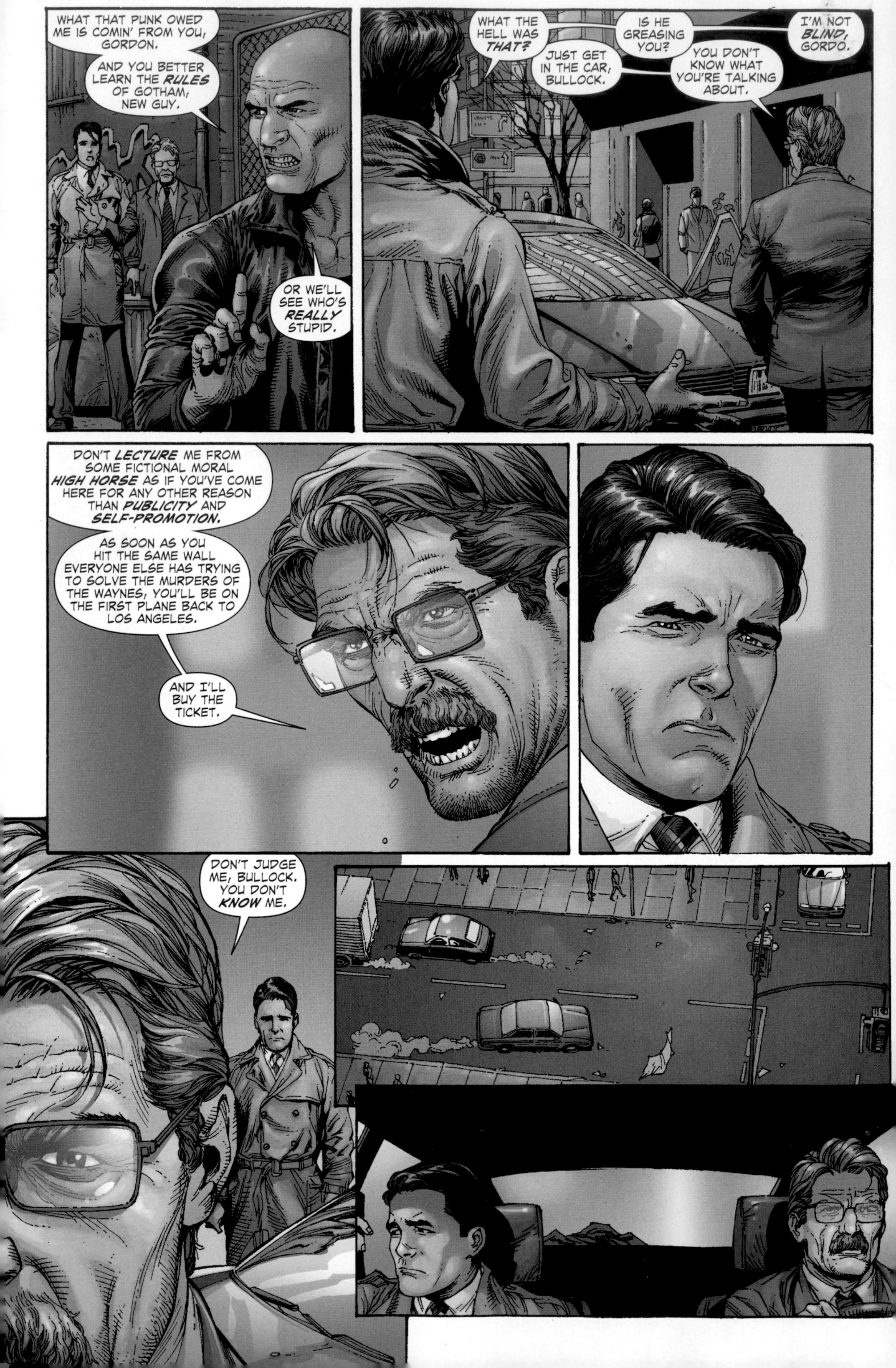
WHAT THAT PUNK OWED ME IS COMIN' FROM YOU, GORDON.
AND YOU BETTER LEARN THE RULES OF GOTHAM, NEW GUY.
OR WE'LL SEE WHO'S REALLY STUPID.
WHAT THE HELL WAS THAT?
JUST GET IN THE CAR, BULLOCK.
IS HE GREASING YOU?
YOU DON'T KNOW WHAT YOU'RE TALKING ABOUT.
I'M NOT BLIND, GORDO.
DON'T LECTURE ME FROM SOME FICTIONAL MORAL HIGH HORSE AS IF YOU'VE COME HERE FOR ANY OTHER REASON THAN PUBLICITY AND SELF-PROMOTION.
AS SOON AS YOU HIT THE SAME WALL EVERYONE ELSE HAS TRYING TO SOLVE THE MURDERS OF THE WAYNES, YOU'LL BE ON THE FIRST PLANE BACK TO LOS ANGELES.
AND I'LL BUY THE TICKET.
DON'T JUDGE ME, BULLOCK. YOU DON'T KNOW ME.

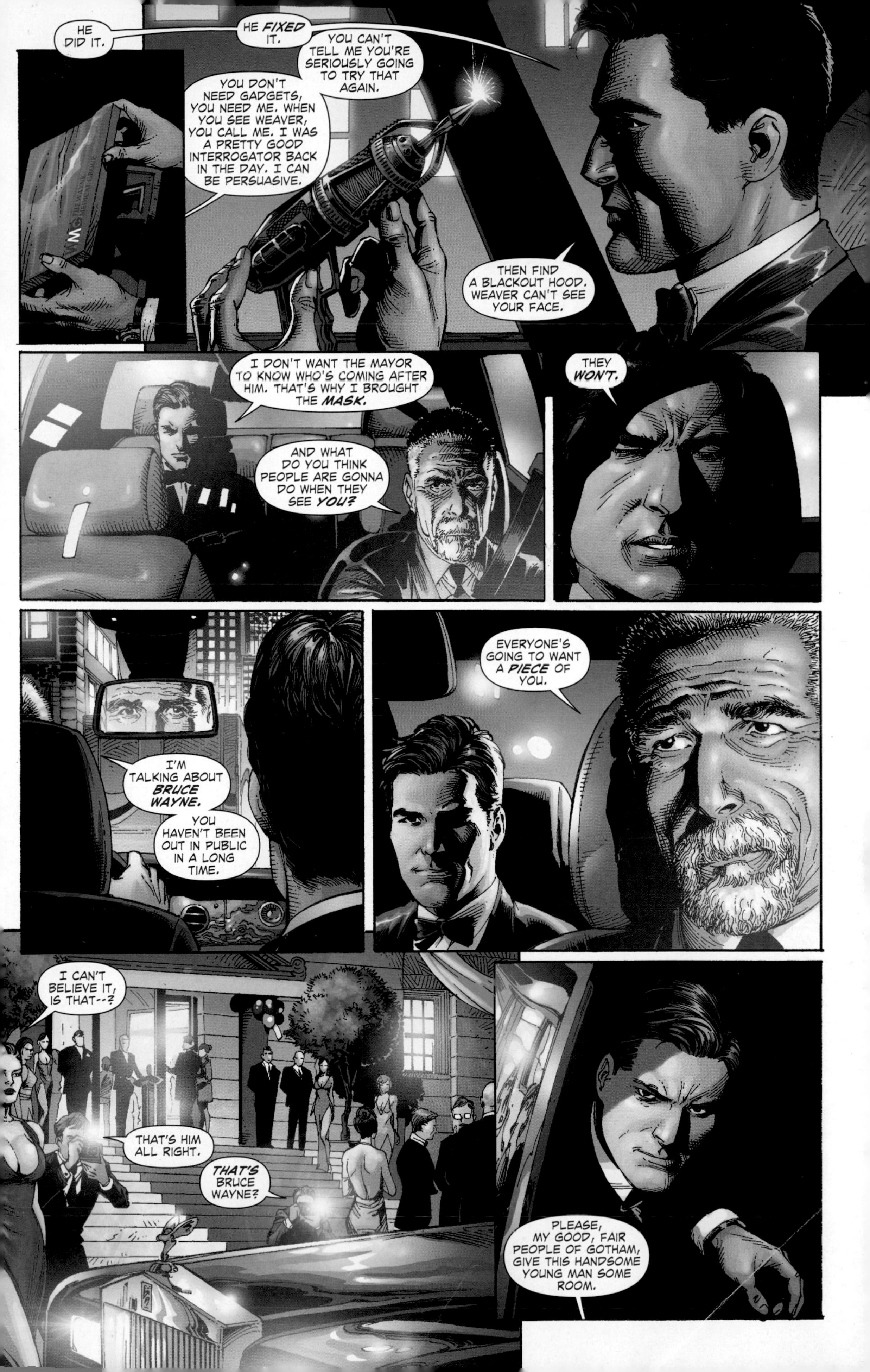

HE DID IT.
HE *FIXED* IT.
YOU CAN'T TELL ME YOU'RE SERIOUSLY GOING TO TRY THAT AGAIN.
YOU DON'T NEED GADGETS, YOU NEED ME. WHEN YOU SEE WEAVER, YOU CALL ME. I WAS A PRETTY GOOD INTERROGATOR BACK IN THE DAY. I CAN BE PERSUASIVE.
THEN FIND A BLACKOUT HOOD. WEAVER CAN'T SEE YOUR FACE.
I DON'T WANT THE MAYOR TO KNOW WHO'S COMING AFTER HIM. THAT'S WHY I BROUGHT THE *MASK.*
AND WHAT DO YOU THINK PEOPLE ARE GONNA DO WHEN THEY SEE *YOU?*
THEY *WON'T.*
I'M TALKING ABOUT *BRUCE WAYNE.*
YOU HAVEN'T BEEN OUT IN PUBLIC IN A LONG TIME.
EVERYONE'S GOING TO WANT A *PIECE* OF YOU.
I CAN'T BELIEVE IT, IS THAT--?
THAT'S HIM ALL RIGHT.
THAT'S BRUCE WAYNE?
PLEASE, MY GOOD, FAIR PEOPLE OF GOTHAM, GIVE THIS HANDSOME YOUNG MAN SOME ROOM.

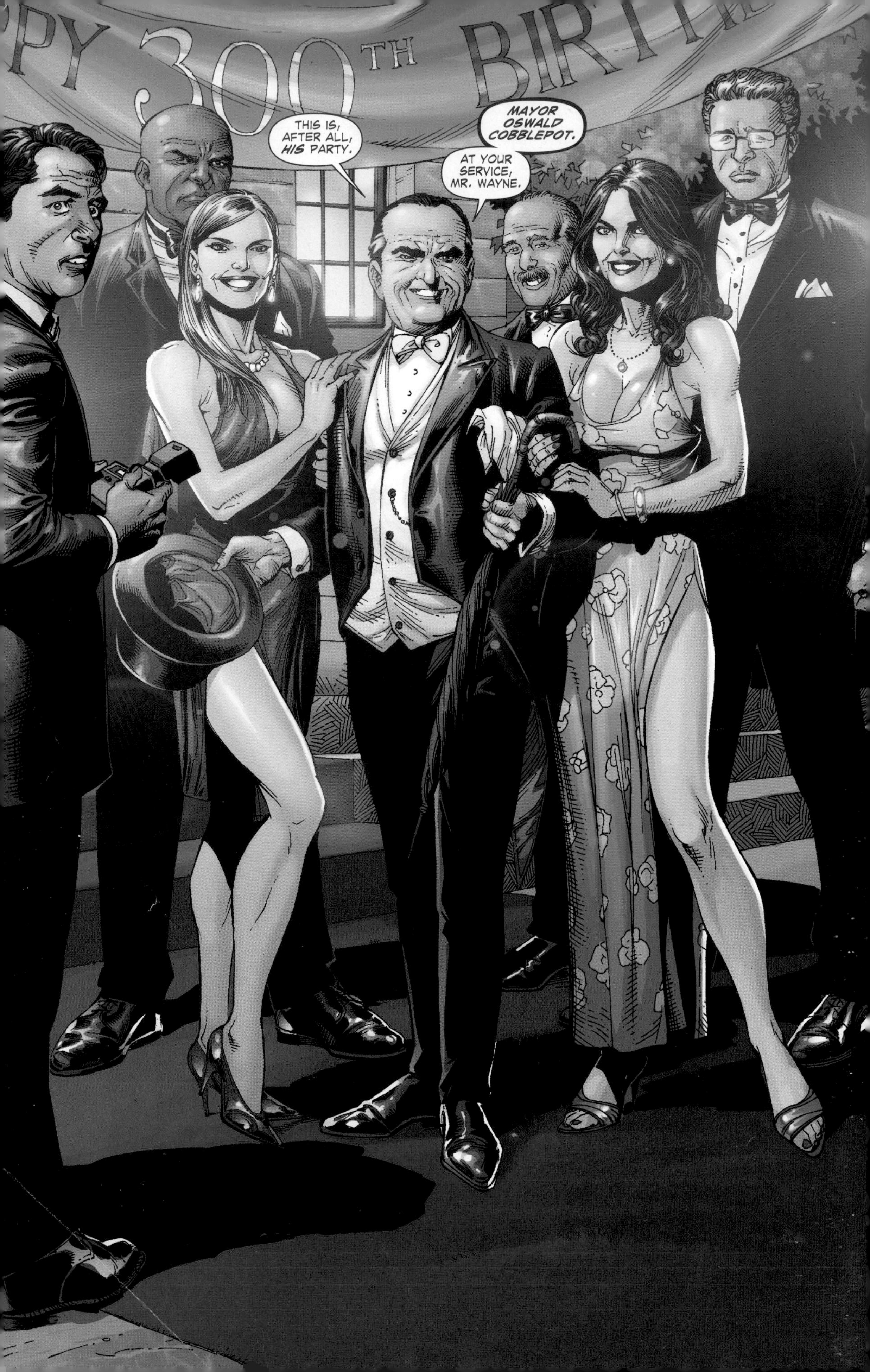

PPY 300TH BIRTH
THIS IS, AFTER ALL, HIS PARTY.
MAYOR OSWALD COBBLEPOT.
AT YOUR SERVICE, MR. WAYNE.

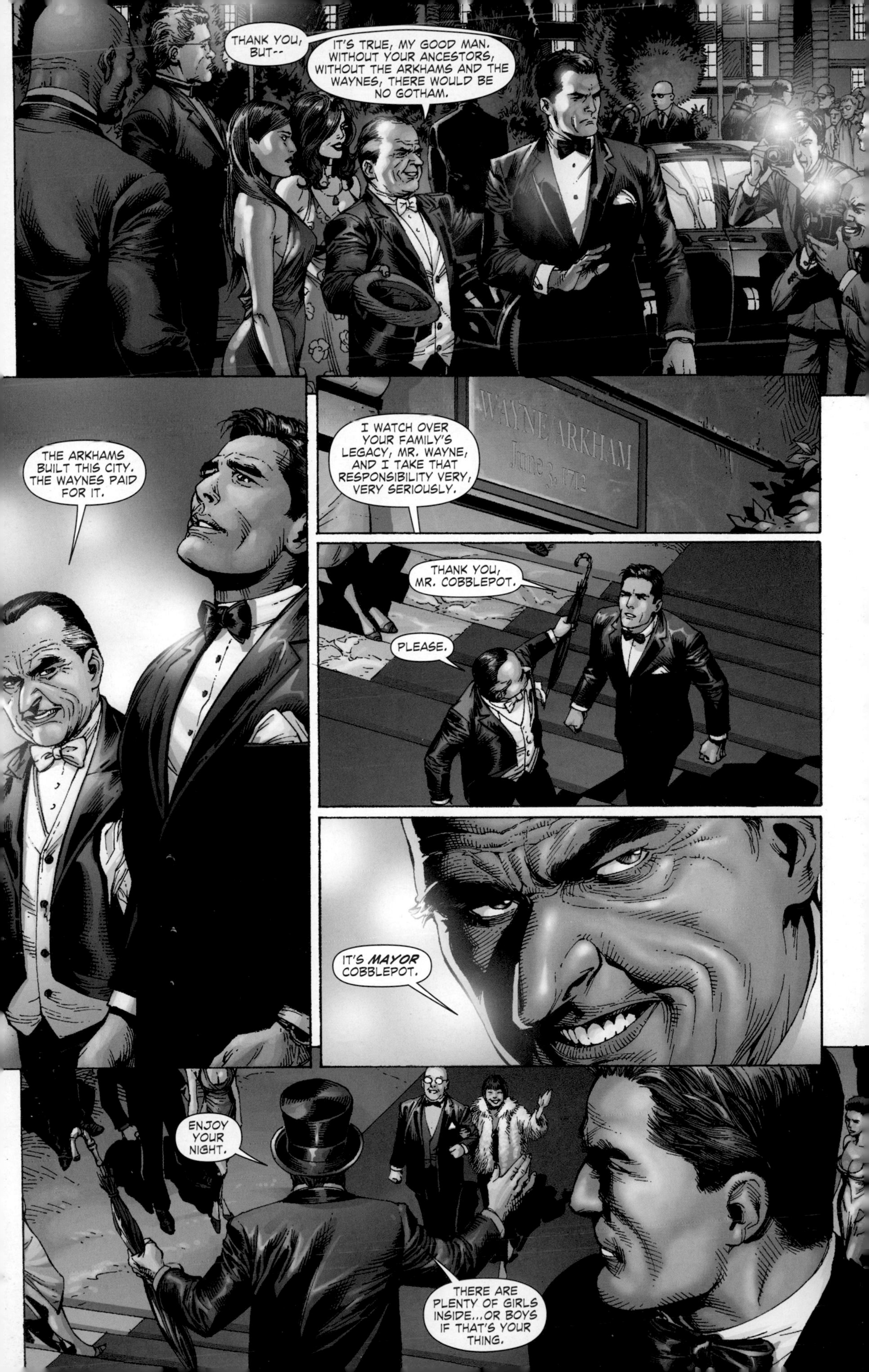
THANK YOU, BUT--
IT'S TRUE, MY GOOD MAN. WITHOUT YOUR ANCESTORS, WITHOUT THE ARKHAMS AND THE WAYNES, THERE WOULD BE NO GOTHAM.
THE ARKHAMS BUILT THIS CITY. THE WAYNES PAID FOR IT.
WAYNE ARKHAM
June 3, 1712
I WATCH OVER YOUR FAMILY'S LEGACY, MR. WAYNE, AND I TAKE THAT RESPONSIBILITY VERY, VERY SERIOUSLY.
THANK YOU, MR. COBBLEPOT.
PLEASE.
IT'S MAYOR COBBLEPOT.
ENJOY YOUR NIGHT.
THERE ARE PLENTY OF GIRLS INSIDE...OR BOYS IF THAT'S YOUR THING.

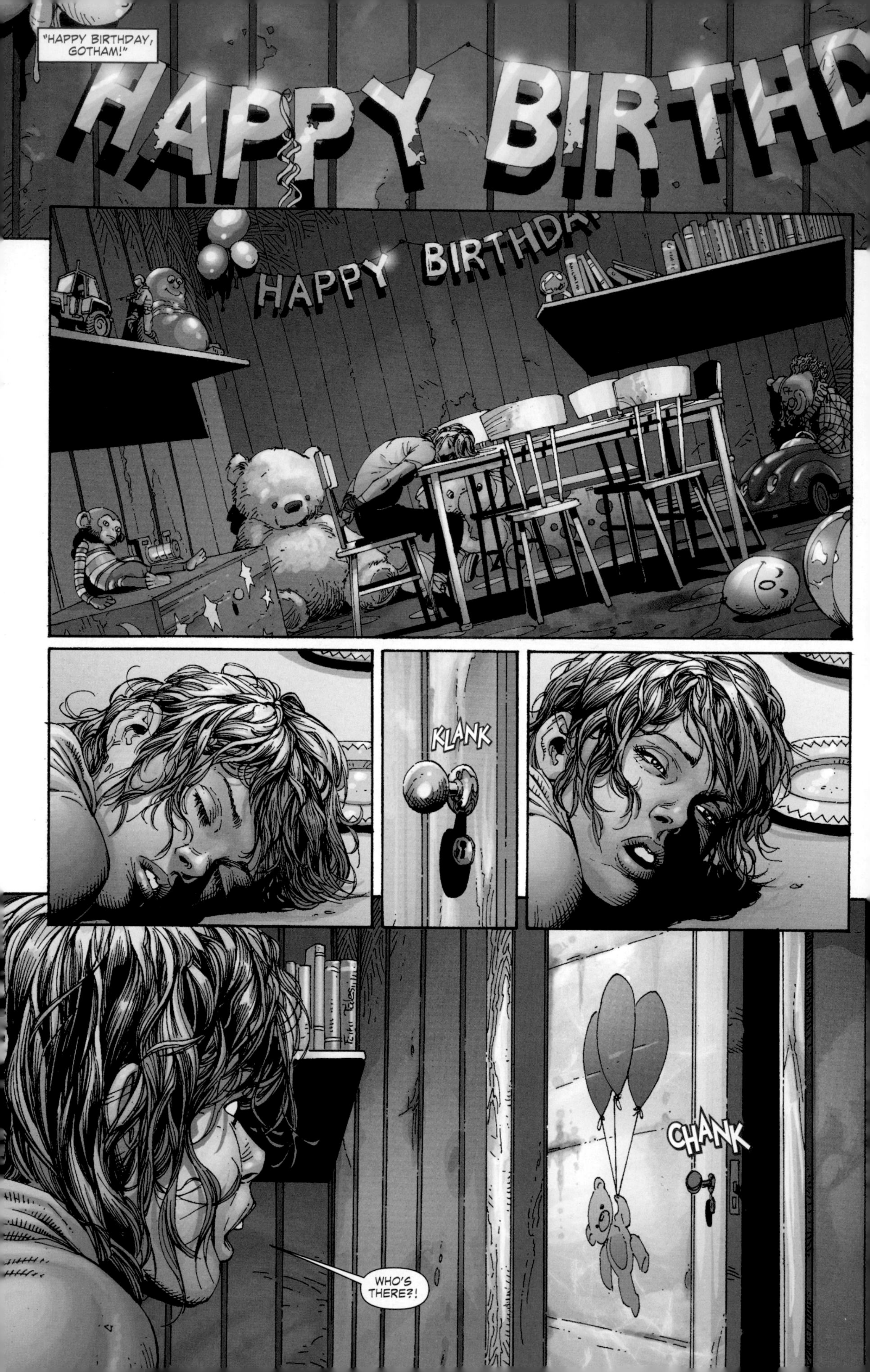
"HAPPY BIRTHDAY, GOTHAM!"
HAPPY BIRTHD
HAPPY BIRTHDA
KLANK
CHANK
WHO'S THERE?!

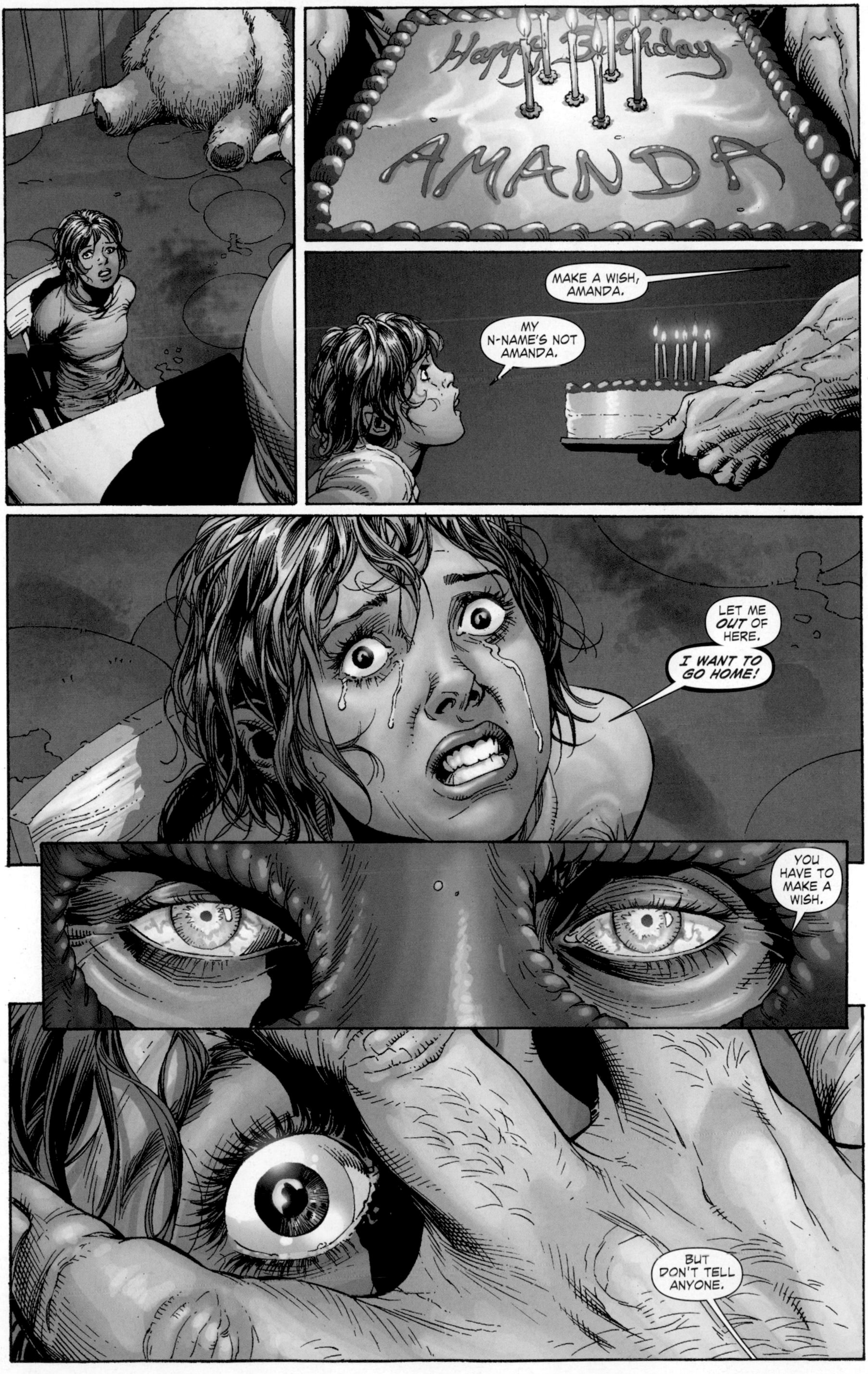
Happy Birthday
AMANDA
MAKE A WISH, AMANDA.
MY N-NAME'S NOT AMANDA.
LET ME *OUT* OF HERE.
I WANT TO GO HOME!
YOU HAVE TO MAKE A WISH.
BUT DON'T TELL ANYONE.

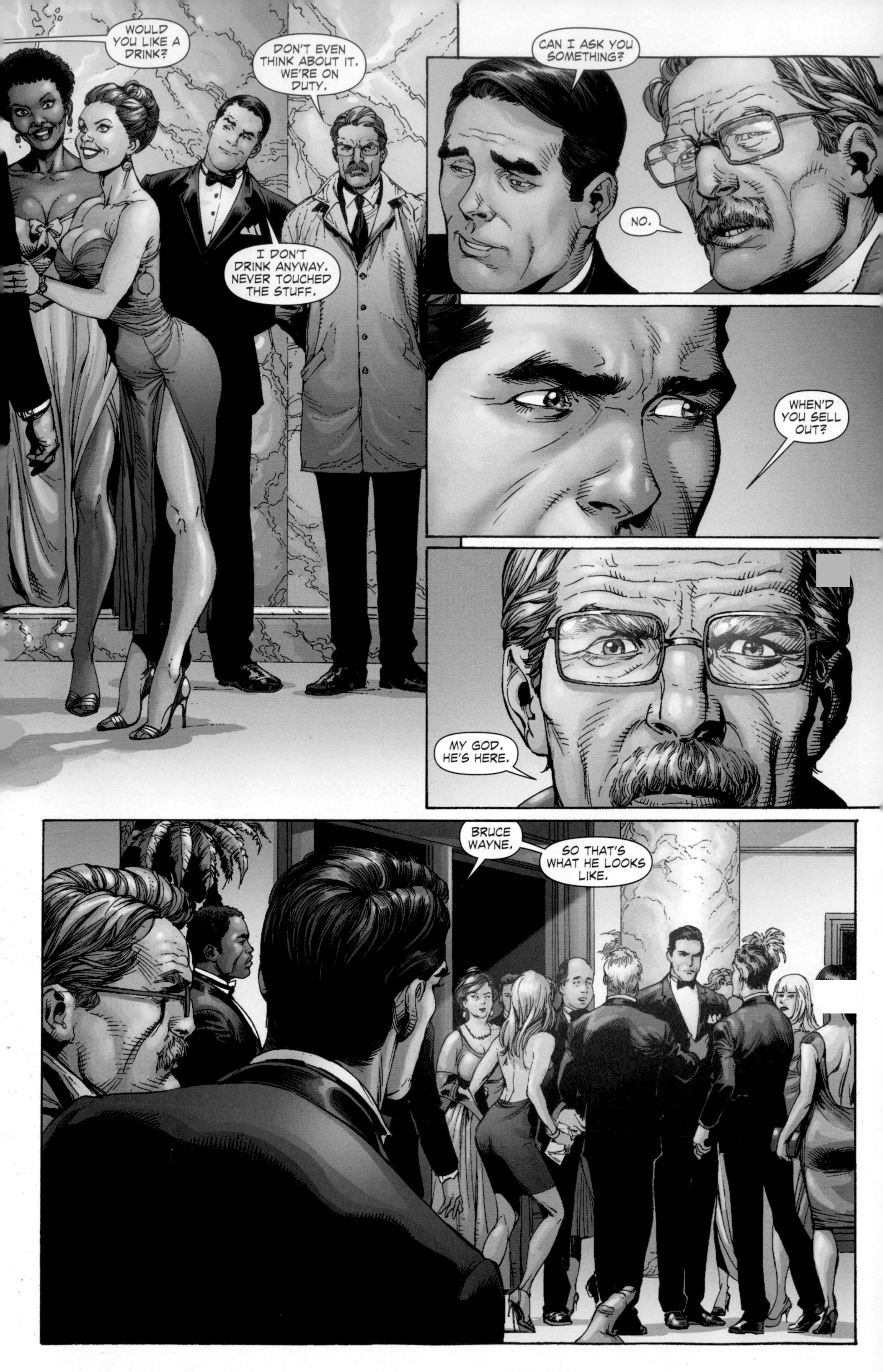
WOULD YOU LIKE A DRINK?
DON'T EVEN THINK ABOUT IT. WE'RE ON DUTY.
I DON'T DRINK ANYWAY. NEVER TOUCHED THE STUFF.
CAN I ASK YOU SOMETHING?
NO.
WHEN'D YOU SELL OUT?
MY GOD. HE'S HERE.
BRUCE WAYNE.
SO THAT'S WHAT HE LOOKS LIKE.

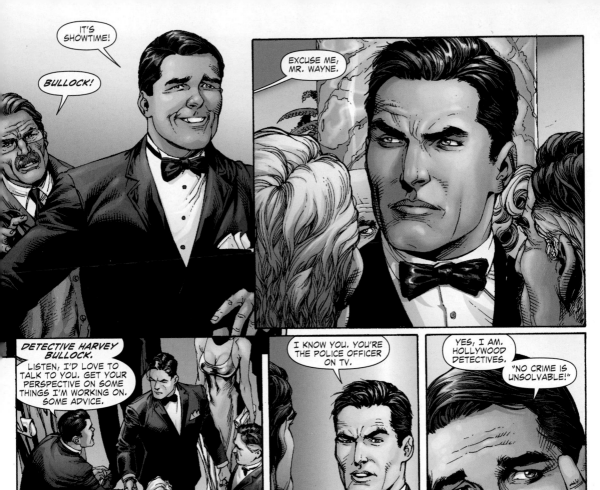

IT'S SHOWTIME!

BULLOCK!

EXCUSE ME, MR. WAYNE.

DETECTIVE HARVEY BULLOCK.
LISTEN, I'D LOVE TO TALK TO YOU. GET YOUR PERSPECTIVE ON SOME THINGS I'M WORKING ON. SOME ADVICE.

I KNOW YOU. YOU'RE THE POLICE OFFICER ON TV.

YES, I AM. HOLLYWOOD DETECTIVES.

"NO CRIME IS UNSOLVABLE!"

THEY JUST CANCELLED THAT, DIDN'T THEY?

PRICK.

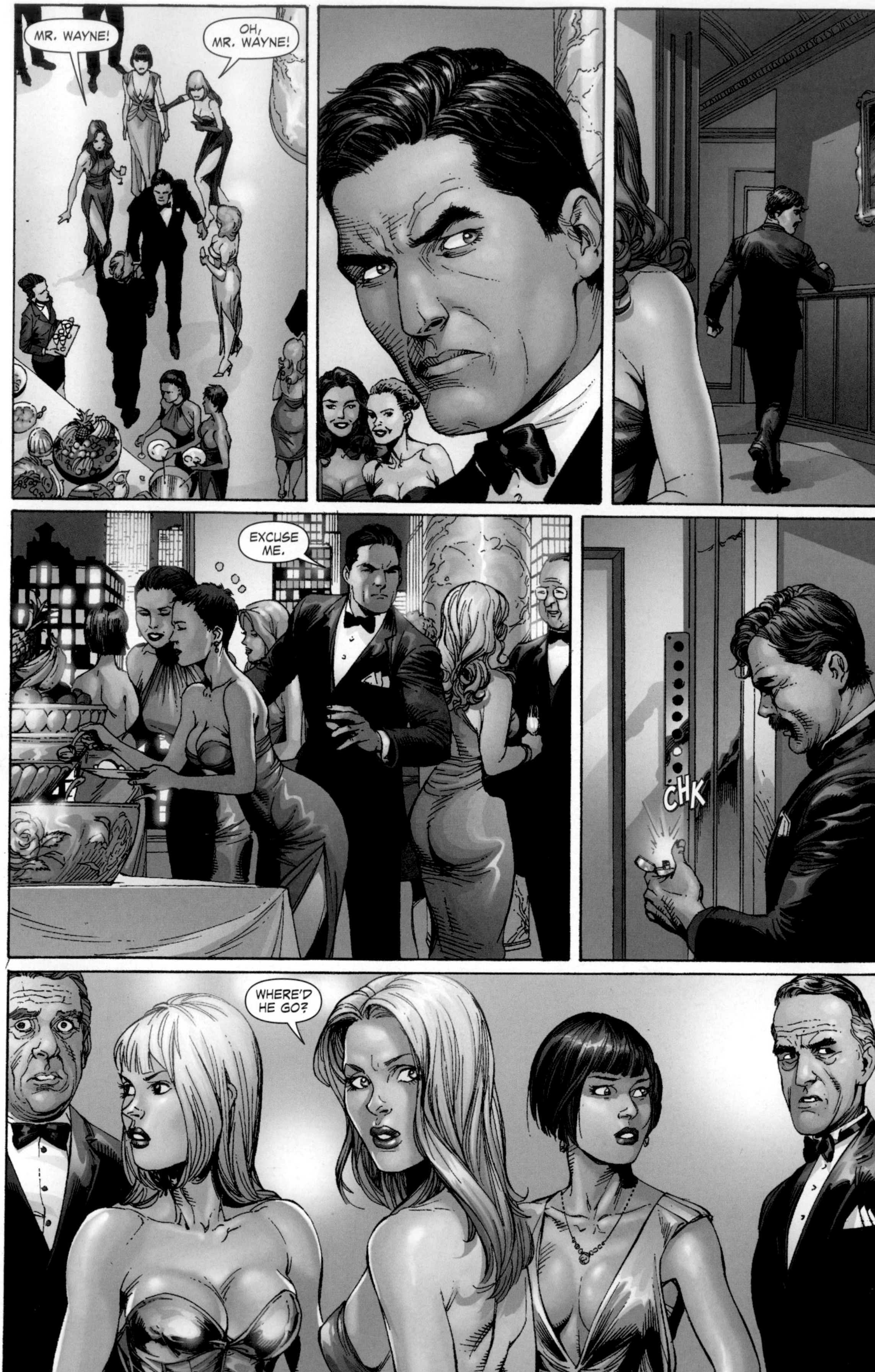
MR. WAYNE!
OH, MR. WAYNE!
EXCUSE ME.
CHK
WHERE'D HE GO?

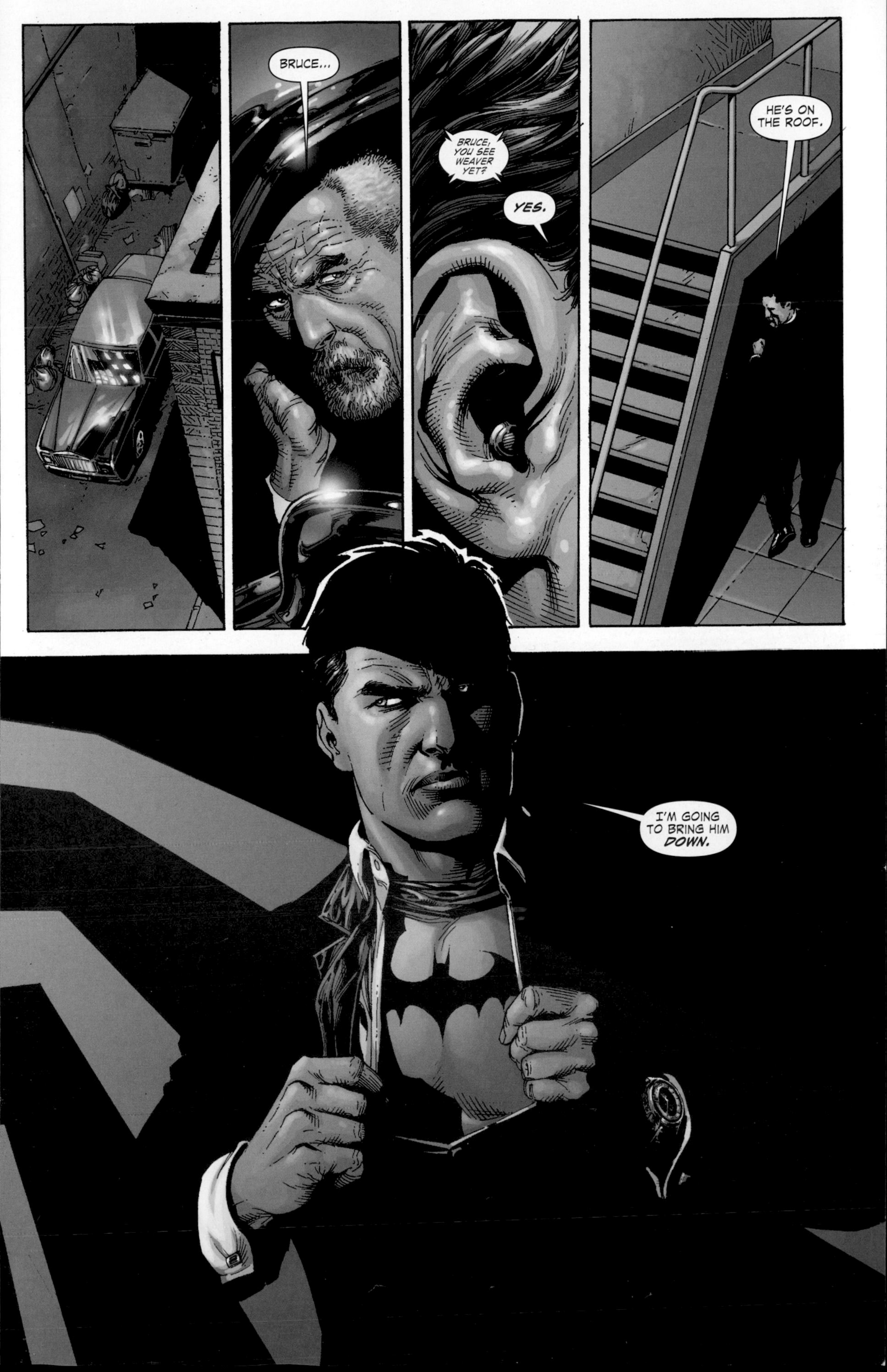
BRUCE...
BRUCE, YOU SEE WEAVER YET?
YES.
HE'S ON THE ROOF.
I'M GOING TO BRING HIM *DOWN.*

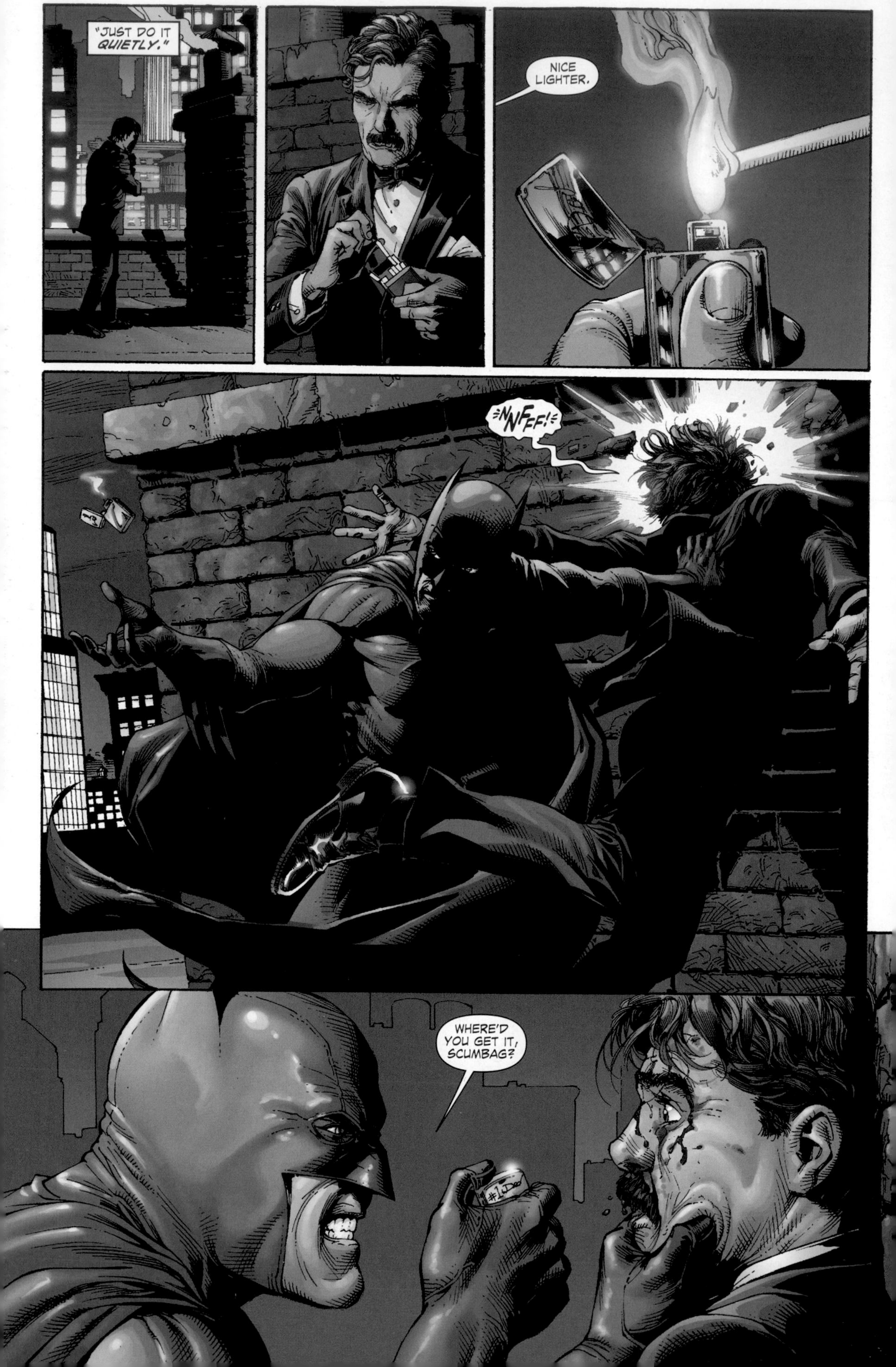
"JUST DO IT QUIETLY."
NICE LIGHTER.
NNFFF!
WHERE'D YOU GET IT, SCUMBAG?

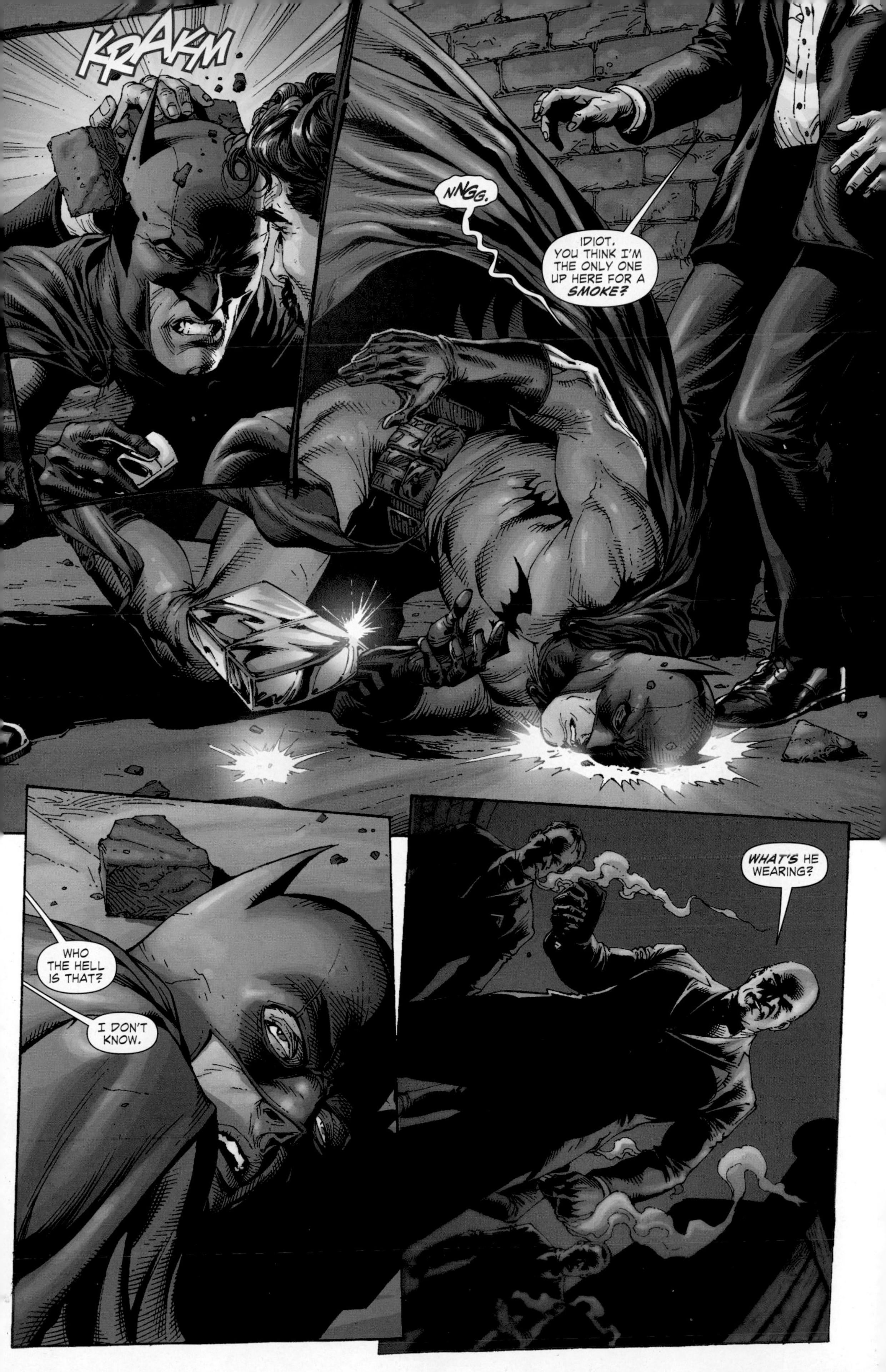
KRAKM
NNGG.
IDIOT. YOU THINK I'M THE ONLY ONE UP HERE FOR A SMOKE?
WHO THE HELL IS THAT?
I DON'T KNOW.
WHAT'S HE WEARING?

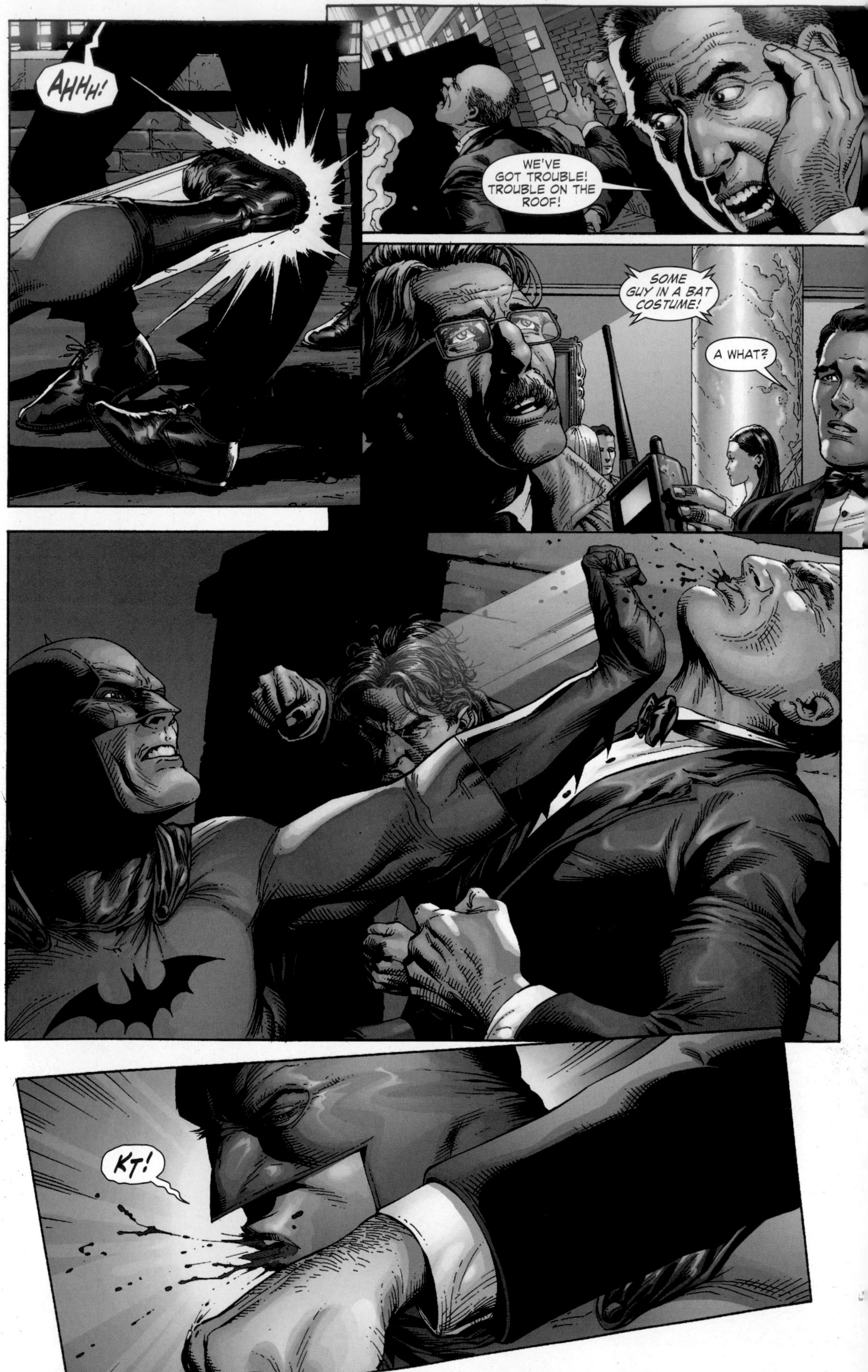
AHHH!
WE'VE GOT TROUBLE! TROUBLE ON THE ROOF!
SOME GUY IN A BAT COSTUME!
A WHAT?
KT!

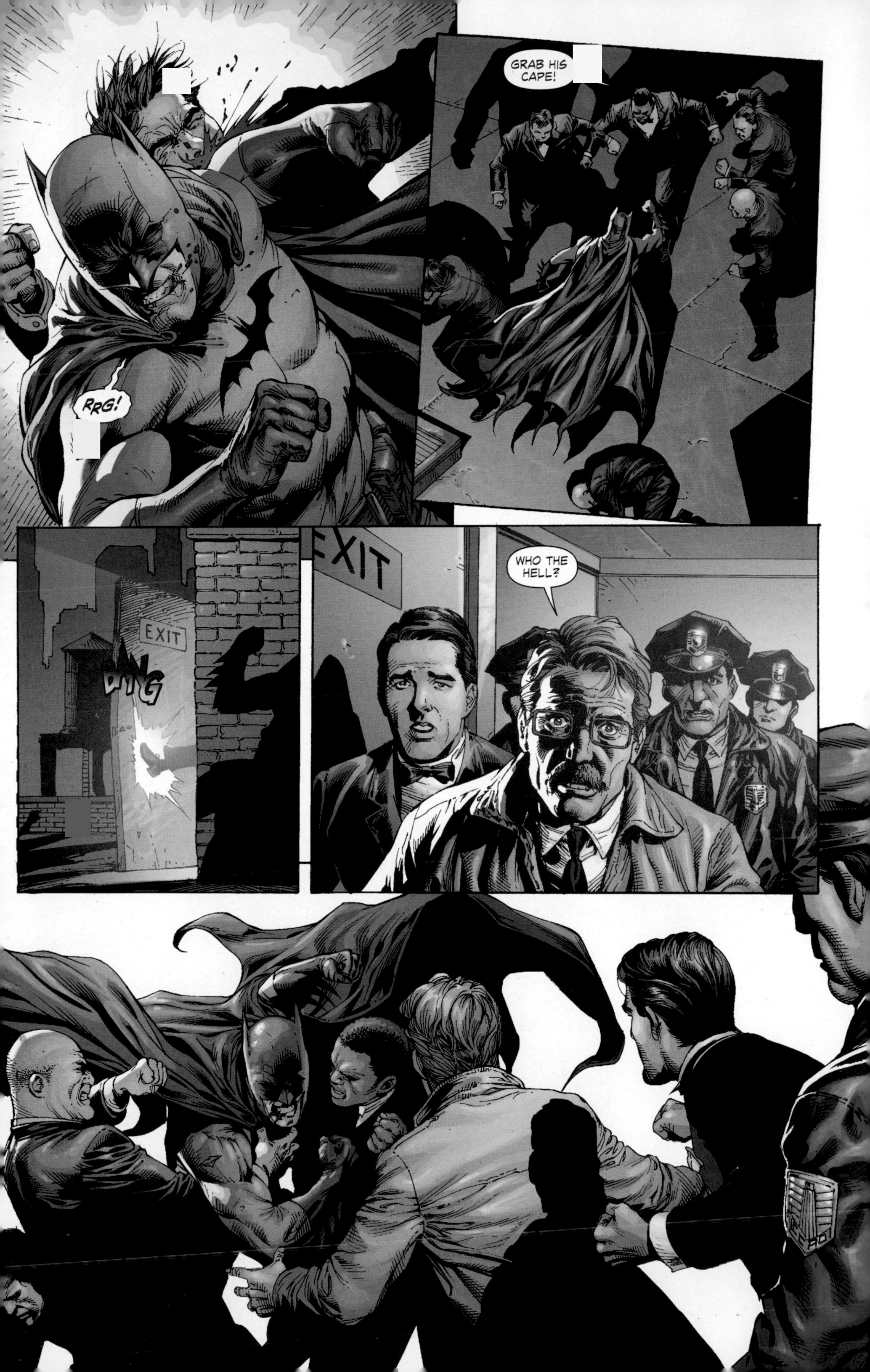
RRG!
GRAB HIS CAPE!
EXIT
BANG
EXIT
WHO THE HELL?

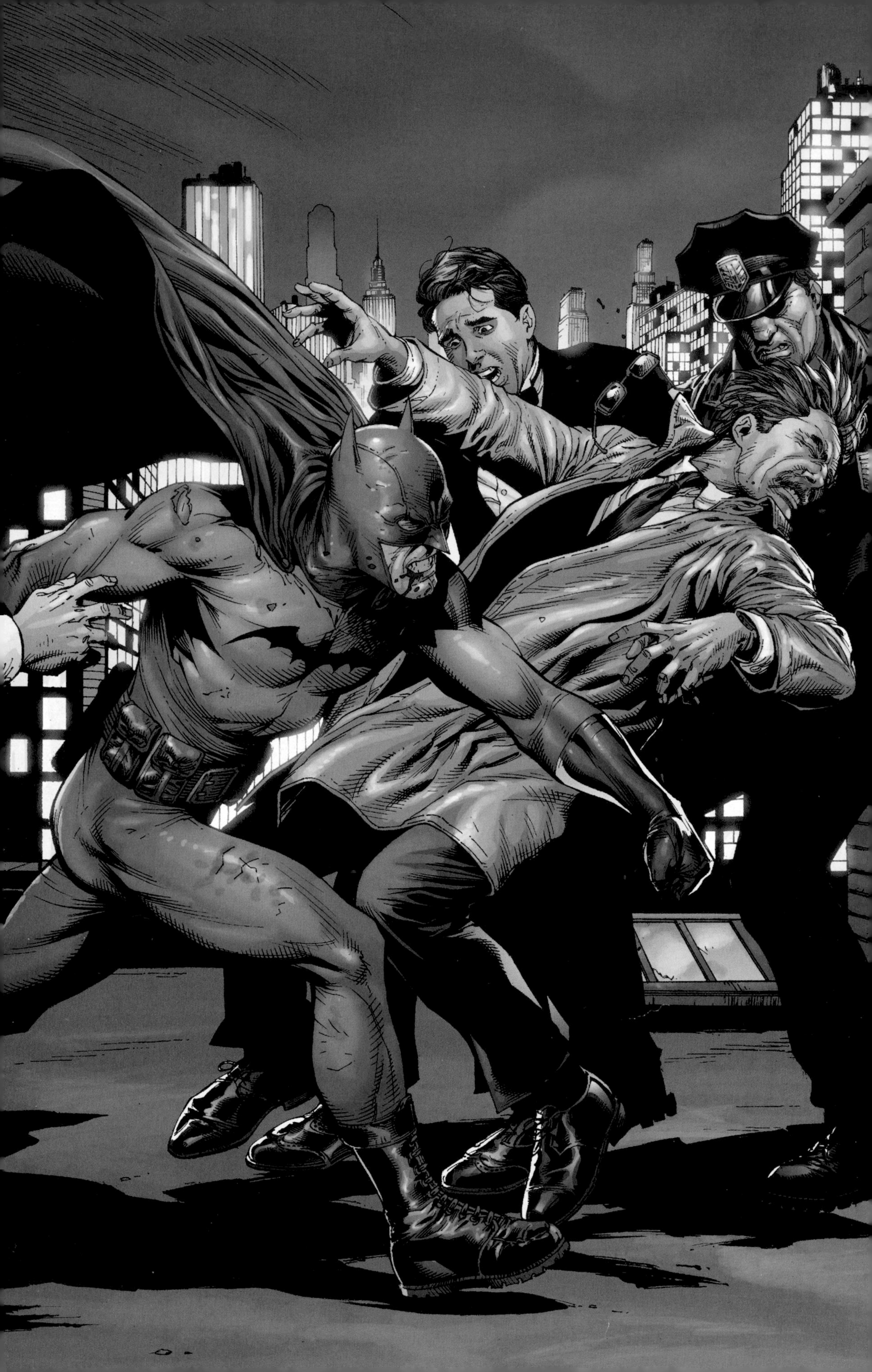

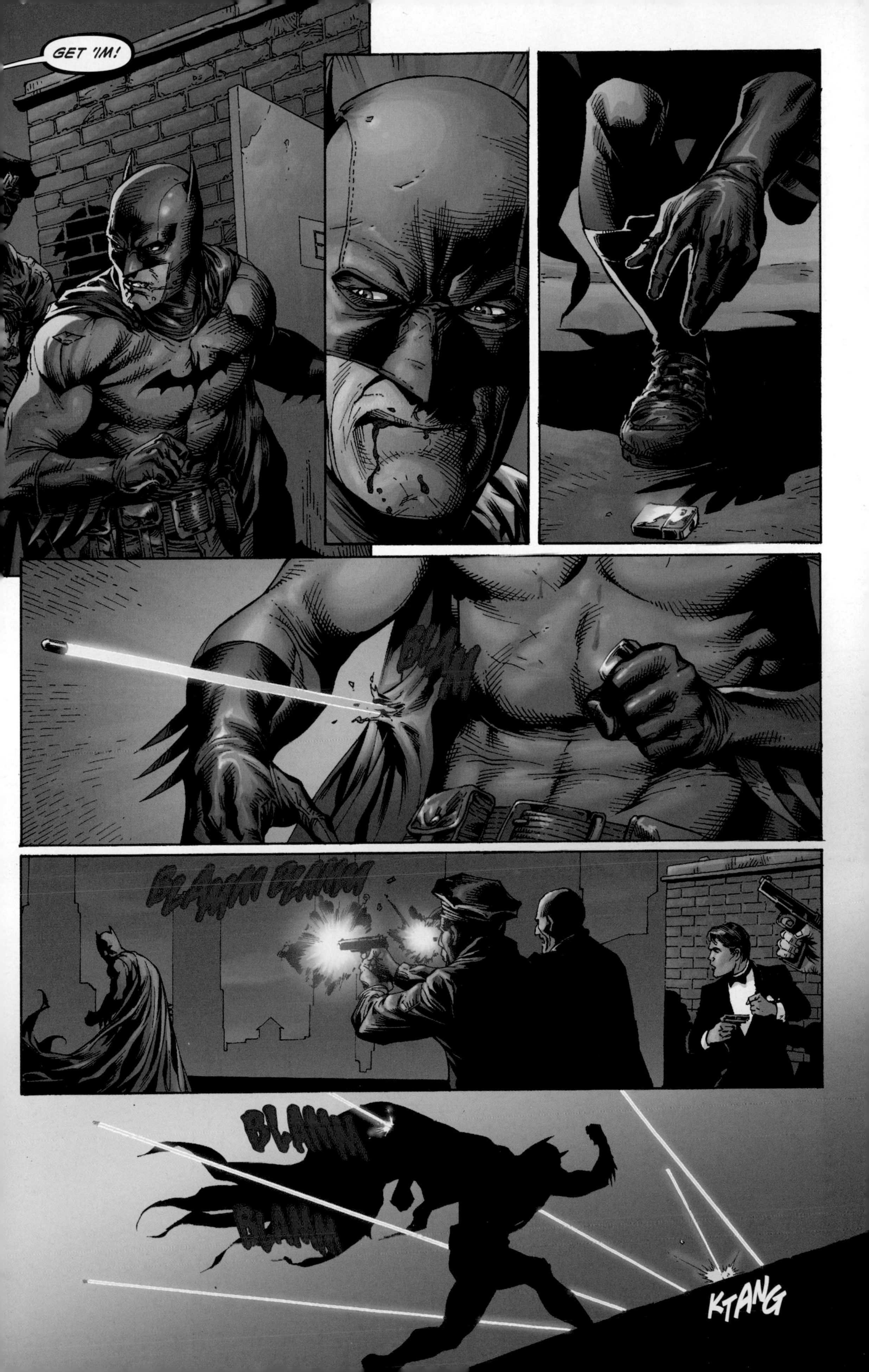
GET 'IM!
BLAMM
BLAMM BLAMM
BLAMM
BLAMM
KTANG

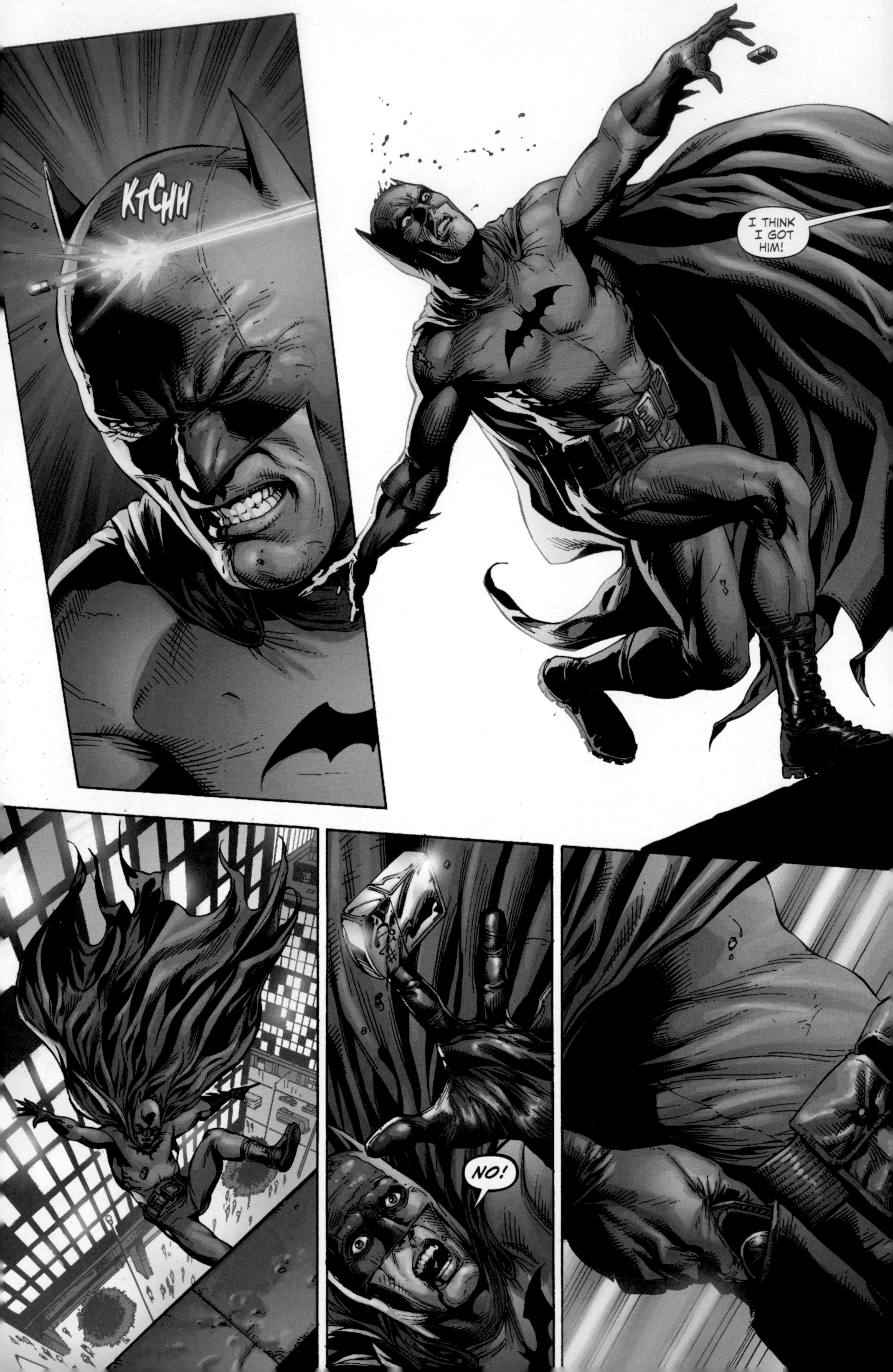
KTCHH
I THINK I GOT HIM!
NO!

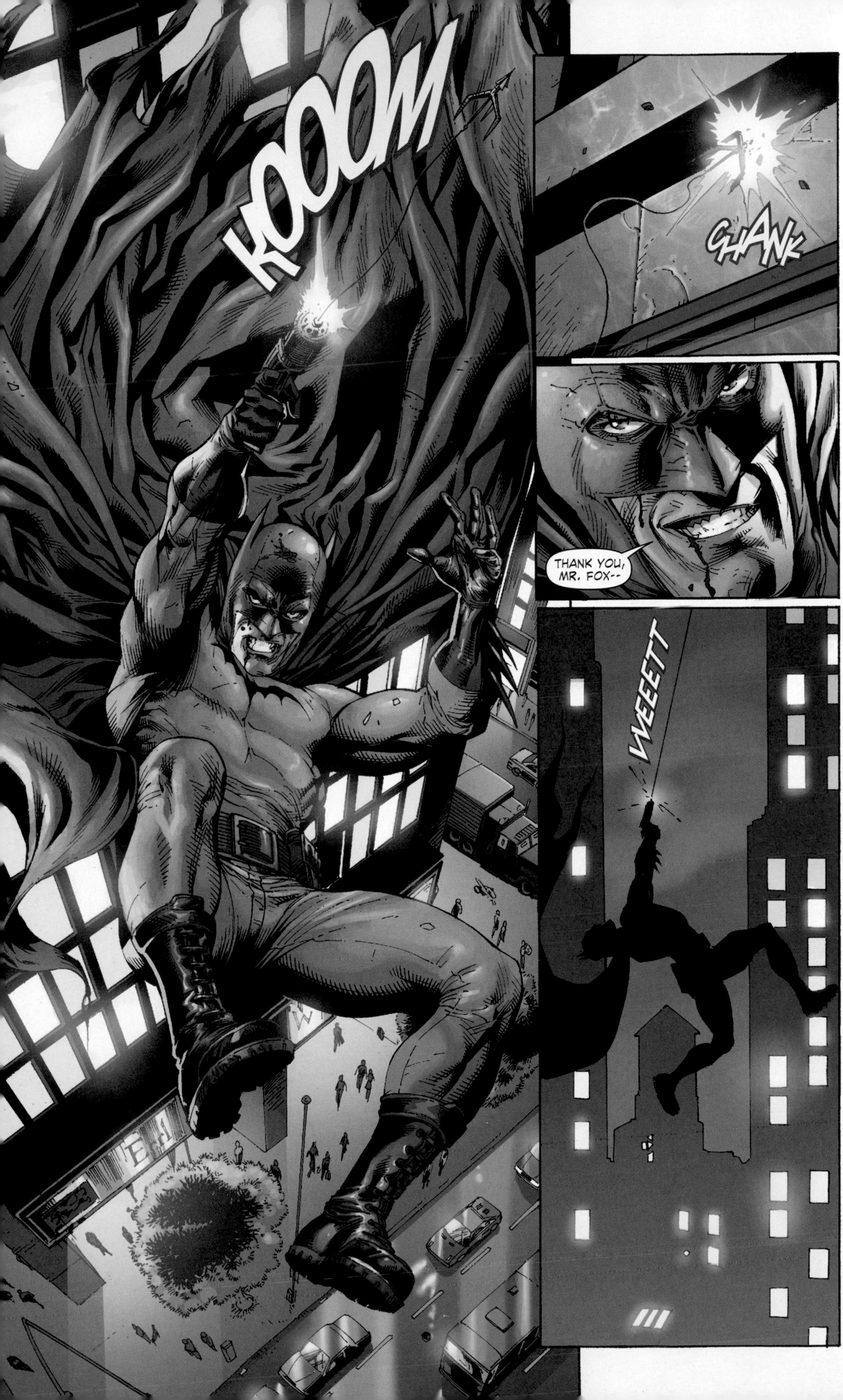
KOOOM
CHANK
THANK YOU, MR. FOX--
WEEETT

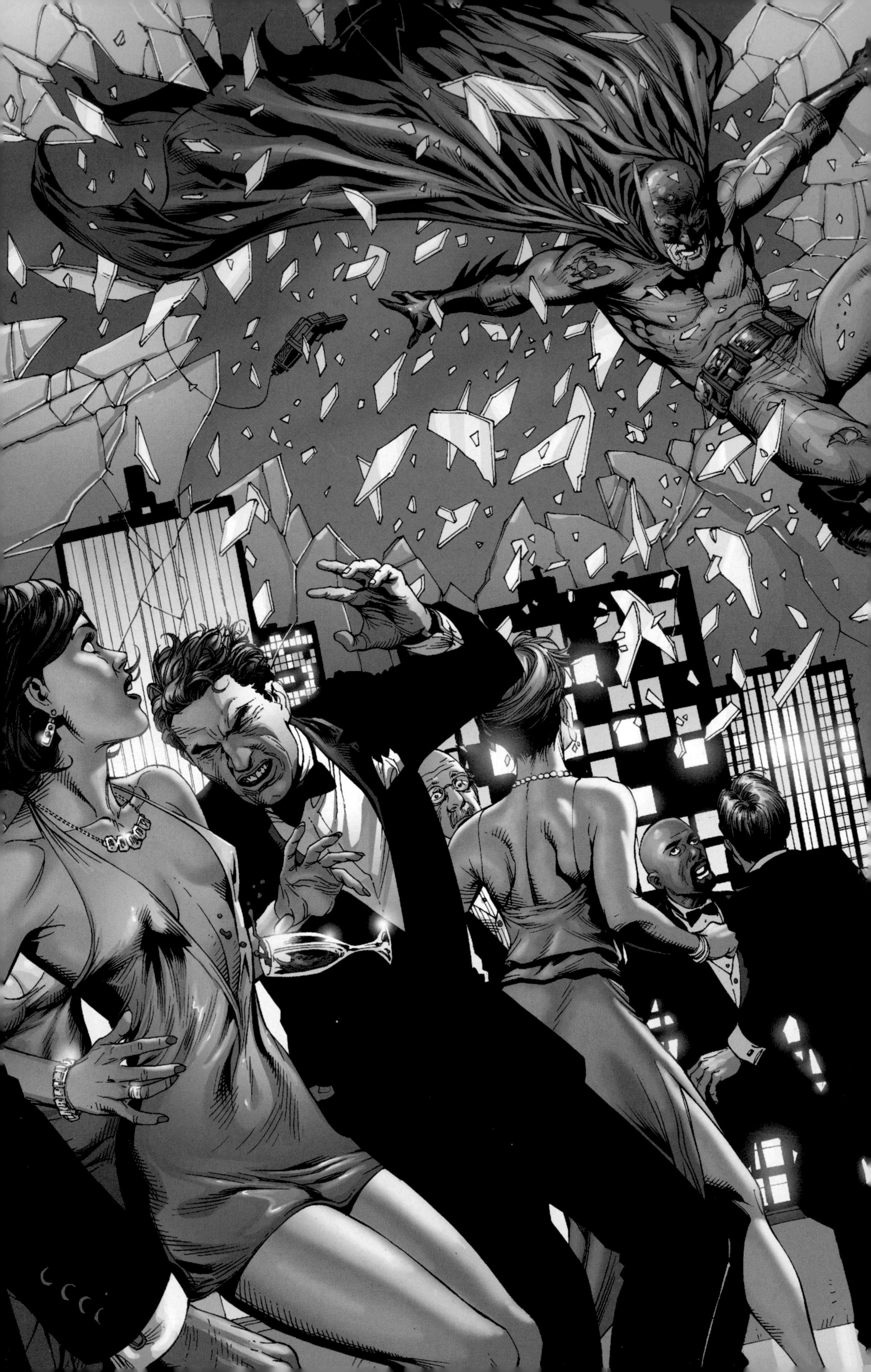

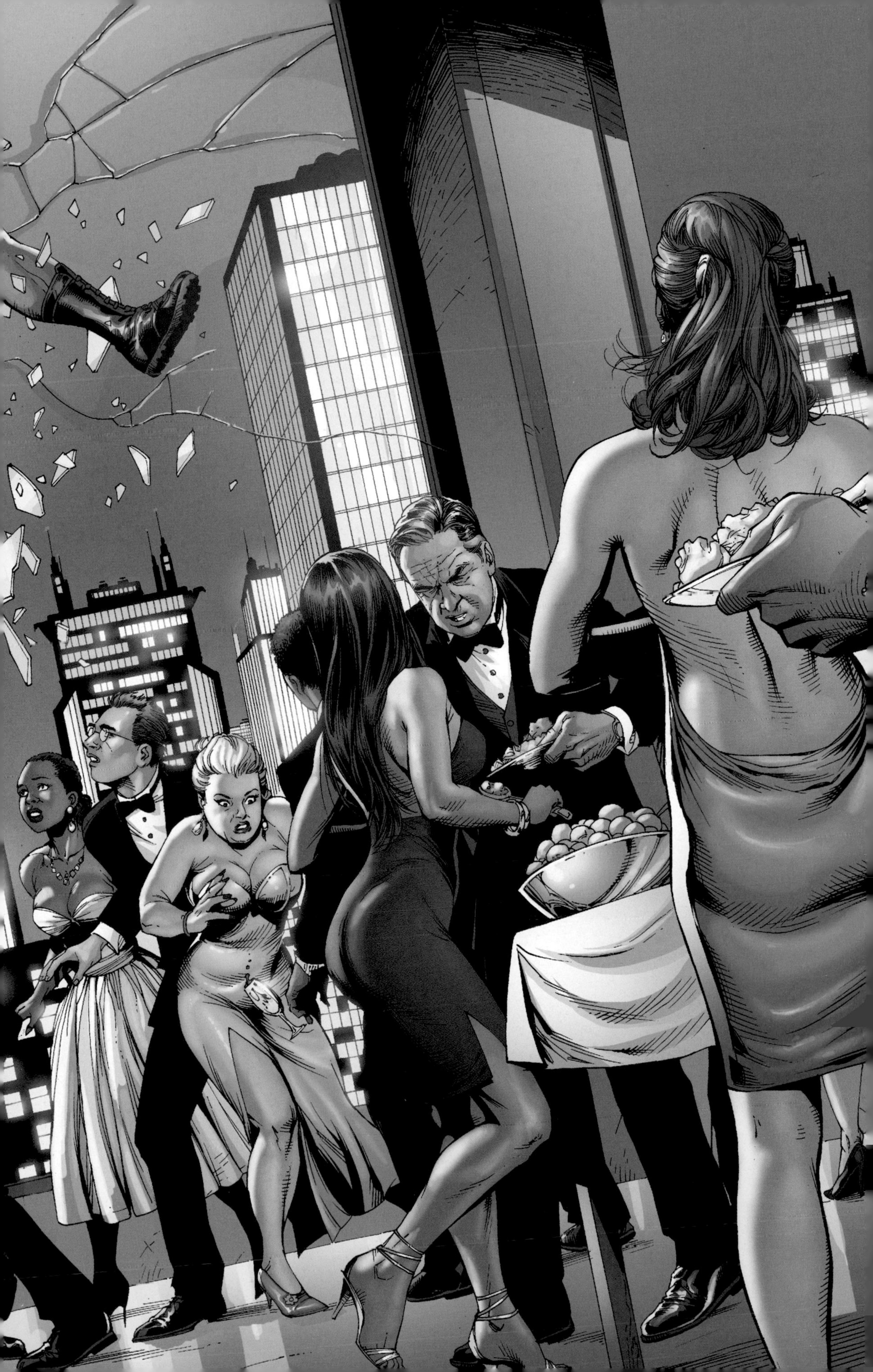

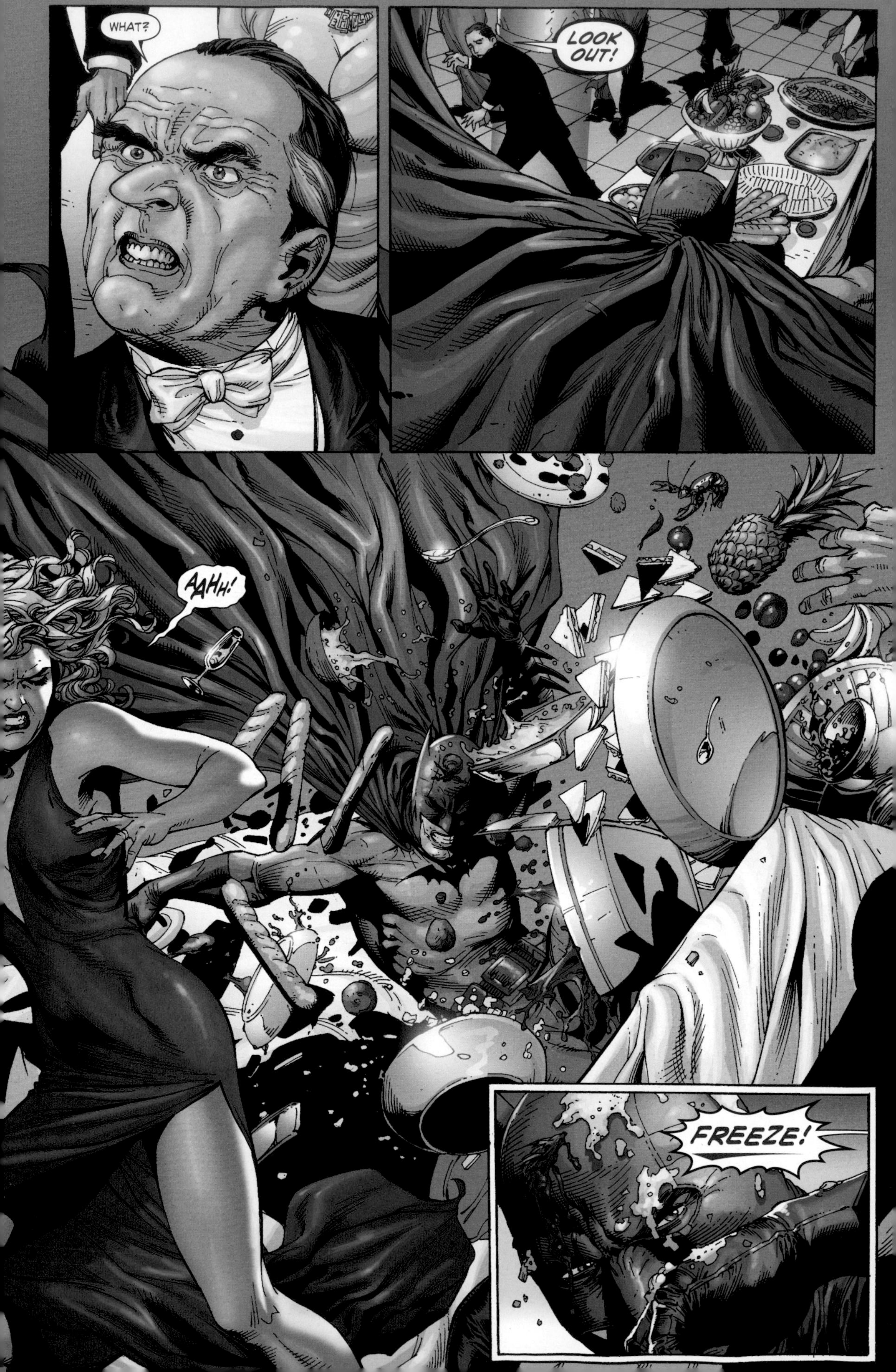
WHAT?
LOOK OUT!
AAHH!
FREEZE!

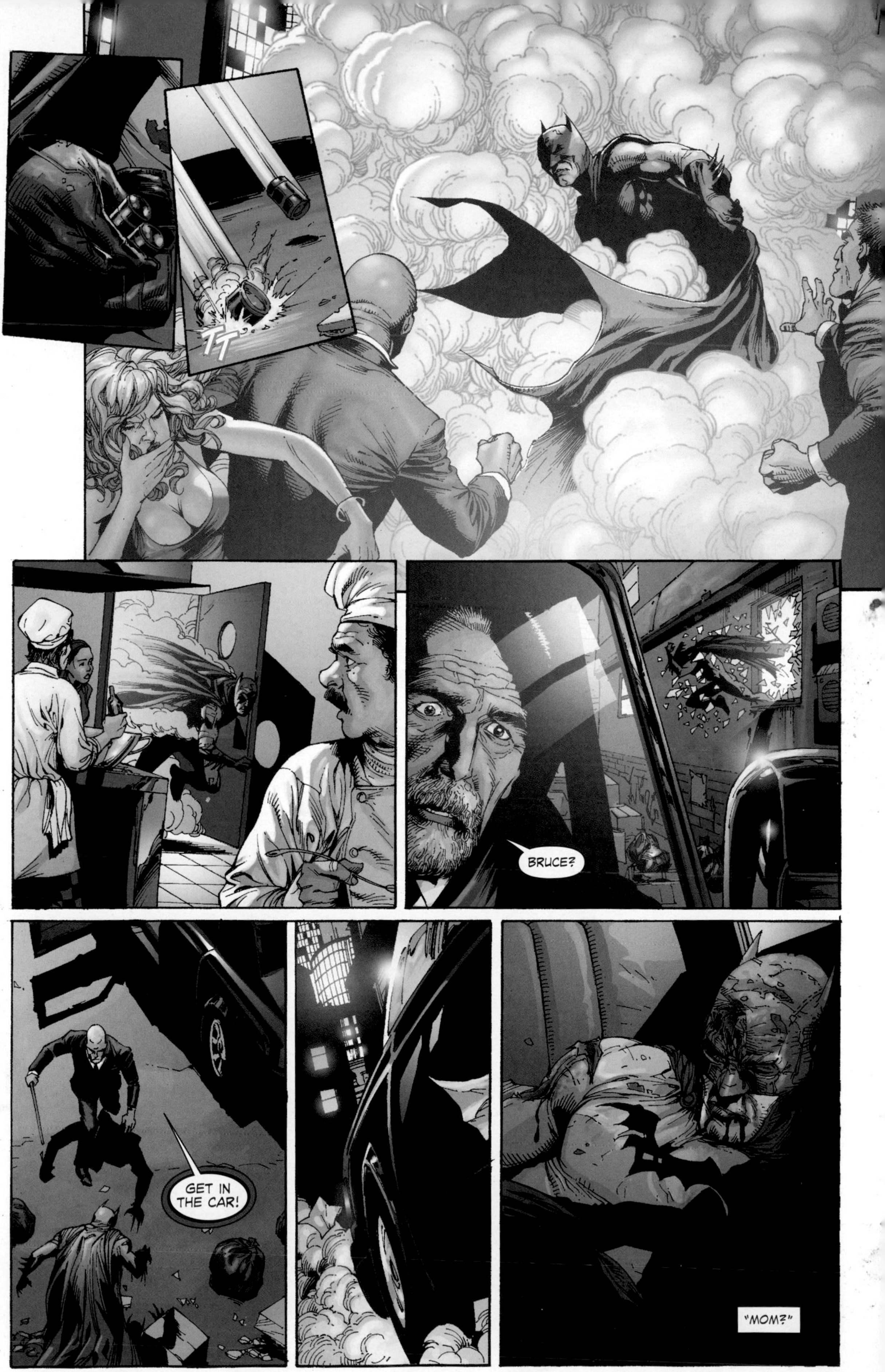
TT
BRUCE?
GET IN THE CAR!
"MOM?"

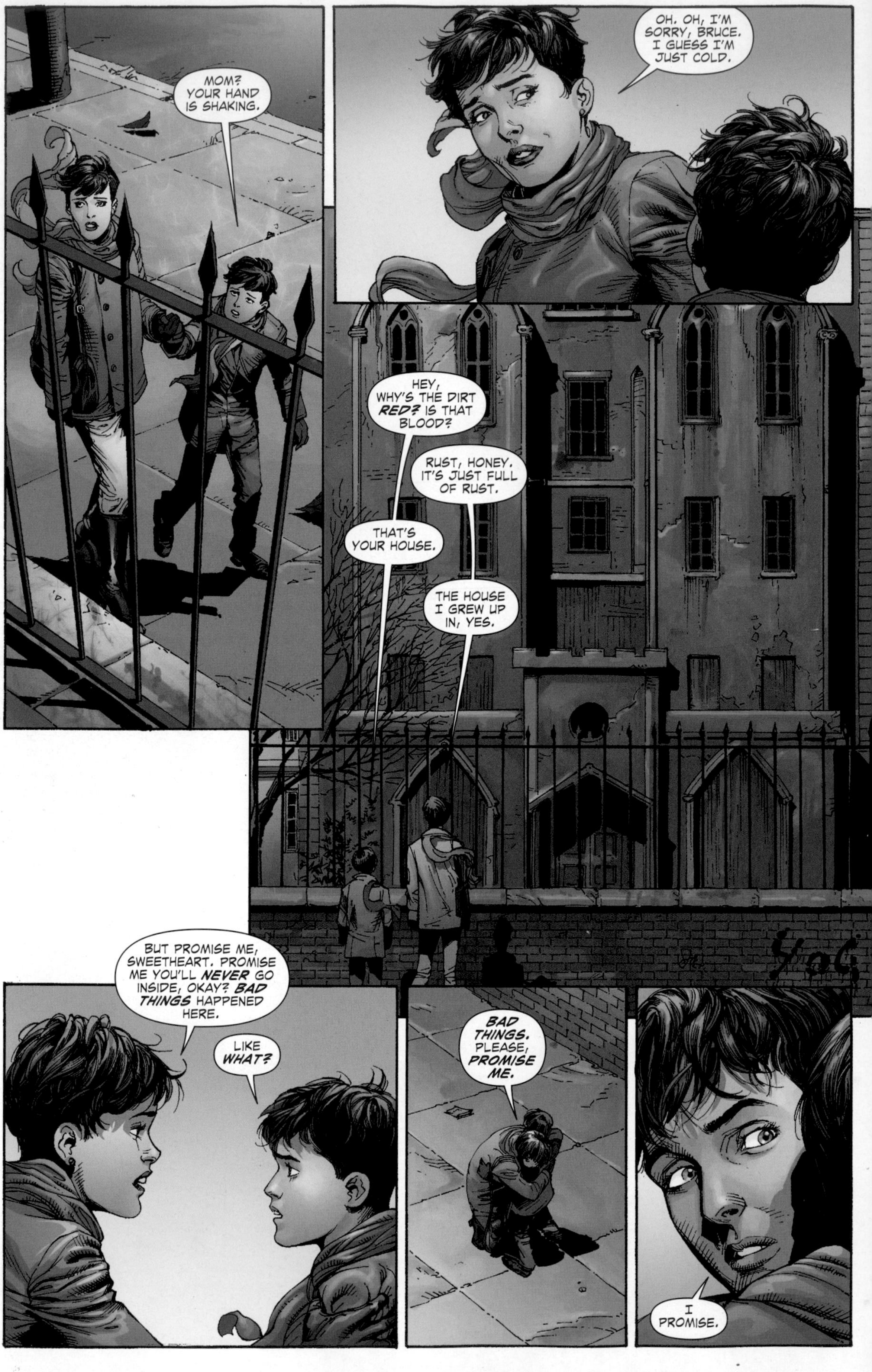
MOM? YOUR HAND IS SHAKING.
OH. OH, I'M SORRY, BRUCE. I GUESS I'M JUST COLD.
HEY, WHY'S THE DIRT RED? IS THAT BLOOD?
RUST, HONEY. IT'S JUST FULL OF RUST.
THAT'S YOUR HOUSE.
THE HOUSE I GREW UP IN, YES.
BUT PROMISE ME, SWEETHEART. PROMISE ME YOU'LL NEVER GO INSIDE, OKAY? BAD THINGS HAPPENED HERE.
LIKE WHAT?
BAD THINGS. PLEASE, PROMISE ME.
I PROMISE.

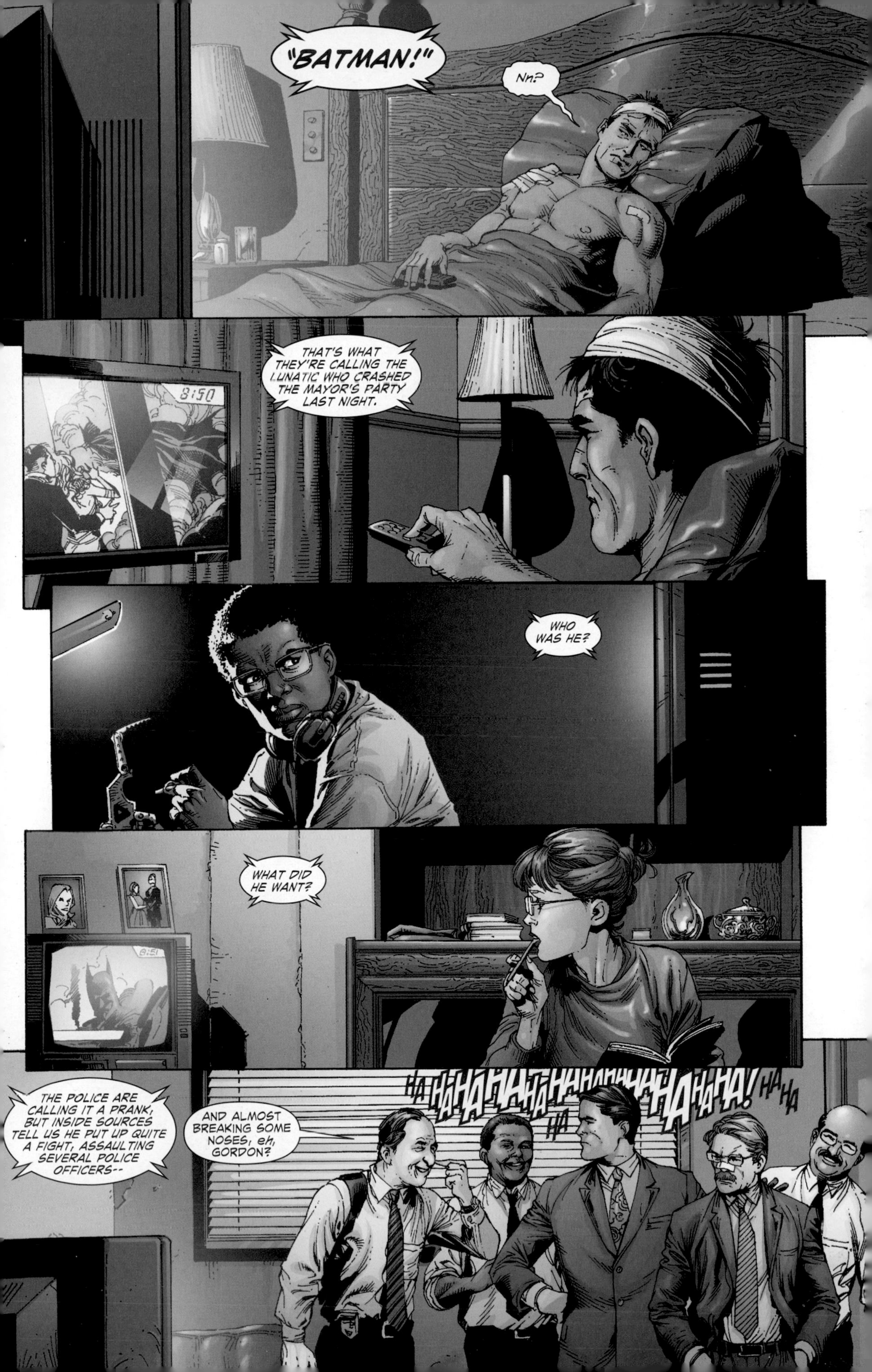
"BATMAN!"
Nn?
THAT'S WHAT THEY'RE CALLING THE LUNATIC WHO CRASHED THE MAYOR'S PARTY LAST NIGHT.
8:50
WHO WAS HE?
WHAT DID HE WANT?
8:51
THE POLICE ARE CALLING IT A PRANK, BUT INSIDE SOURCES TELL US HE PUT UP QUITE A FIGHT, ASSAULTING SEVERAL POLICE OFFICERS--
AND ALMOST BREAKING SOME NOSES, eh, GORDON?
HAHAHAHAHAHAHAHAHAHAHAHAHAHA! HA HA HA

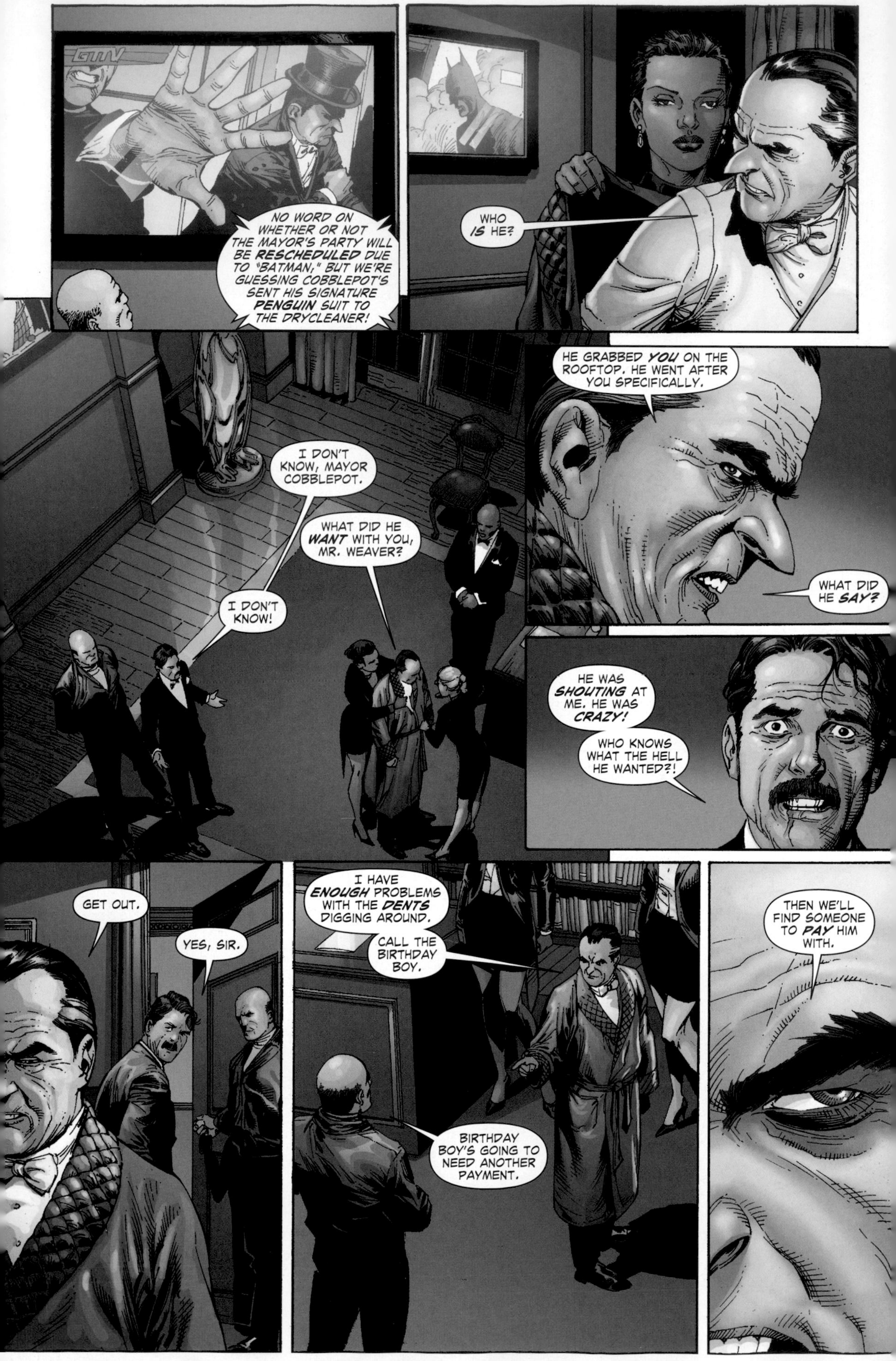
NO WORD ON WHETHER OR NOT THE MAYOR'S PARTY WILL BE RESCHEDULED DUE TO "BATMAN," BUT WE'RE GUESSING COBBLEPOT'S SENT HIS SIGNATURE PENGUIN SUIT TO THE DRYCLEANER!
WHO IS HE?
I DON'T KNOW, MAYOR COBBLEPOT.
WHAT DID HE WANT WITH YOU, MR. WEAVER?
I DON'T KNOW!
HE GRABBED YOU ON THE ROOFTOP. HE WENT AFTER YOU SPECIFICALLY.
WHAT DID HE SAY?
HE WAS SHOUTING AT ME. HE WAS CRAZY!
WHO KNOWS WHAT THE HELL HE WANTED?!
GET OUT.
YES, SIR.
I HAVE ENOUGH PROBLEMS WITH THE DENTS DIGGING AROUND.
CALL THE BIRTHDAY BOY.
BIRTHDAY BOY'S GOING TO NEED ANOTHER PAYMENT.
THEN WE'LL FIND SOMEONE TO PAY HIM WITH.

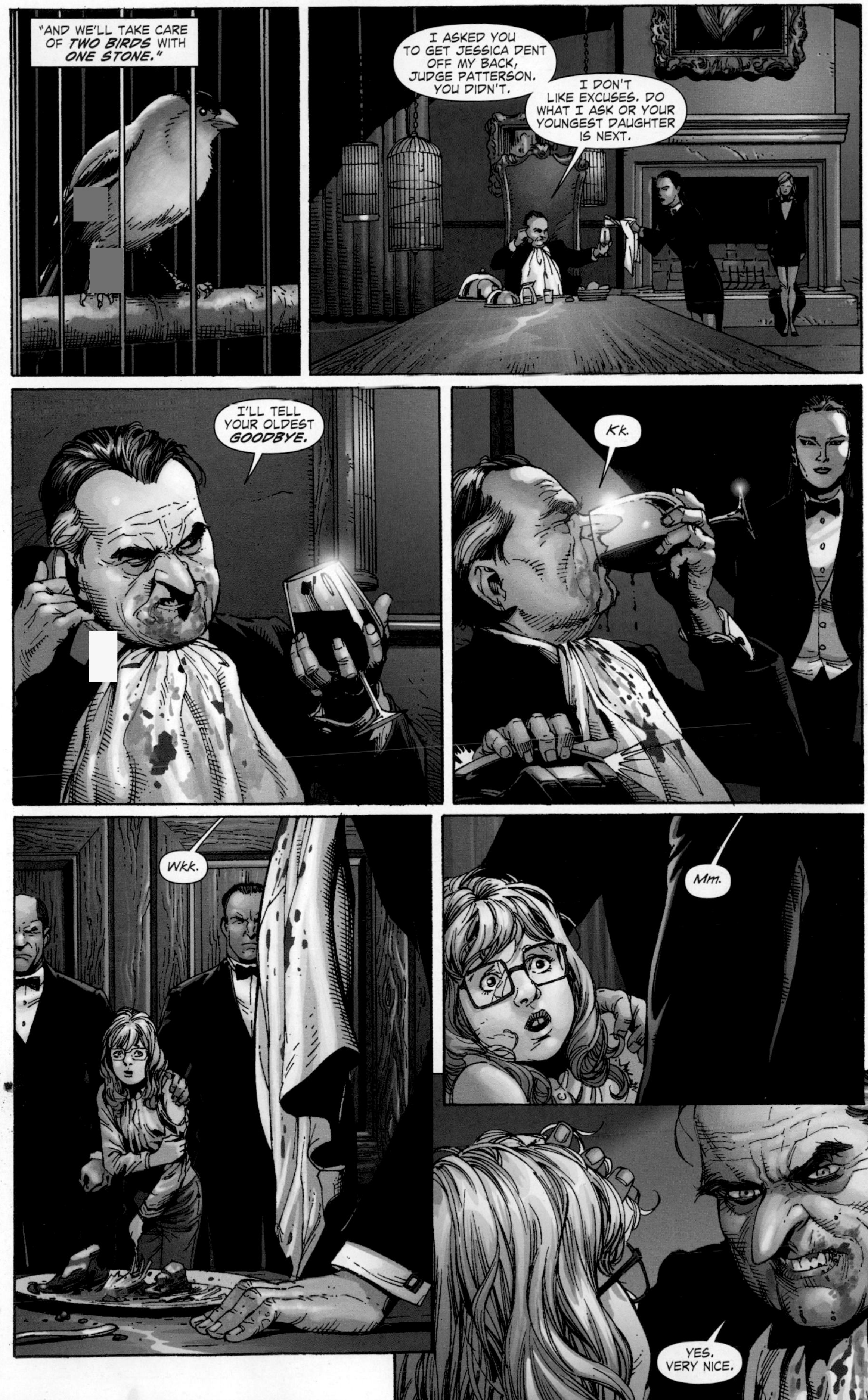
"AND WE'LL TAKE CARE OF TWO BIRDS WITH ONE STONE."
I ASKED YOU TO GET JESSICA DENT OFF MY BACK, JUDGE PATTERSON. YOU DIDN'T.
I DON'T LIKE EXCUSES. DO WHAT I ASK OR YOUR YOUNGEST DAUGHTER IS NEXT.
I'LL TELL YOUR OLDEST GOODBYE.
Kk.
Wkk.
Mm.
YES. VERY NICE.

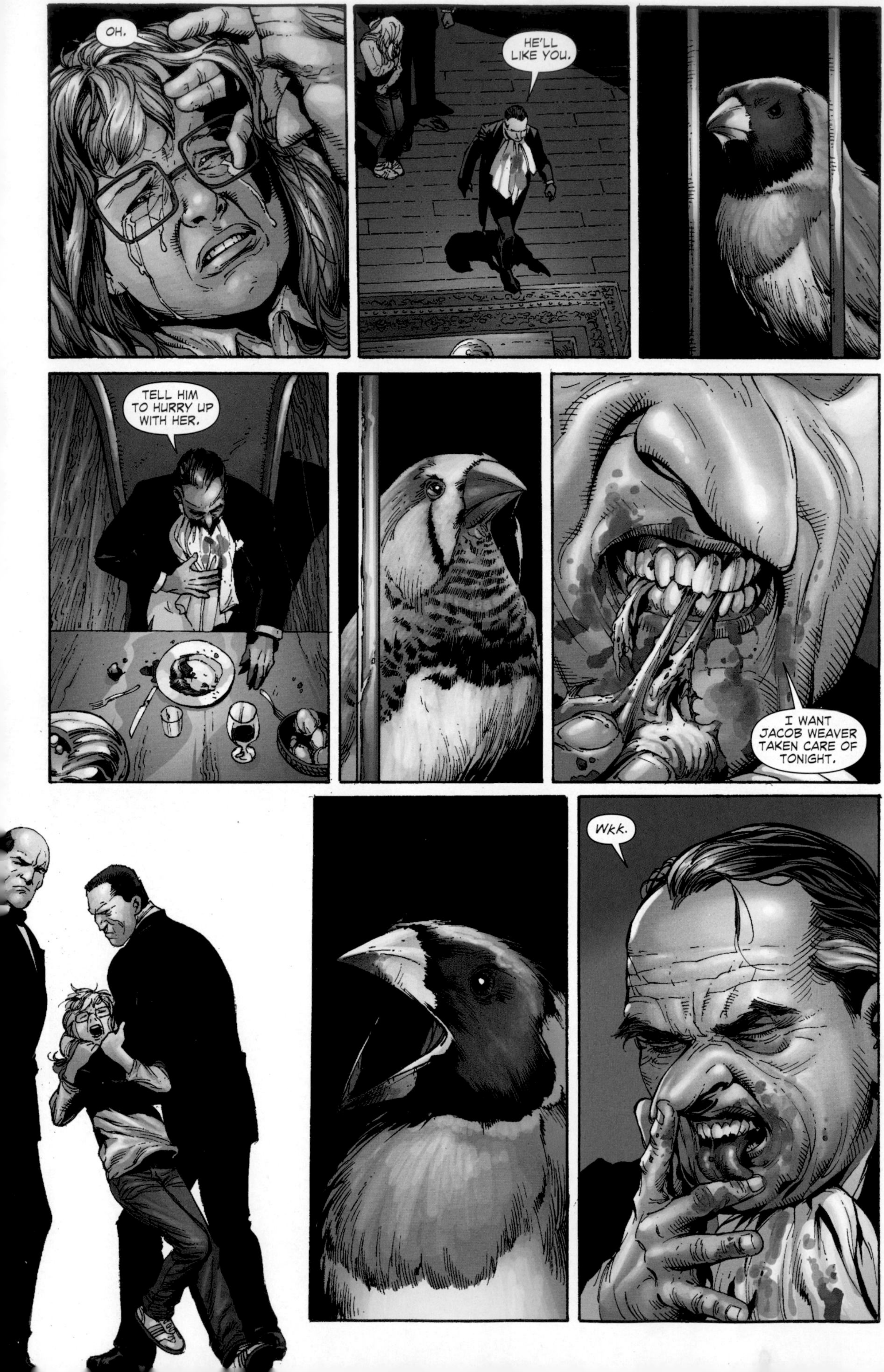
OH.
HE'LL LIKE YOU.
TELL HIM TO HURRY UP WITH HER.
I WANT JACOB WEAVER TAKEN CARE OF TONIGHT.
Wkk.

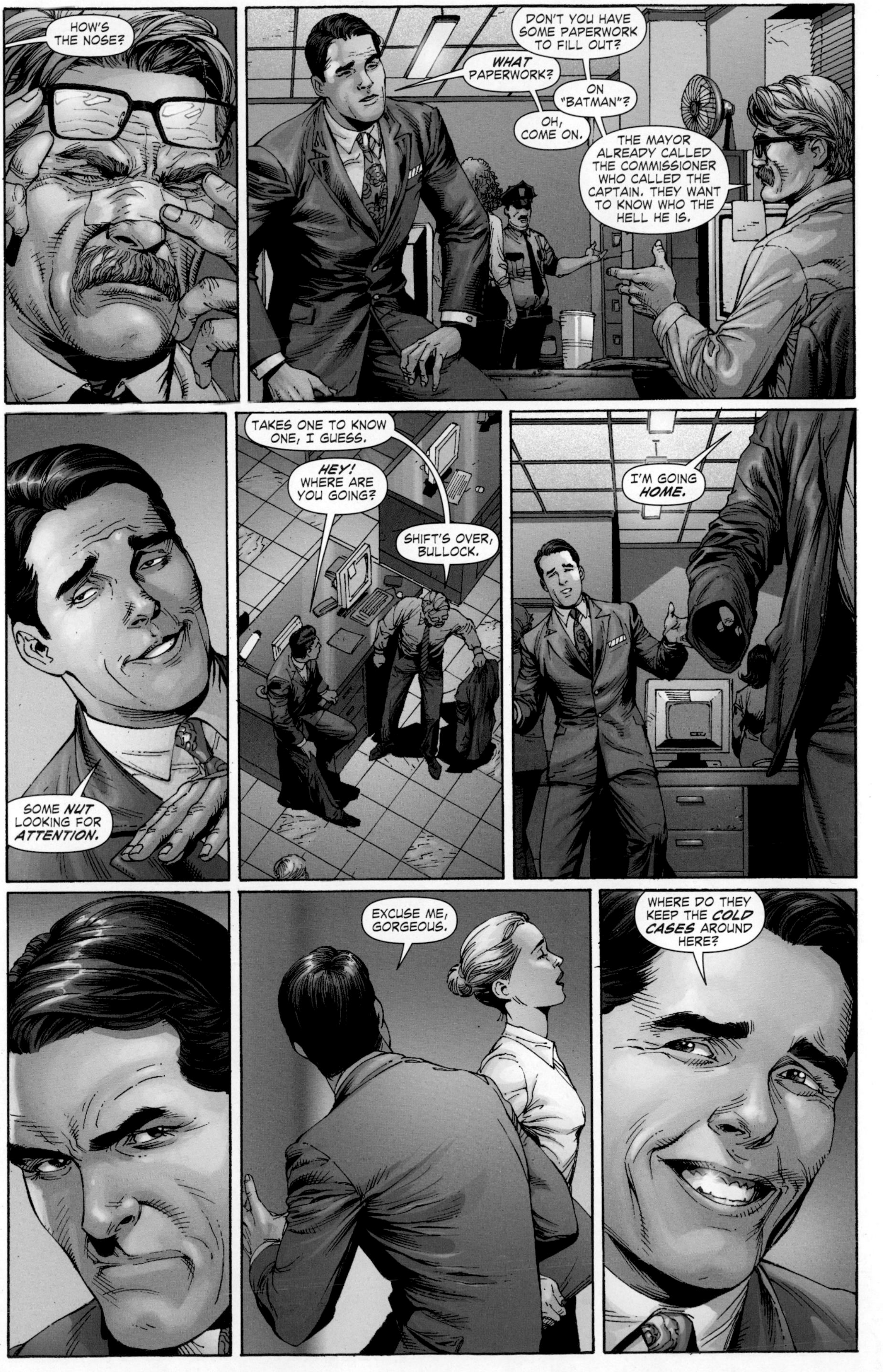
HOW'S THE NOSE?
DON'T YOU HAVE SOME PAPERWORK TO FILL OUT?
WHAT PAPERWORK?
ON "BATMAN"?
OH, COME ON.
THE MAYOR ALREADY CALLED THE COMMISSIONER WHO CALLED THE CAPTAIN. THEY WANT TO KNOW WHO THE HELL HE IS.
SOME NUT LOOKING FOR ATTENTION.
TAKES ONE TO KNOW ONE, I GUESS.
HEY! WHERE ARE YOU GOING?
SHIFT'S OVER, BULLOCK.
I'M GOING HOME.
EXCUSE ME, GORGEOUS.
WHERE DO THEY KEEP THE COLD CASES AROUND HERE?

I LOVE YOU, BRUCE.

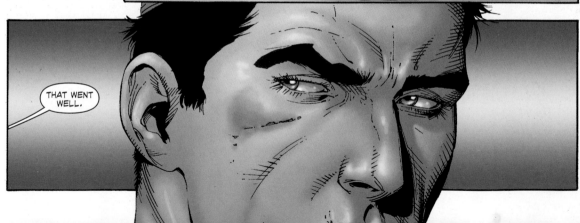

THAT WENT WELL.

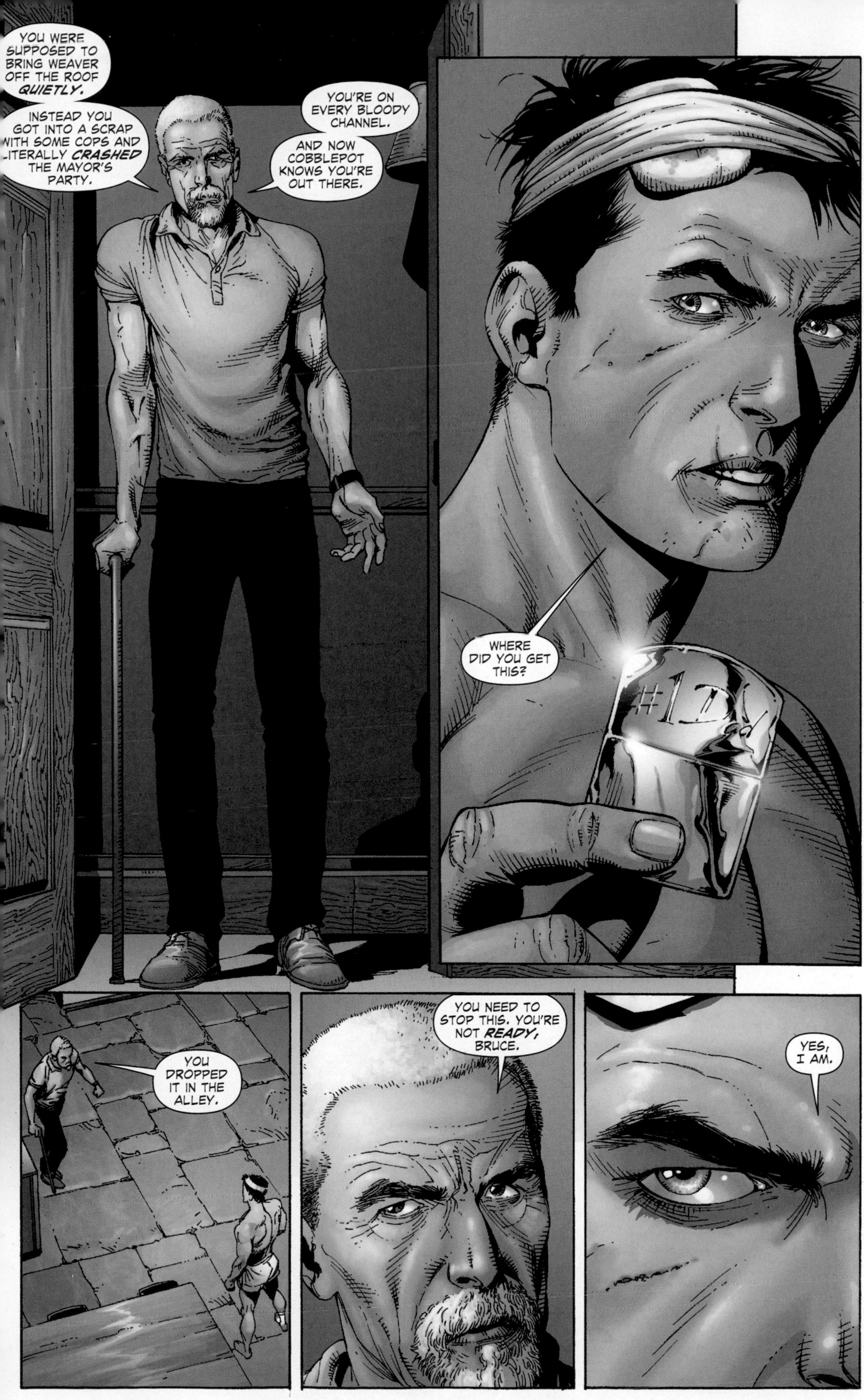
YOU WERE SUPPOSED TO BRING WEAVER OFF THE ROOF *QUIETLY.*
INSTEAD YOU GOT INTO A SCRAP WITH SOME COPS AND LITERALLY *CRASHED* THE MAYOR'S PARTY.
YOU'RE ON EVERY BLOODY CHANNEL.
AND NOW COBBLEPOT KNOWS YOU'RE OUT THERE.
WHERE DID YOU GET THIS?
YOU DROPPED IT IN THE ALLEY.
YOU NEED TO STOP THIS. YOU'RE NOT *READY,* BRUCE.
YES, I AM.

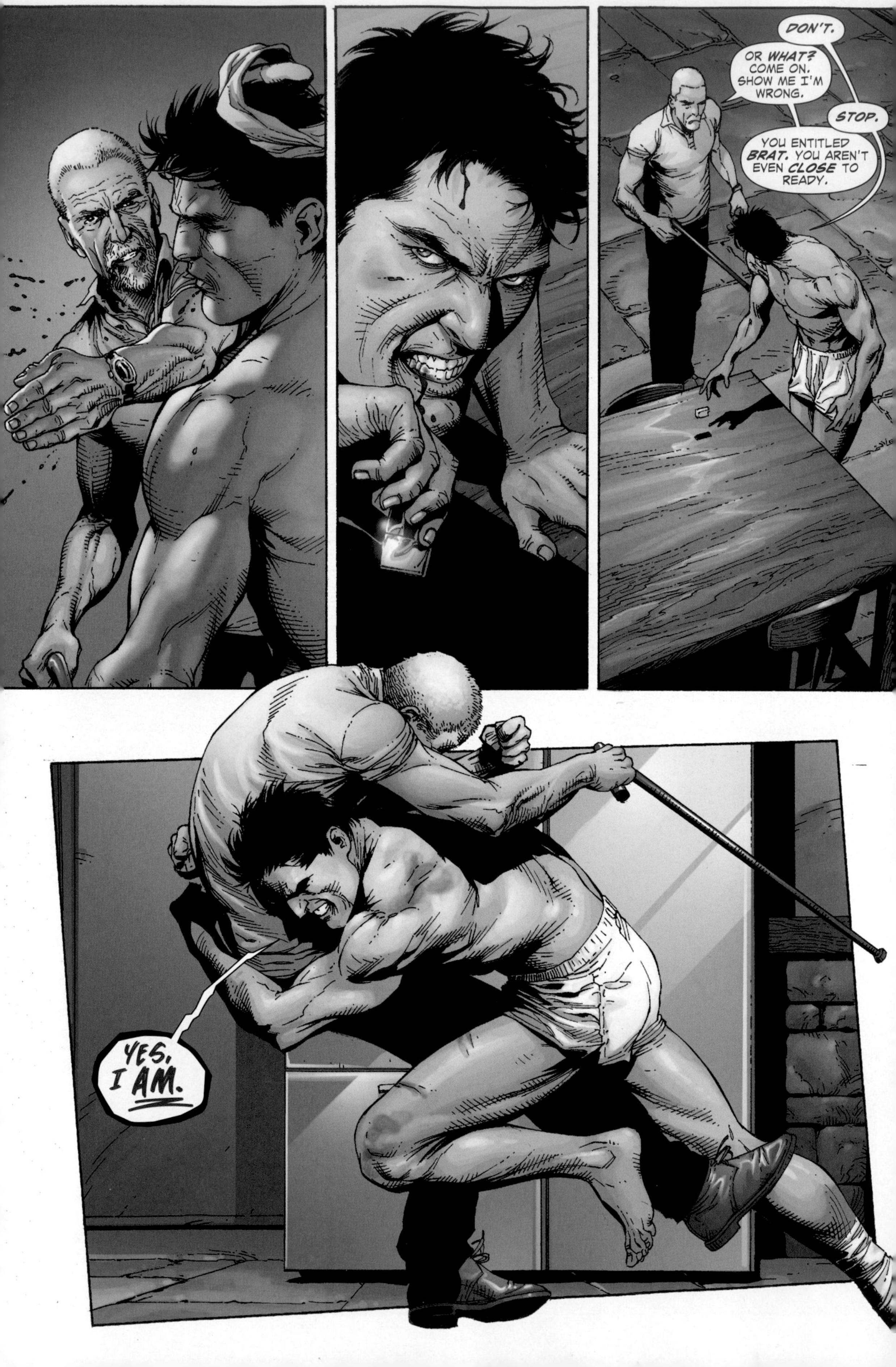
DON'T.
OR WHAT? COME ON. SHOW ME I'M WRONG.
STOP.
YOU ENTITLED BRAT. YOU AREN'T EVEN CLOSE TO READY.
YES, I AM.

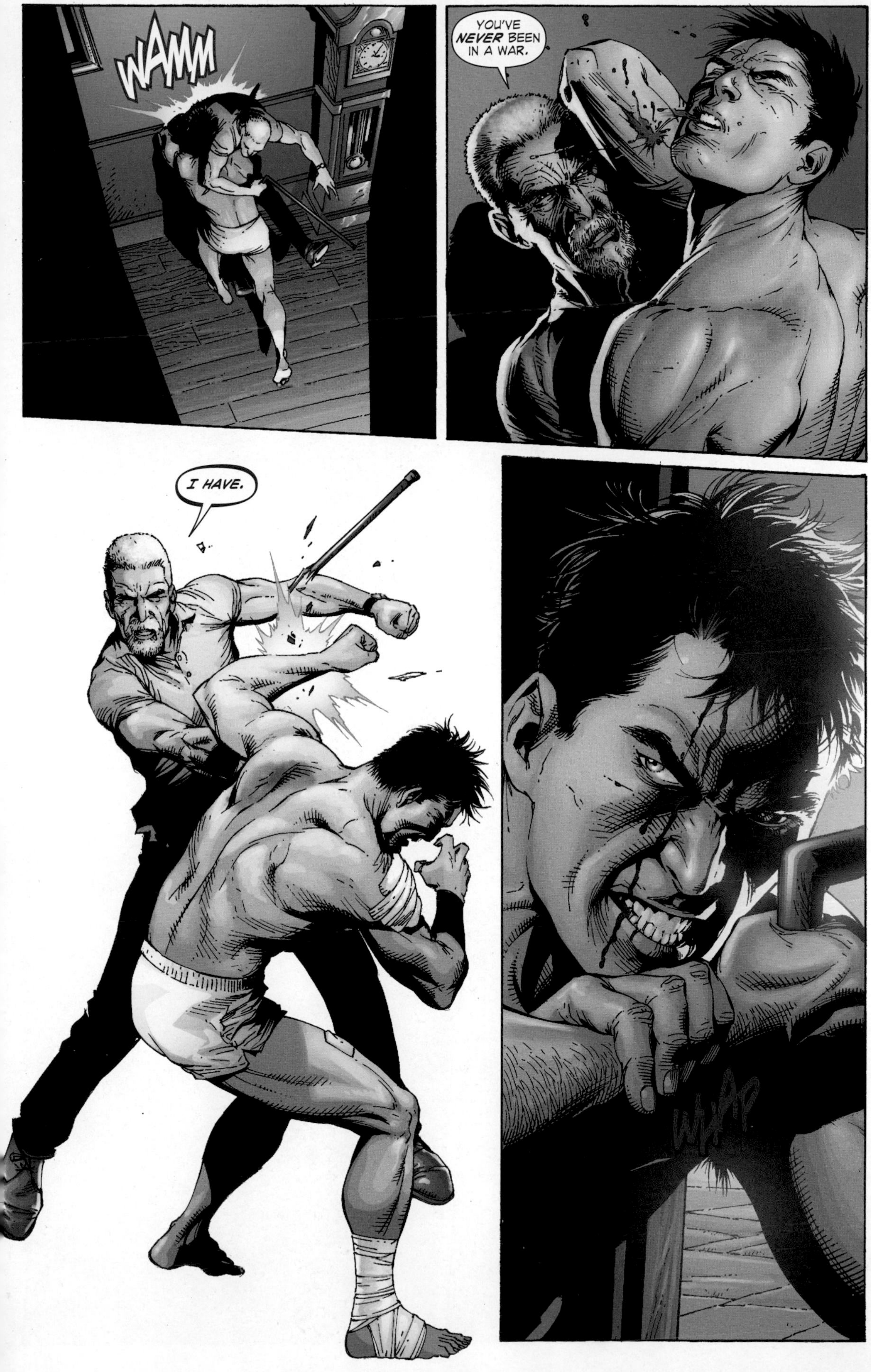
WAMM
YOU'VE NEVER BEEN IN A WAR.
I HAVE.

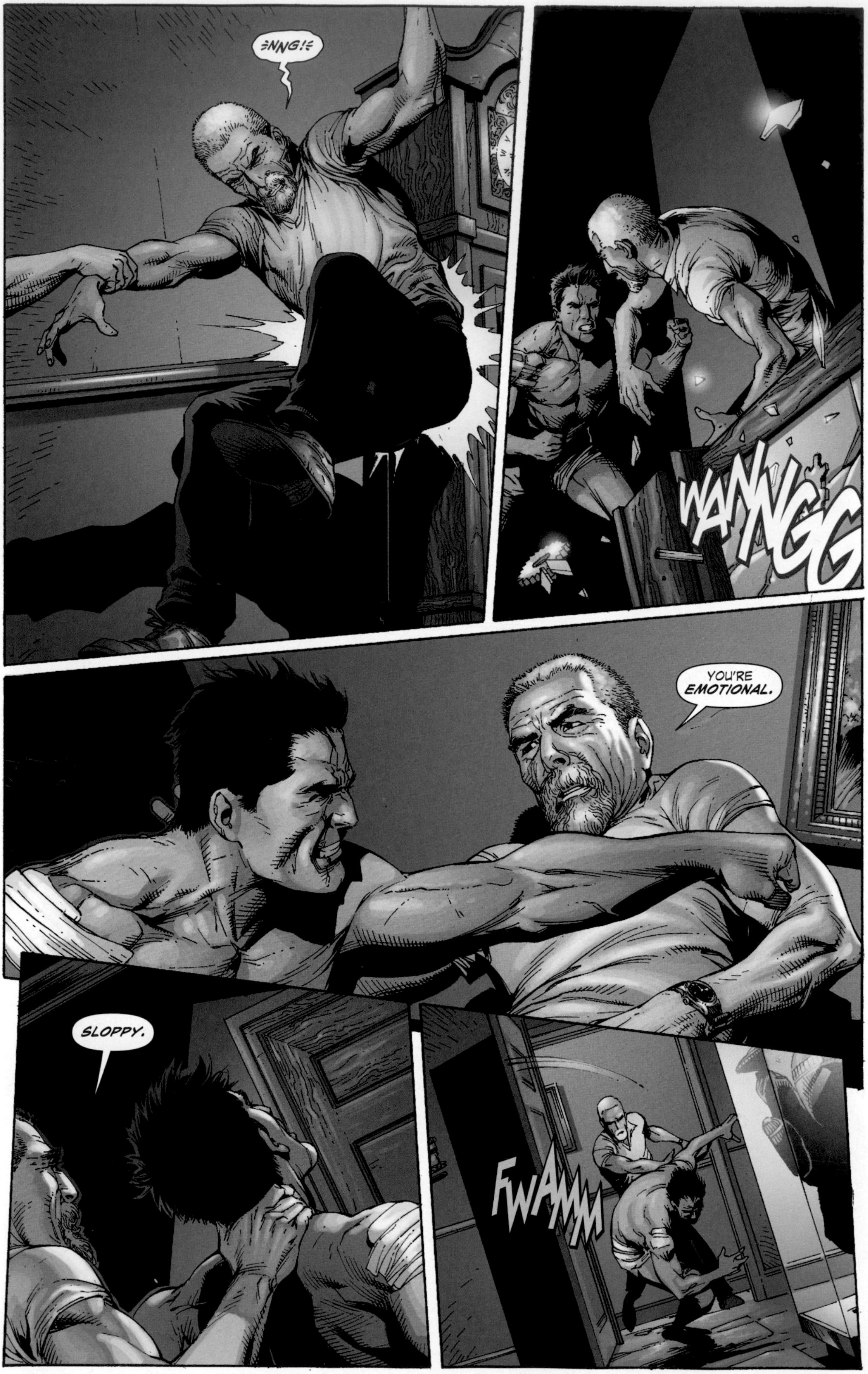

NNG!
WANNGG
YOU'RE EMOTIONAL.
SLOPPY.
FWAMM

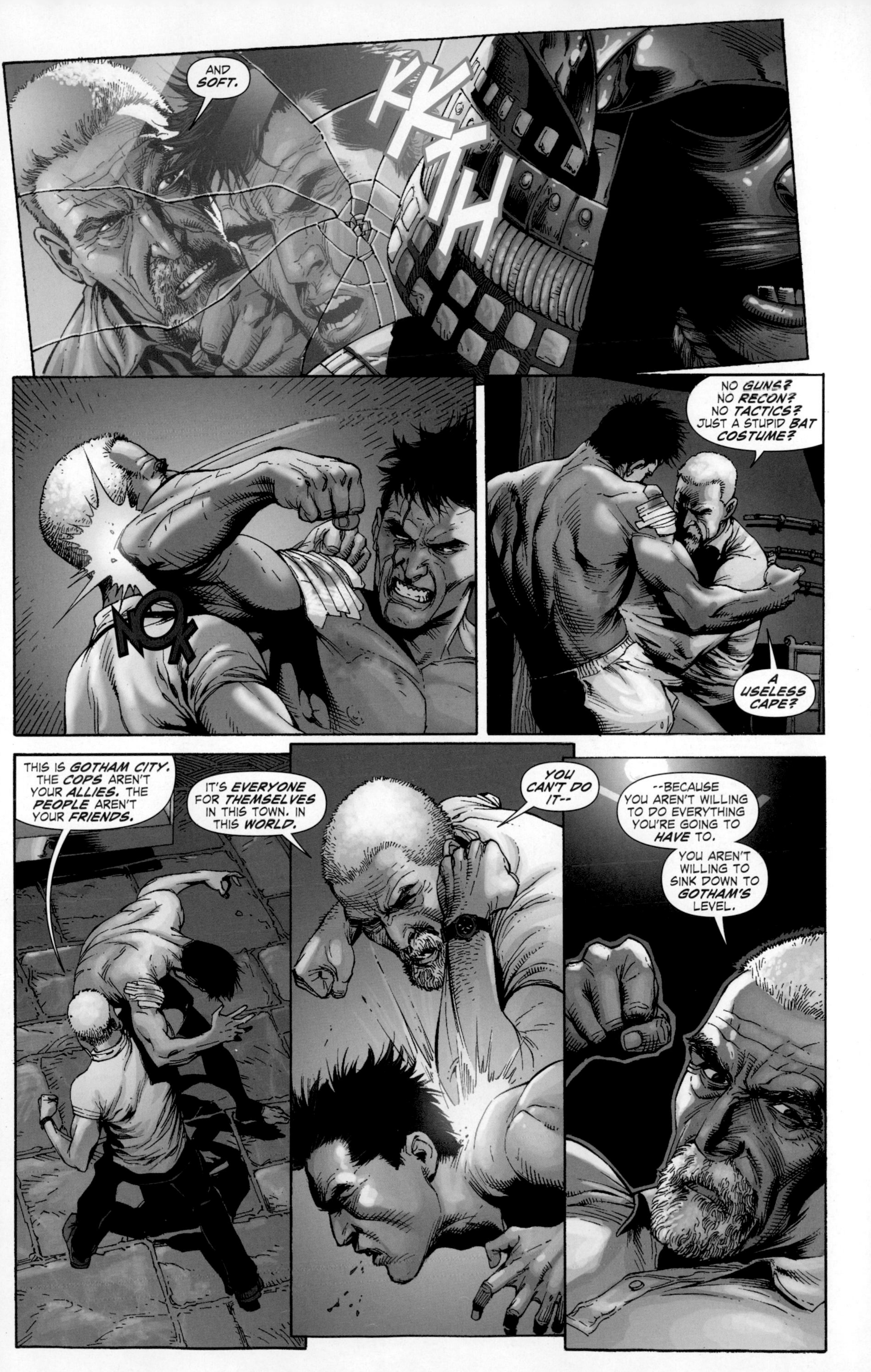
AND SOFT.
KKTH
NOK
NO GUNS? NO RECON? NO TACTICS? JUST A STUPID BAT COSTUME?
A USELESS CAPE?
THIS IS GOTHAM CITY. THE COPS AREN'T YOUR ALLIES. THE PEOPLE AREN'T YOUR FRIENDS.
IT'S EVERYONE FOR THEMSELVES IN THIS TOWN. IN THIS WORLD.
YOU CAN'T DO IT--
--BECAUSE YOU AREN'T WILLING TO DO EVERYTHING YOU'RE GOING TO HAVE TO.
YOU AREN'T WILLING TO SINK DOWN TO GOTHAM'S LEVEL.

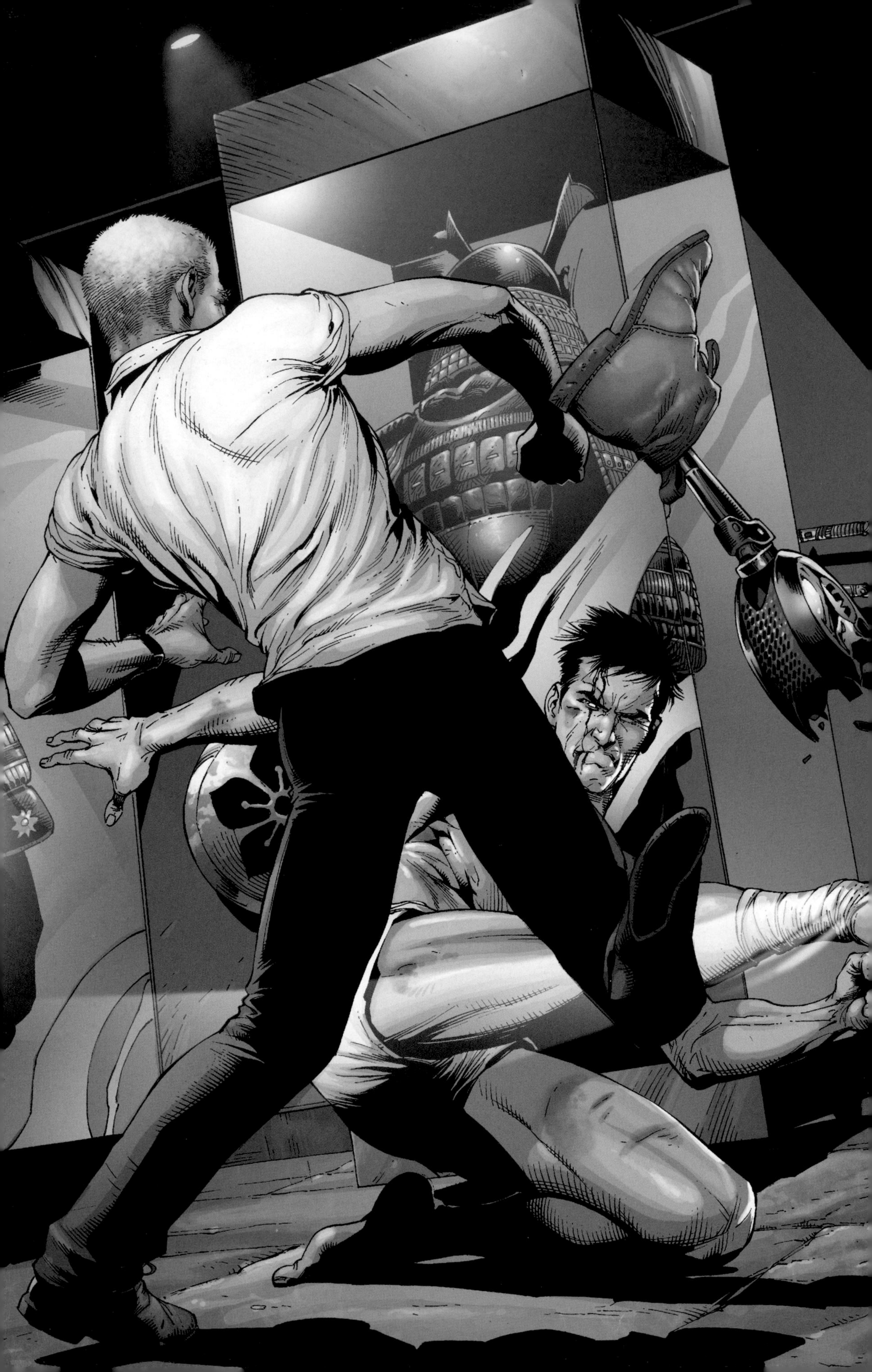

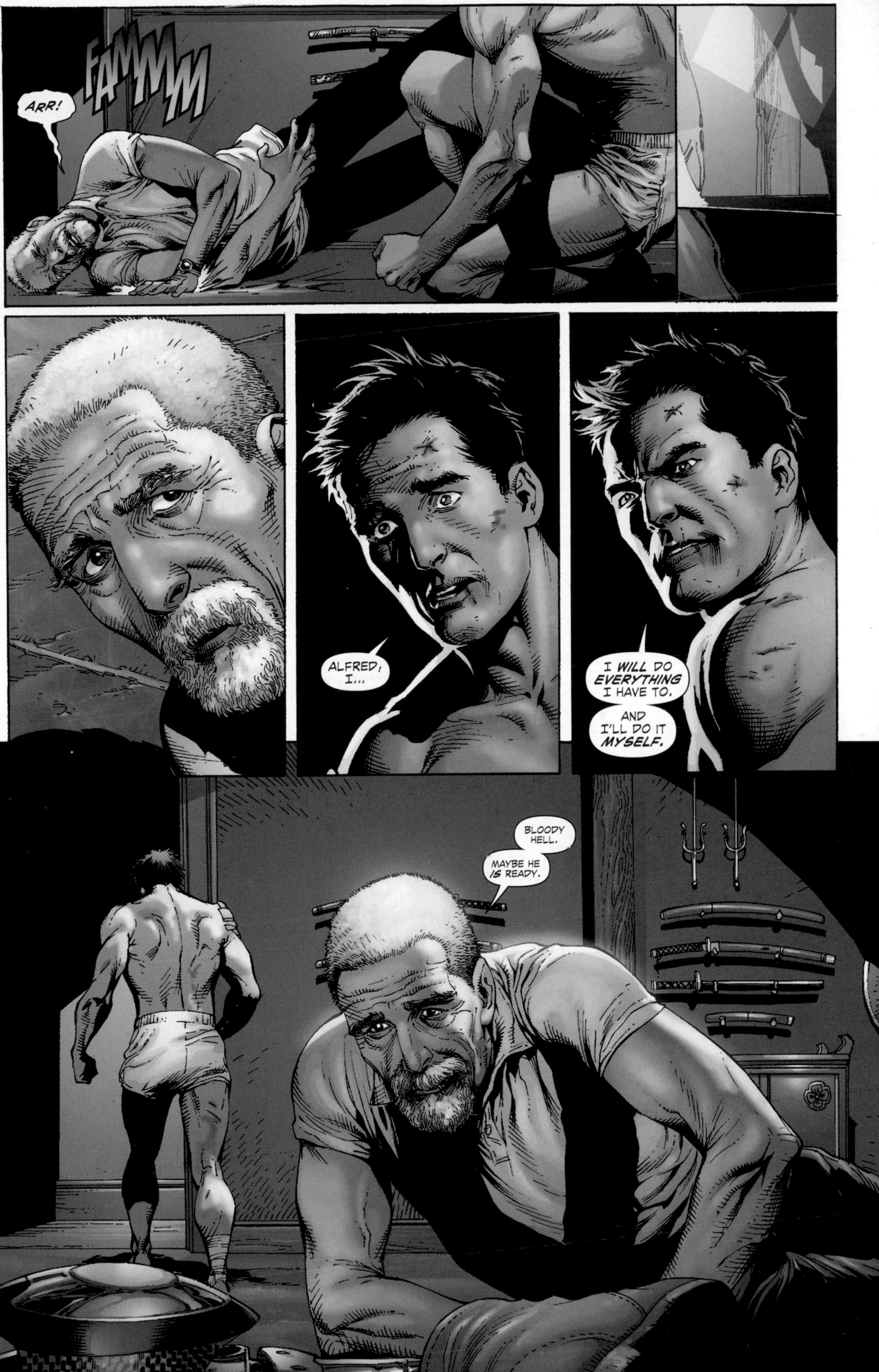
FAMMM
ARR!
ALFRED, I...
I WILL DO EVERYTHING I HAVE TO.
AND I'LL DO IT MYSELF.
BLOODY HELL.
MAYBE HE IS READY.

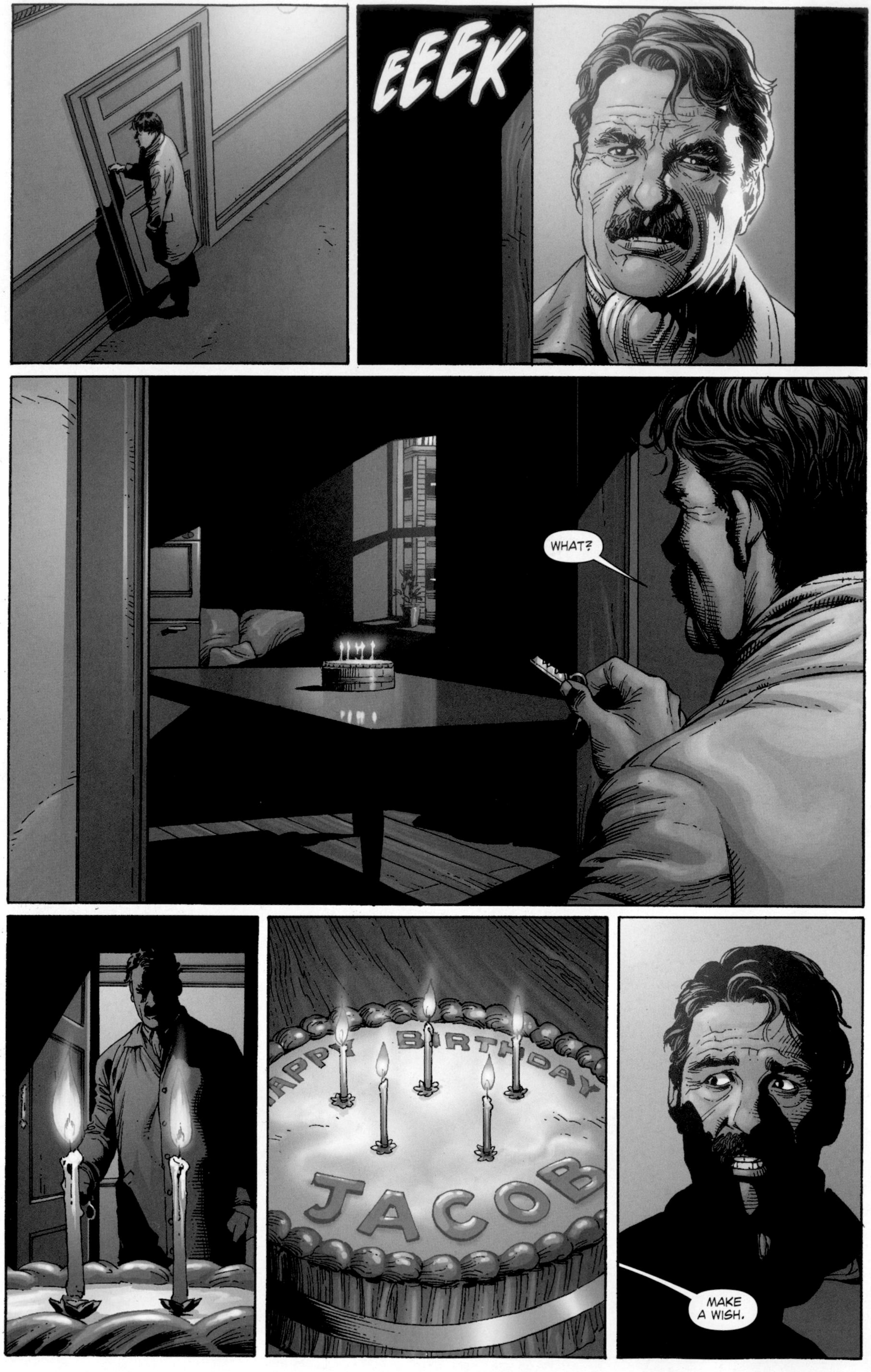
EEEK
WHAT?
HAPPY BIRTHDAY
JACOB
MAKE A WISH.

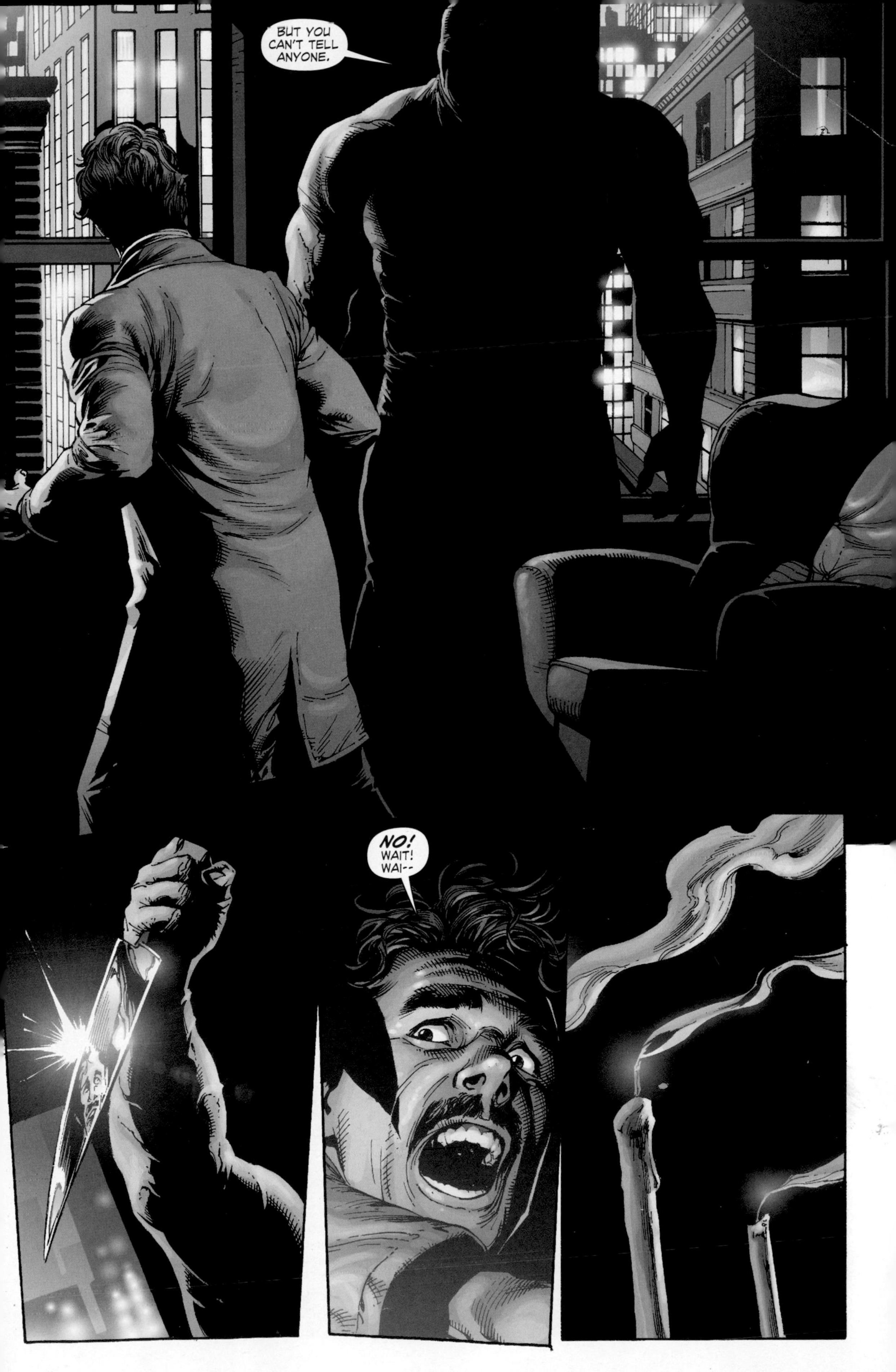
BUT YOU CAN'T TELL ANYONE.
NO! WAIT! WAI--

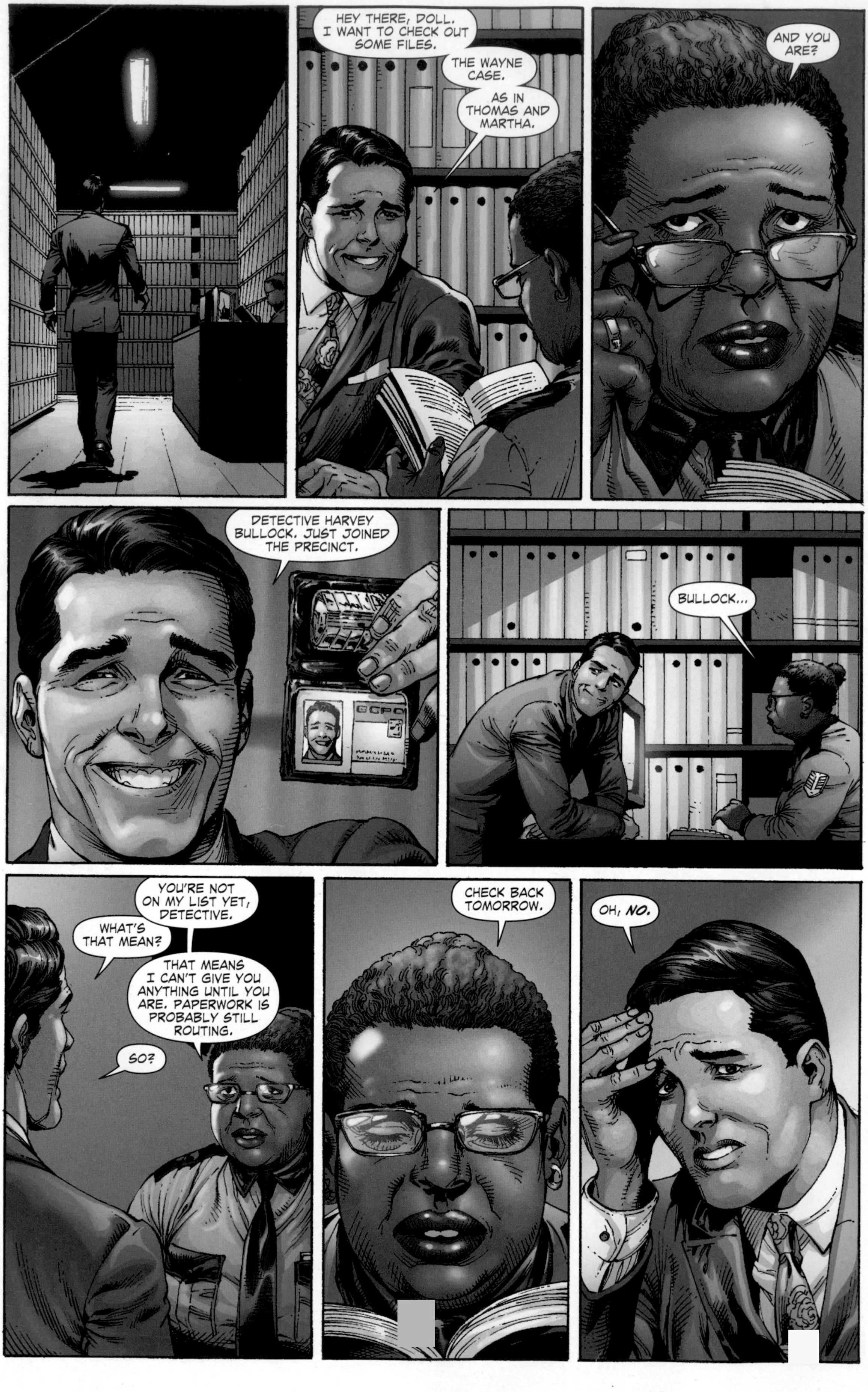
HEY THERE, DOLL. I WANT TO CHECK OUT SOME FILES.
THE WAYNE CASE.
AS IN THOMAS AND MARTHA.
AND YOU ARE?
DETECTIVE HARVEY BULLOCK. JUST JOINED THE PRECINCT.
GCPD
BULLOCK...
YOU'RE NOT ON MY LIST YET, DETECTIVE.
WHAT'S THAT MEAN?
THAT MEANS I CAN'T GIVE YOU ANYTHING UNTIL YOU ARE. PAPERWORK IS PROBABLY STILL ROUTING.
SO?
CHECK BACK TOMORROW.
OH, NO.

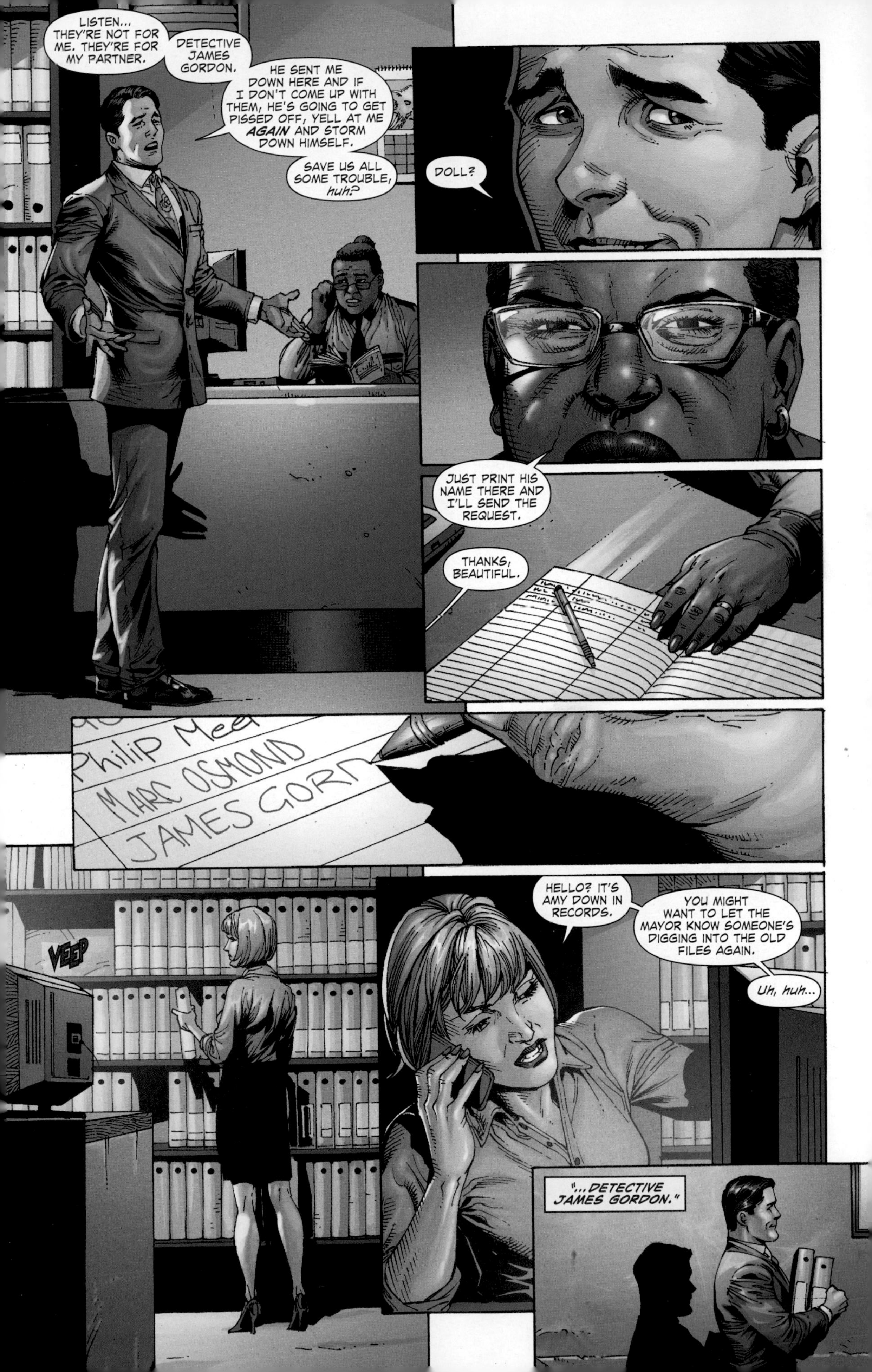

LISTEN... THEY'RE NOT FOR ME. THEY'RE FOR MY PARTNER.
DETECTIVE JAMES GORDON.
HE SENT ME DOWN HERE AND IF I DON'T COME UP WITH THEM, HE'S GOING TO GET PISSED OFF, YELL AT ME AGAIN AND STORM DOWN HIMSELF.
SAVE US ALL SOME TROUBLE, huh?
DOLL?
JUST PRINT HIS NAME THERE AND I'LL SEND THE REQUEST.
THANKS, BEAUTIFUL.
Philip Mee
MARC OSMOND
JAMES GORD
VEEP
HELLO? IT'S AMY DOWN IN RECORDS.
YOU MIGHT WANT TO LET THE MAYOR KNOW SOMEONE'S DIGGING INTO THE OLD FILES AGAIN.
Uh, huh...
"...DETECTIVE JAMES GORDON."

BARBARA?

I'M SORRY I'M LATE.

...BARBARA?

BZZD

HELLO?

HEY, DAD.

BARBARA? WHERE ARE YOU?

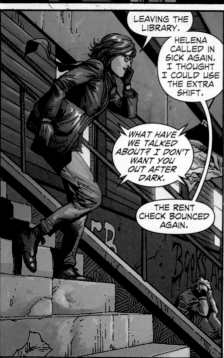

LEAVING THE LIBRARY.

HELENA CALLED IN SICK AGAIN. I THOUGHT I COULD USE THE EXTRA SHIFT.

WHAT HAVE WE TALKED ABOUT? I DON'T WANT YOU OUT AFTER DARK.

THE RENT CHECK BOUNCED AGAIN.

...BARBARA, I...

DON'T WORRY ABOUT IT, DAD.

WE'RE IN THIS TOGETHER.

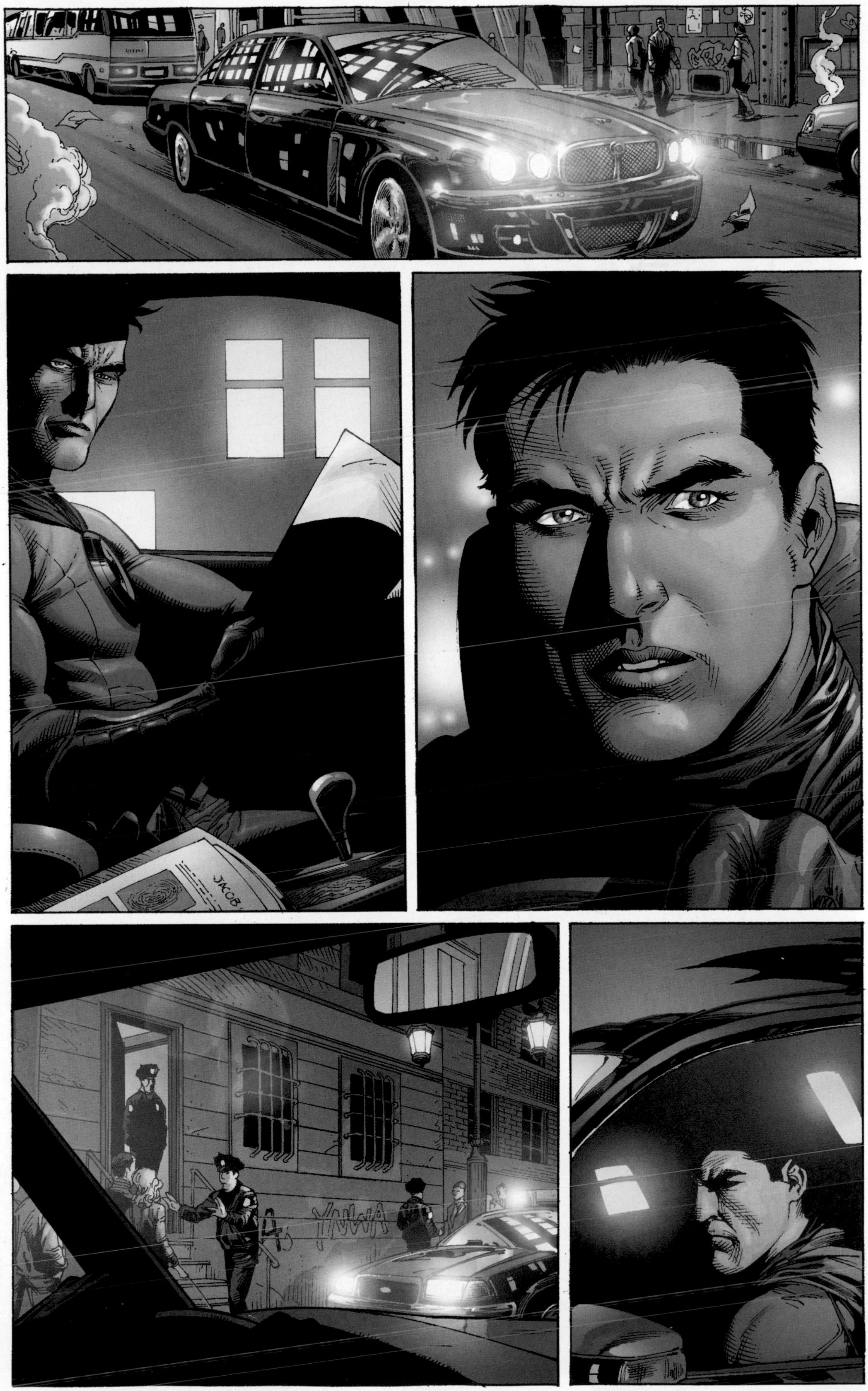
JACOB
YNWA

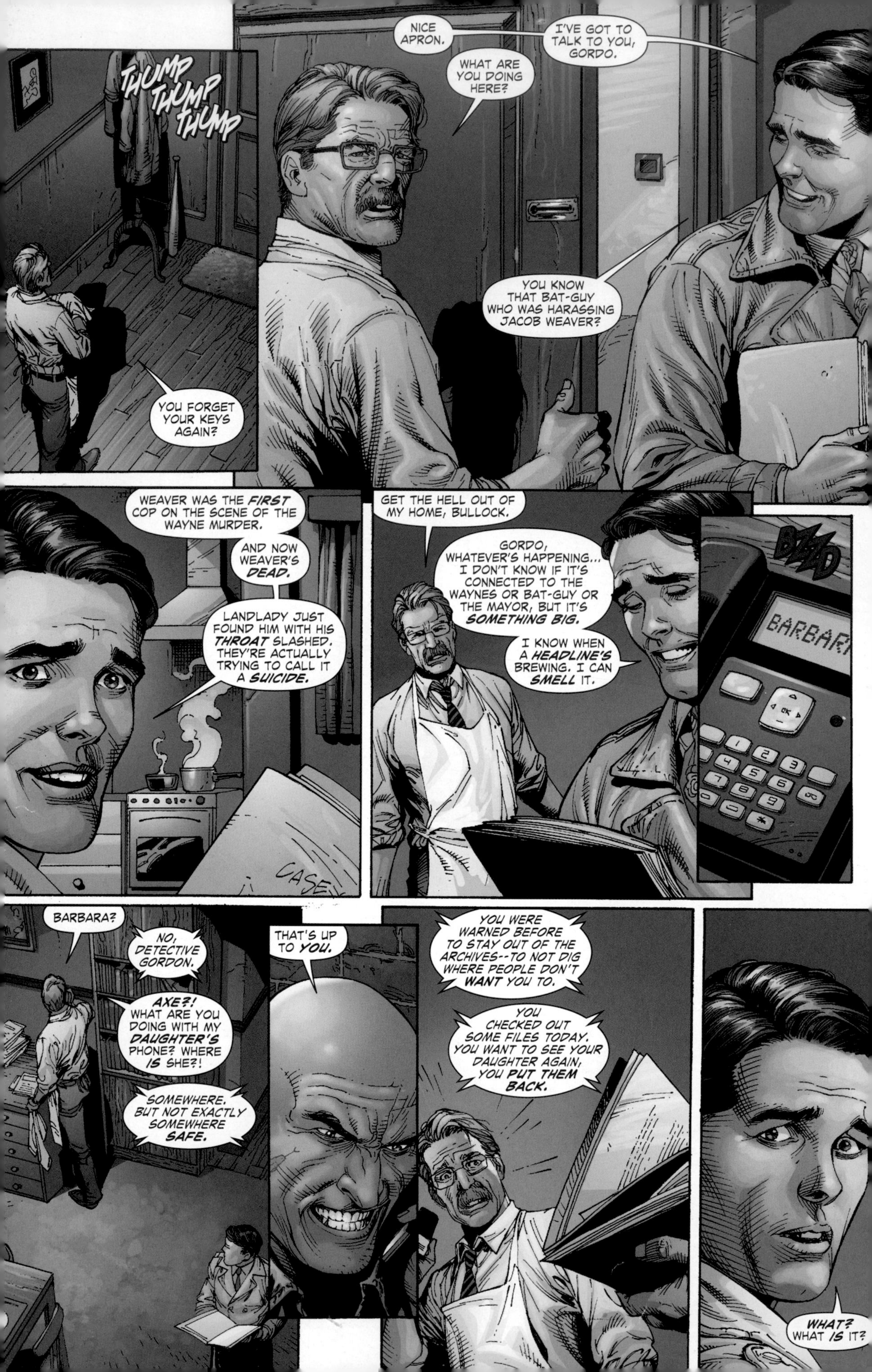
THUMP THUMP THUMP
YOU FORGET YOUR KEYS AGAIN?
NICE APRON.
I'VE GOT TO TALK TO YOU, GORDO.
WHAT ARE YOU DOING HERE?
YOU KNOW THAT BAT-GUY WHO WAS HARASSING JACOB WEAVER?
WEAVER WAS THE FIRST COP ON THE SCENE OF THE WAYNE MURDER.
AND NOW WEAVER'S DEAD.
LANDLADY JUST FOUND HIM WITH HIS THROAT SLASHED. THEY'RE ACTUALLY TRYING TO CALL IT A SUICIDE.
GET THE HELL OUT OF MY HOME, BULLOCK.
GORDO, WHATEVER'S HAPPENING... I DON'T KNOW IF IT'S CONNECTED TO THE WAYNES OR BAT-GUY OR THE MAYOR, BUT IT'S SOMETHING BIG.
I KNOW WHEN A HEADLINE'S BREWING. I CAN SMELL IT.
BZZZ
BARBARA?
NO, DETECTIVE GORDON.
AXE?! WHAT ARE YOU DOING WITH MY DAUGHTER'S PHONE? WHERE IS SHE?!
SOMEWHERE. BUT NOT EXACTLY SOMEWHERE SAFE.
THAT'S UP TO YOU.
YOU WERE WARNED BEFORE TO STAY OUT OF THE ARCHIVES--TO NOT DIG WHERE PEOPLE DON'T WANT YOU TO.
YOU CHECKED OUT SOME FILES TODAY. YOU WANT TO SEE YOUR DAUGHTER AGAIN, YOU PUT THEM BACK.
WHAT? WHAT IS IT?

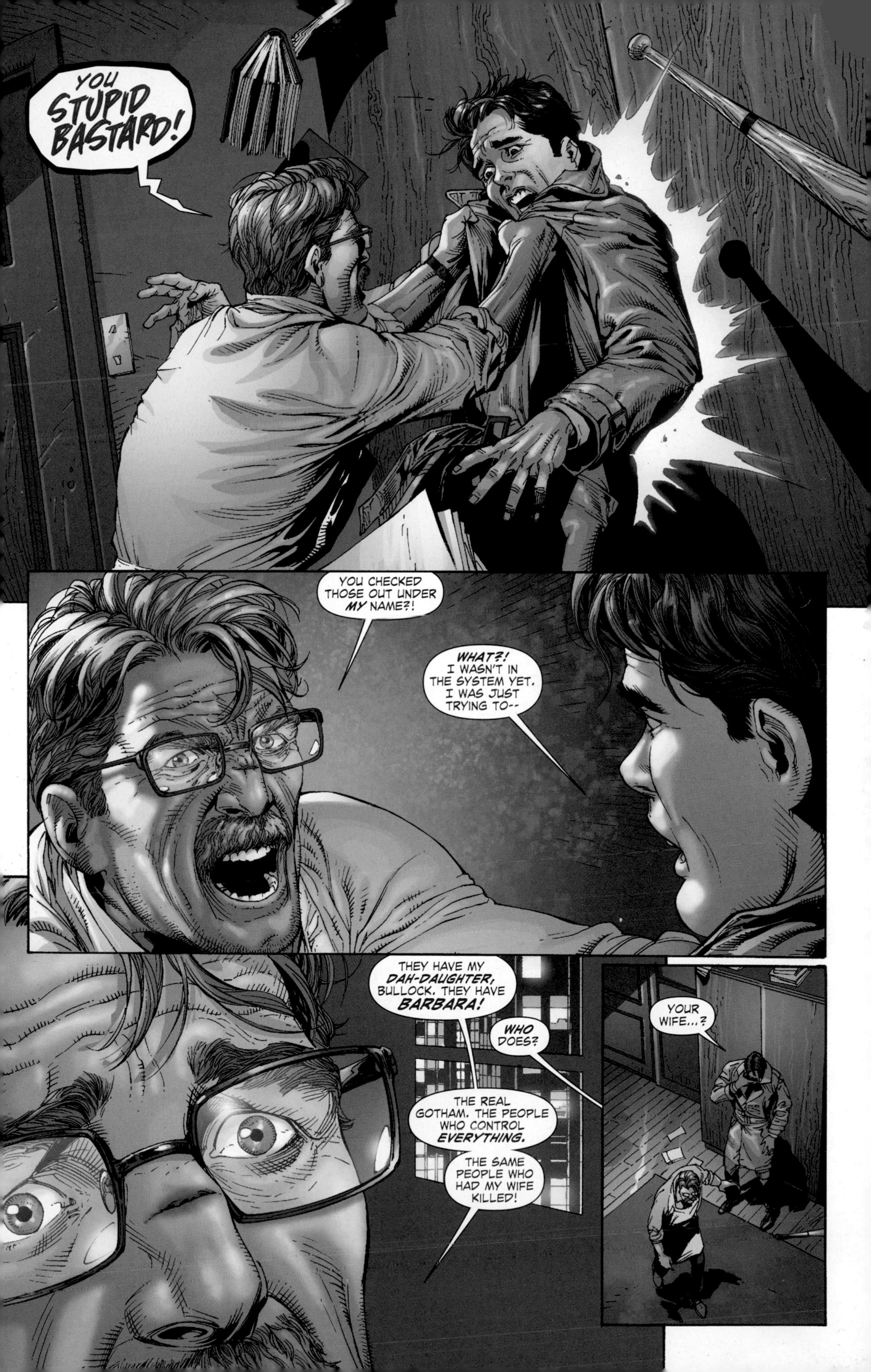
YOU STUPID BASTARD!
YOU CHECKED THOSE OUT UNDER MY NAME?!
WHAT?! I WASN'T IN THE SYSTEM YET. I WAS JUST TRYING TO--
THEY HAVE MY DAH-DAUGHTER, BULLOCK. THEY HAVE BARBARA!
WHO DOES?
THE REAL GOTHAM. THE PEOPLE WHO CONTROL EVERYTHING.
THE SAME PEOPLE WHO HAD MY WIFE KILLED!
YOUR WIFE...?

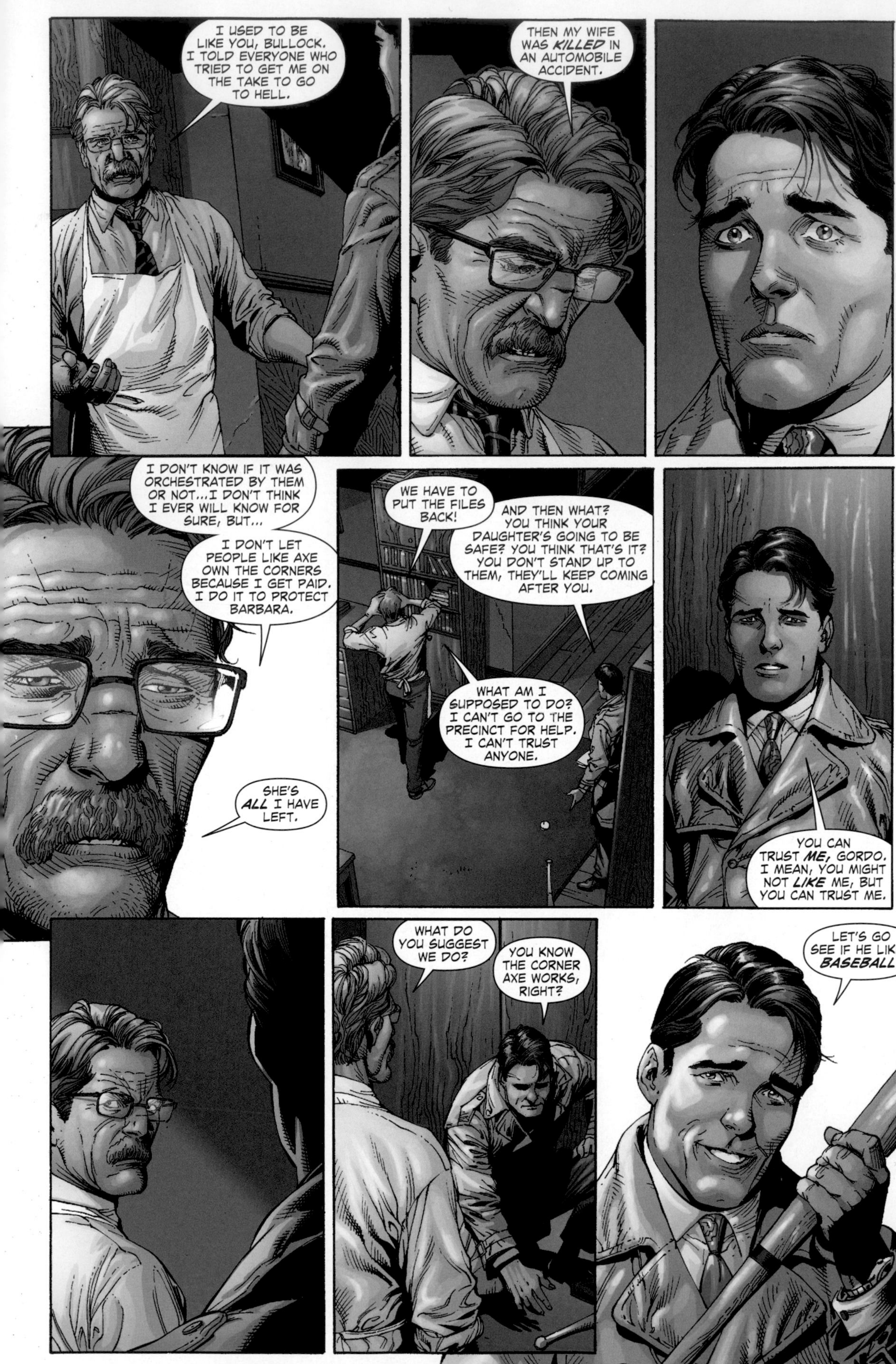
I USED TO BE LIKE YOU, BULLOCK. I TOLD EVERYONE WHO TRIED TO GET ME ON THE TAKE TO GO TO HELL.
THEN MY WIFE WAS KILLED IN AN AUTOMOBILE ACCIDENT.
I DON'T KNOW IF IT WAS ORCHESTRATED BY THEM OR NOT...I DON'T THINK I EVER WILL KNOW FOR SURE, BUT...
I DON'T LET PEOPLE LIKE AXE OWN THE CORNERS BECAUSE I GET PAID. I DO IT TO PROTECT BARBARA.
SHE'S ALL I HAVE LEFT.
WE HAVE TO PUT THE FILES BACK!
AND THEN WHAT? YOU THINK YOUR DAUGHTER'S GOING TO BE SAFE? YOU THINK THAT'S IT? YOU DON'T STAND UP TO THEM, THEY'LL KEEP COMING AFTER YOU.
WHAT AM I SUPPOSED TO DO? I CAN'T GO TO THE PRECINCT FOR HELP. I CAN'T TRUST ANYONE.
YOU CAN TRUST ME, GORDO. I MEAN, YOU MIGHT NOT LIKE ME, BUT YOU CAN TRUST ME.
WHAT DO YOU SUGGEST WE DO?
YOU KNOW THE CORNER AXE WORKS, RIGHT?
LET'S GO SEE IF HE LIKES BASEBALL.

WHERE YOU GOIN', HONEYS?

WE GOTTA GO TO WORK.

I'VE GOT WORK FOR YOU, BABY.

COME BACK!

KRAK

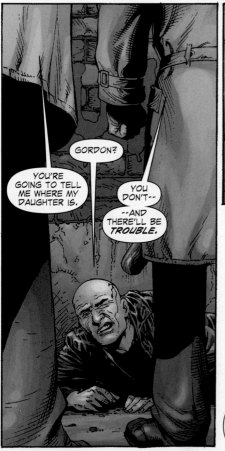

GORDON?

YOU'RE GOING TO TELL ME WHERE MY DAUGHTER IS.

YOU DON'T--

--AND THERE'LL BE TROUBLE.

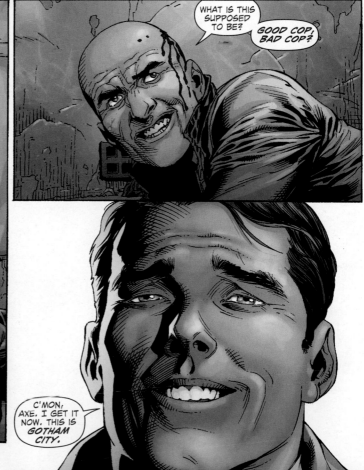

WHAT IS THIS SUPPOSED TO BE? GOOD COP, BAD COP?

C'MON, AXE. I GET IT NOW. THIS IS GOTHAM CITY.

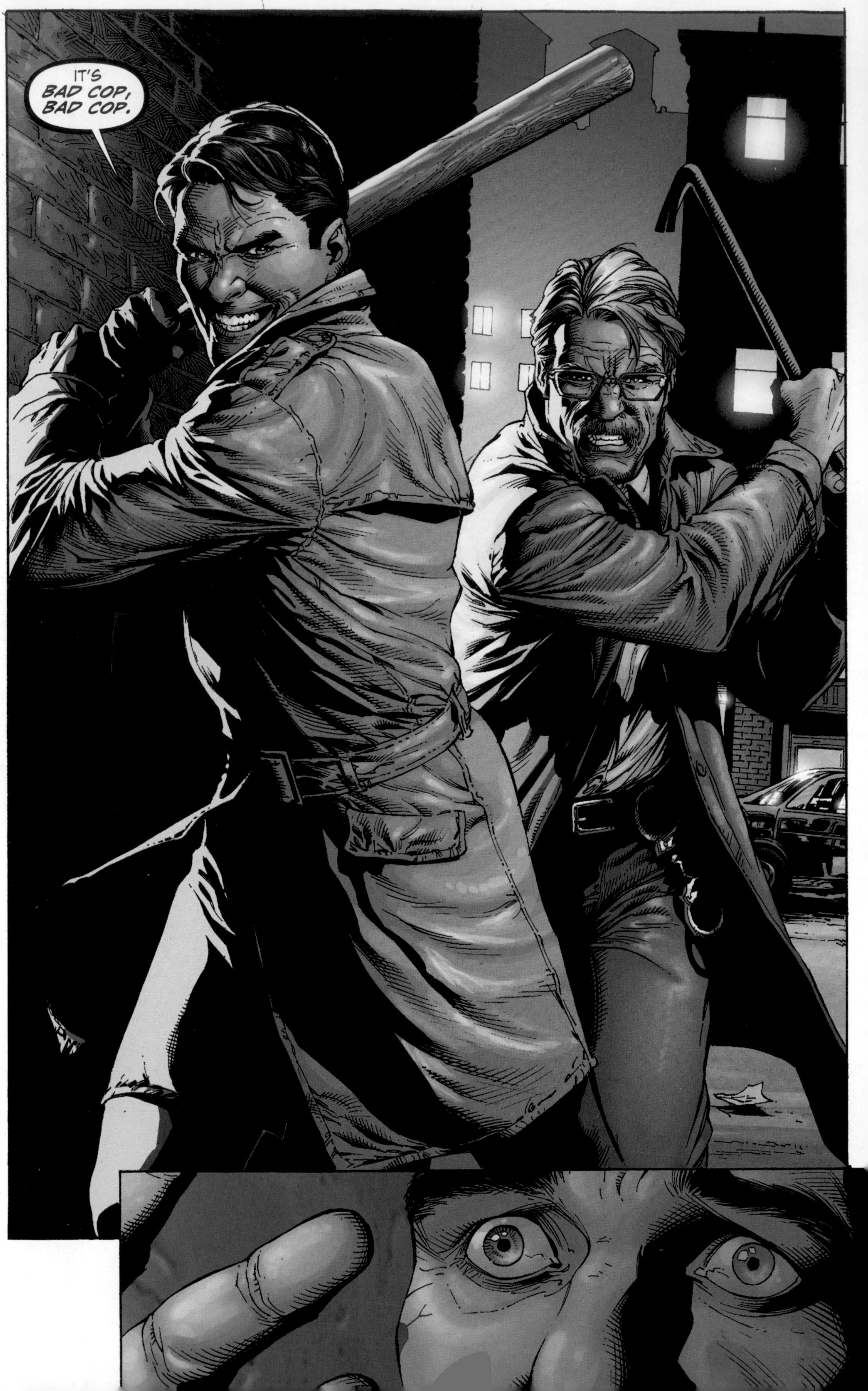
IT'S BAD COP, BAD COP.

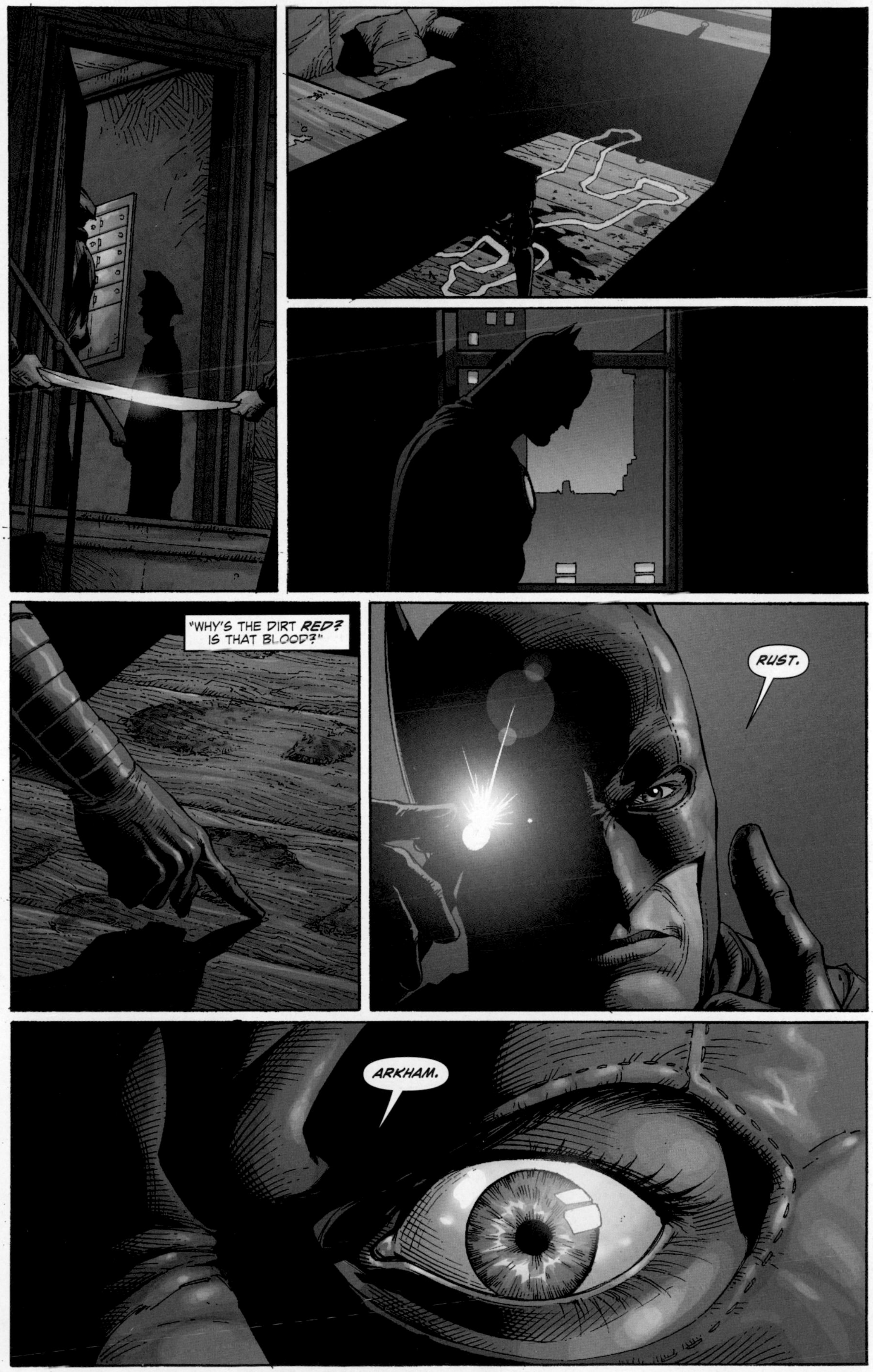
"WHY'S THE DIRT RED? IS THAT BLOOD?"
RUST.
ARKHAM.

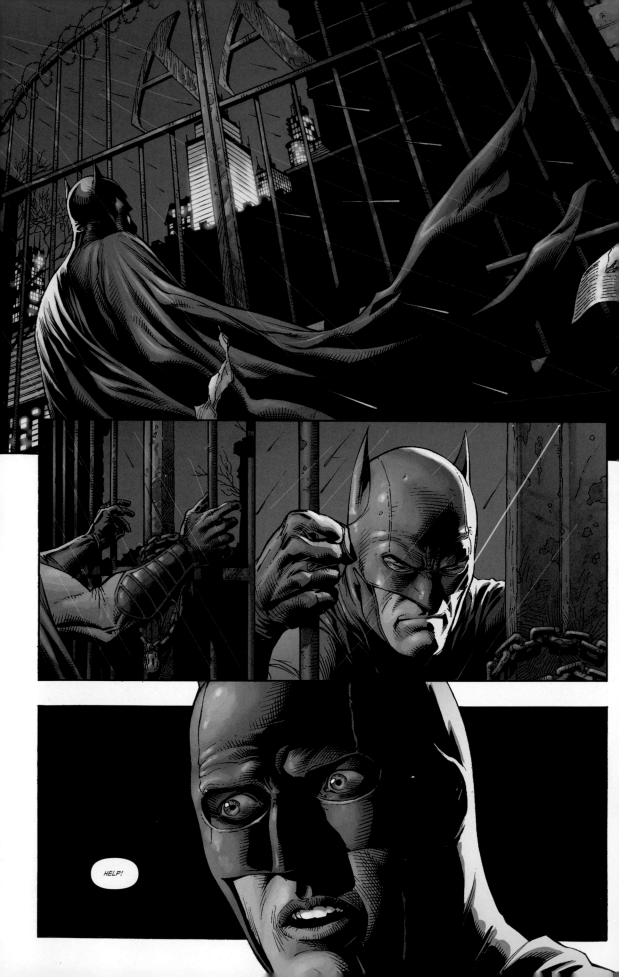

HELP!

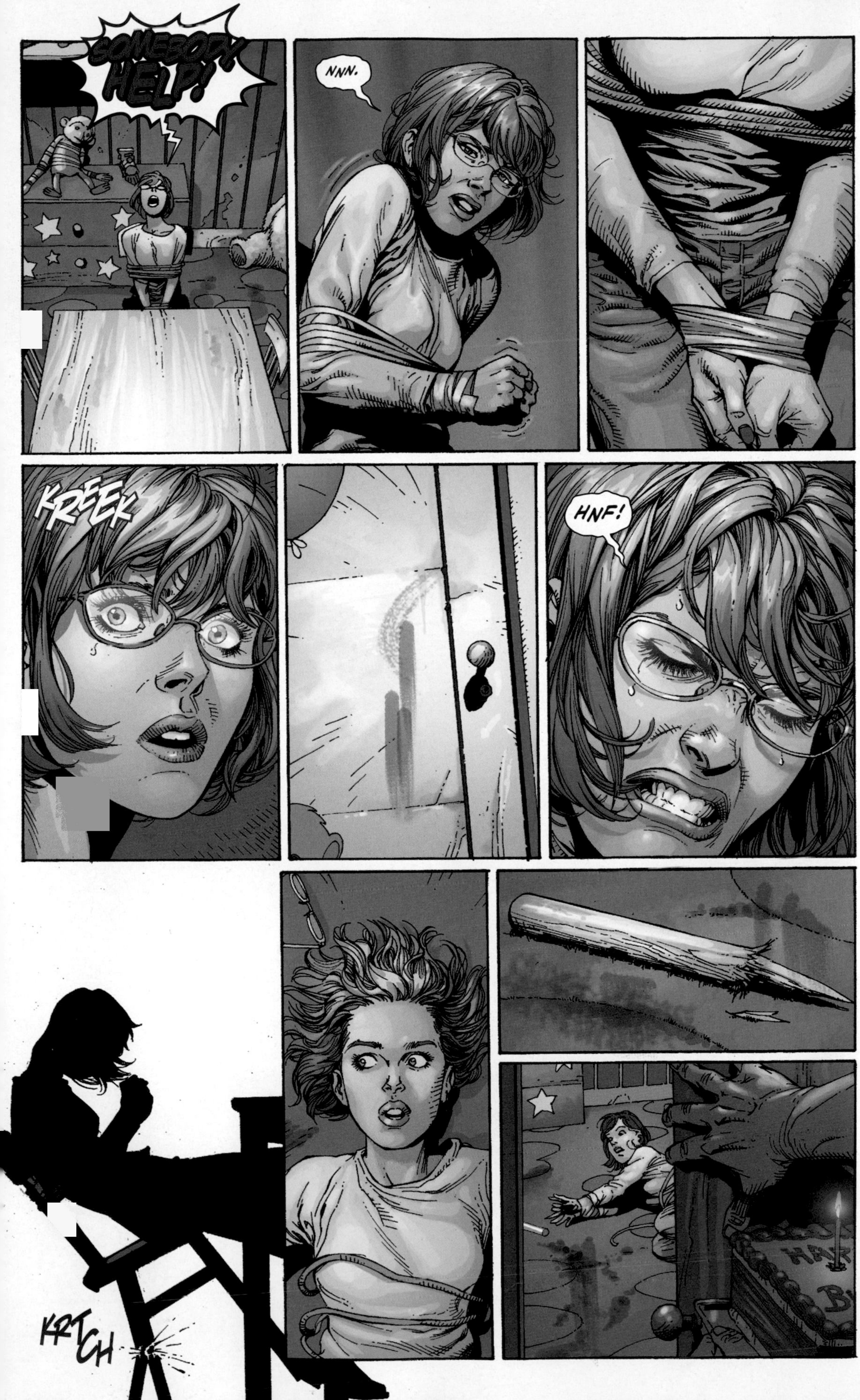
SOMEBODY HELP!
NNN.
KREEK
HNF!
KRTCH

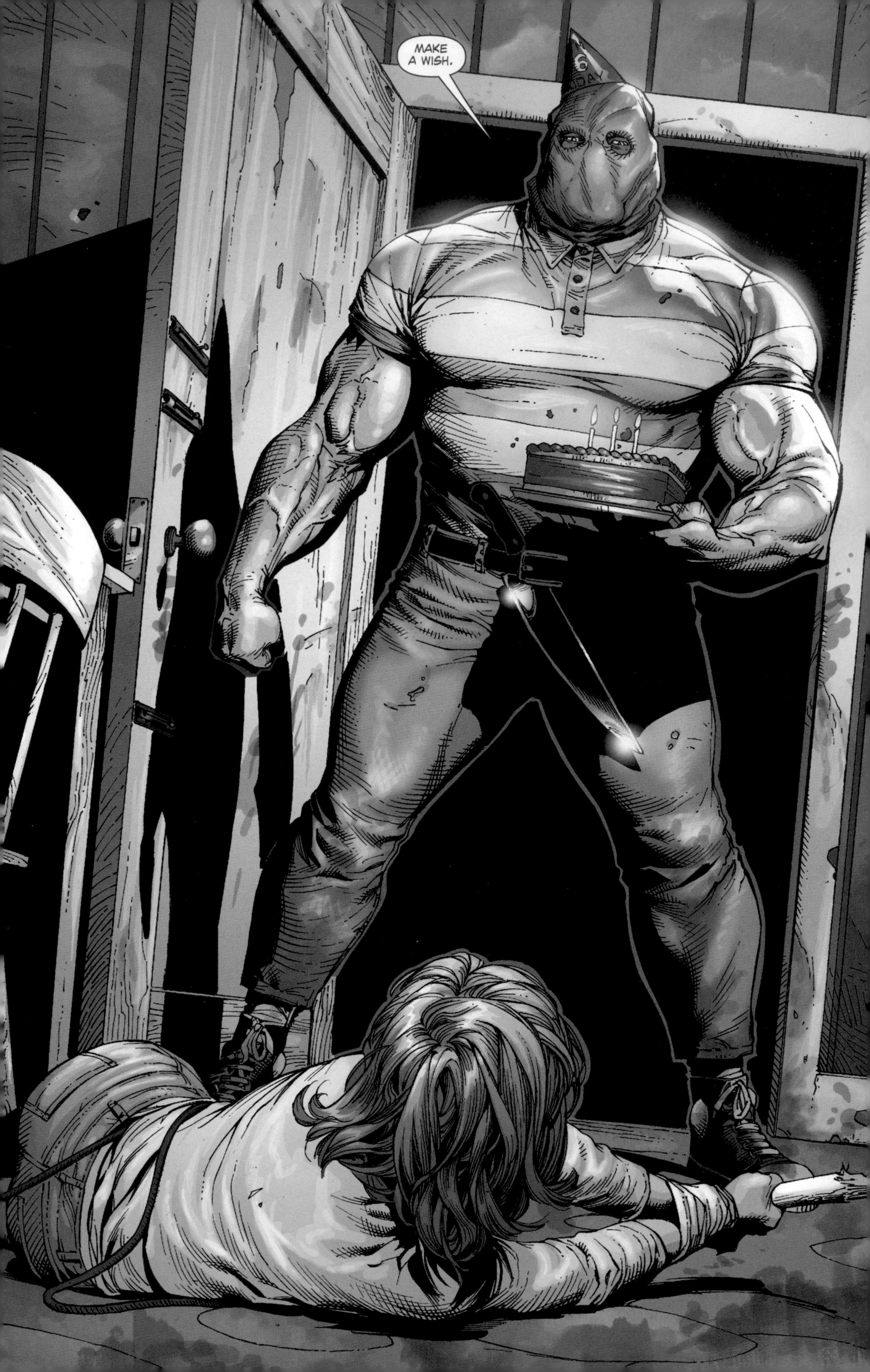
MAKE A WISH.

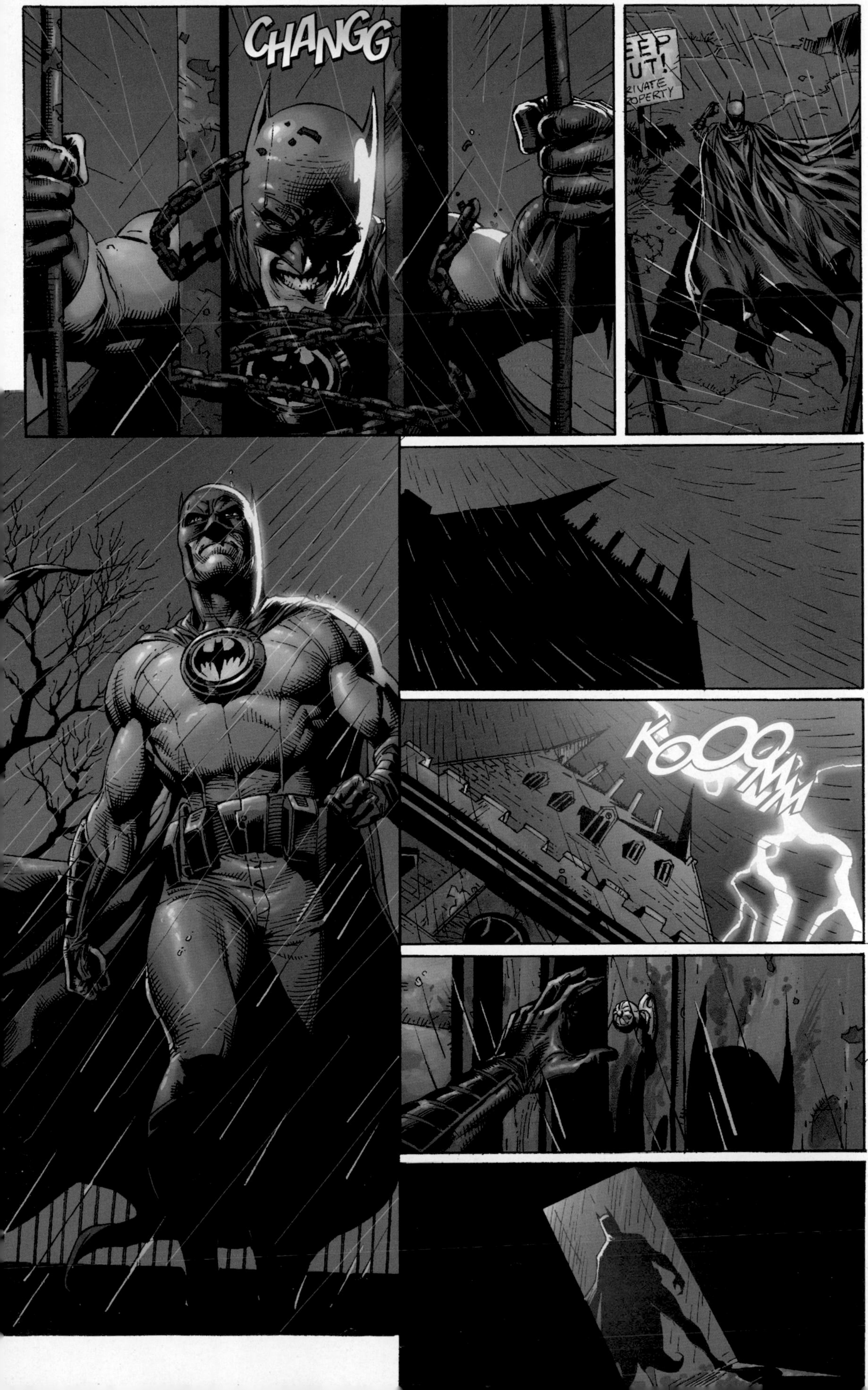
CHANGG
KOOOMM

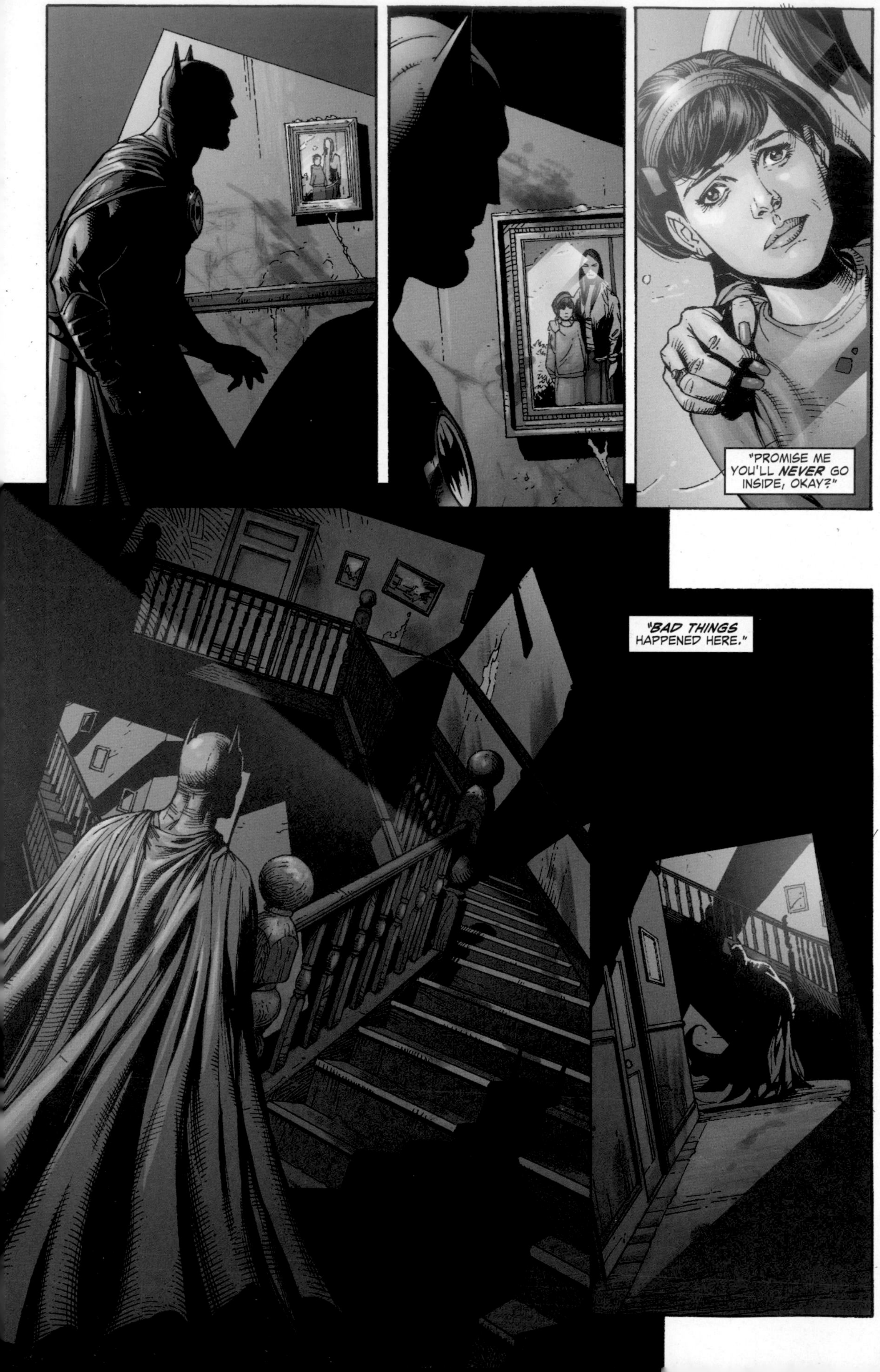
"PROMISE ME YOU'LL NEVER GO INSIDE, OKAY?"
"BAD THINGS HAPPENED HERE."

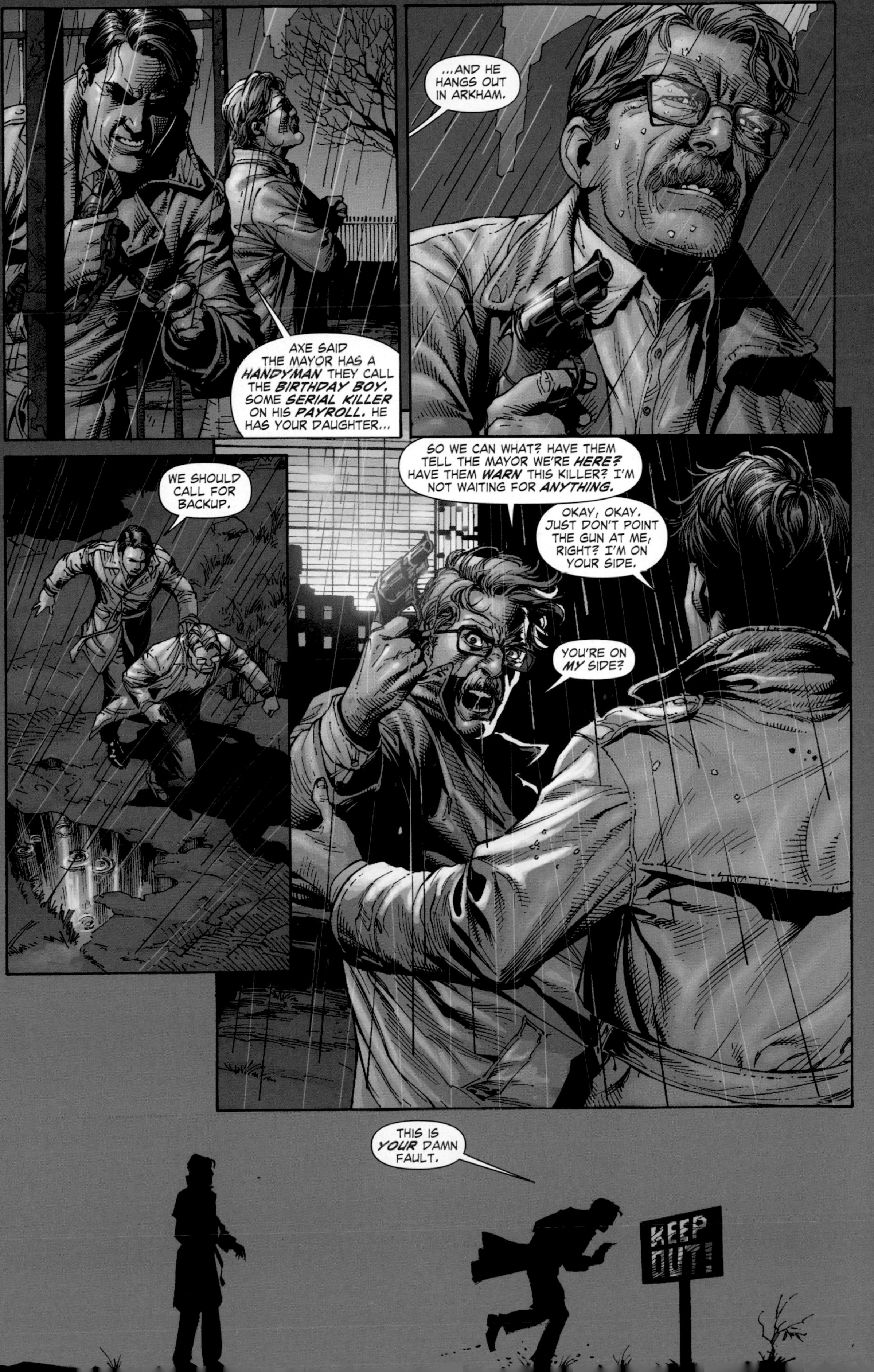
AXE SAID THE MAYOR HAS A HANDYMAN THEY CALL THE BIRTHDAY BOY. SOME SERIAL KILLER ON HIS PAYROLL. HE HAS YOUR DAUGHTER...
...AND HE HANGS OUT IN ARKHAM.
WE SHOULD CALL FOR BACKUP.
SO WE CAN WHAT? HAVE THEM TELL THE MAYOR WE'RE HERE? HAVE THEM WARN THIS KILLER? I'M NOT WAITING FOR ANYTHING.
OKAY, OKAY. JUST DON'T POINT THE GUN AT ME, RIGHT? I'M ON YOUR SIDE.
YOU'RE ON MY SIDE?
THIS IS YOUR DAMN FAULT.
KEEP OUT!

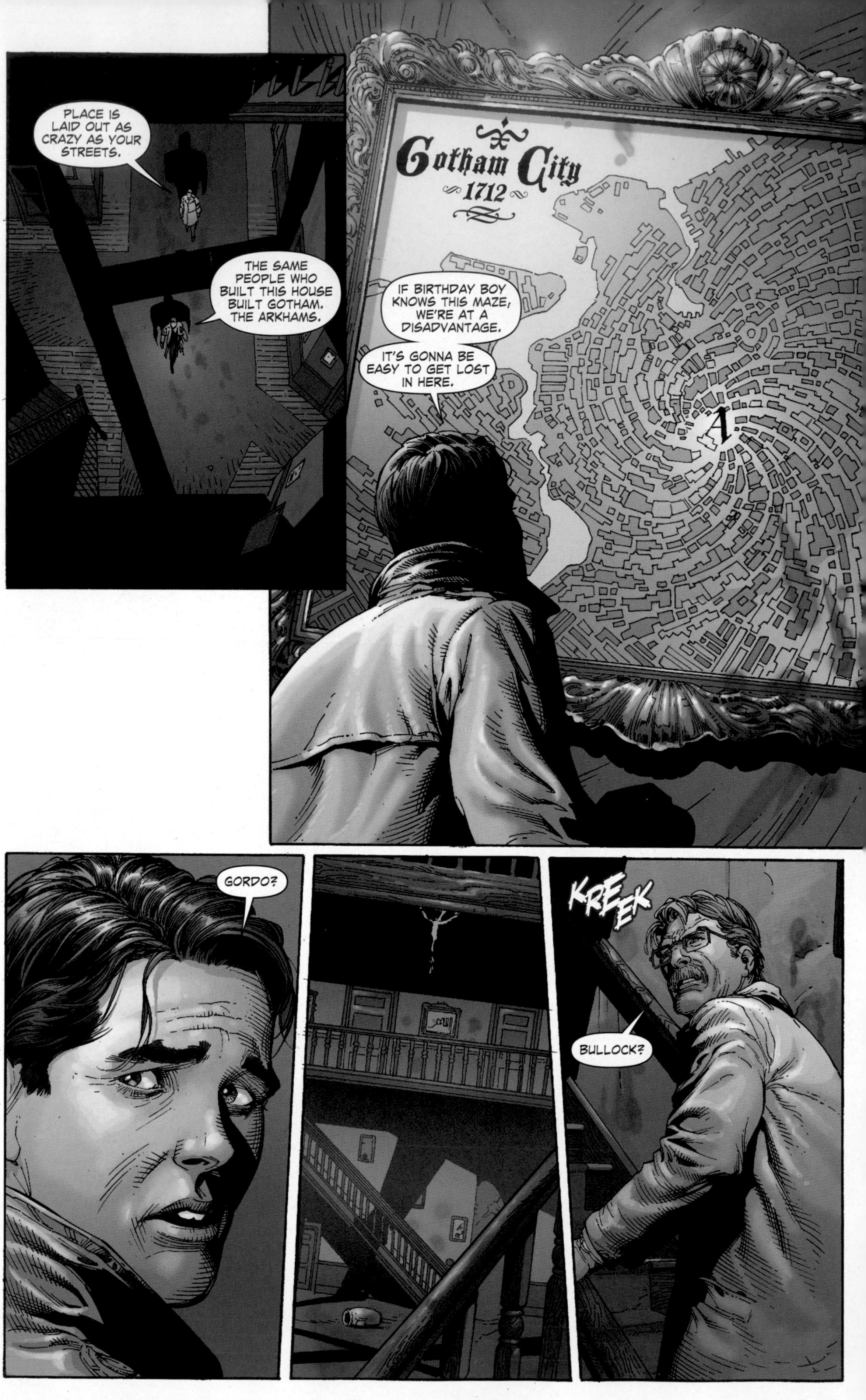
PLACE IS LAID OUT AS CRAZY AS YOUR STREETS.
THE SAME PEOPLE WHO BUILT THIS HOUSE BUILT GOTHAM. THE ARKHAMS.
Gotham City
1712
IF BIRTHDAY BOY KNOWS THIS MAZE, WE'RE AT A DISADVANTAGE.
IT'S GONNA BE EASY TO GET LOST IN HERE.
GORDO?
KREEK
BULLOCK?

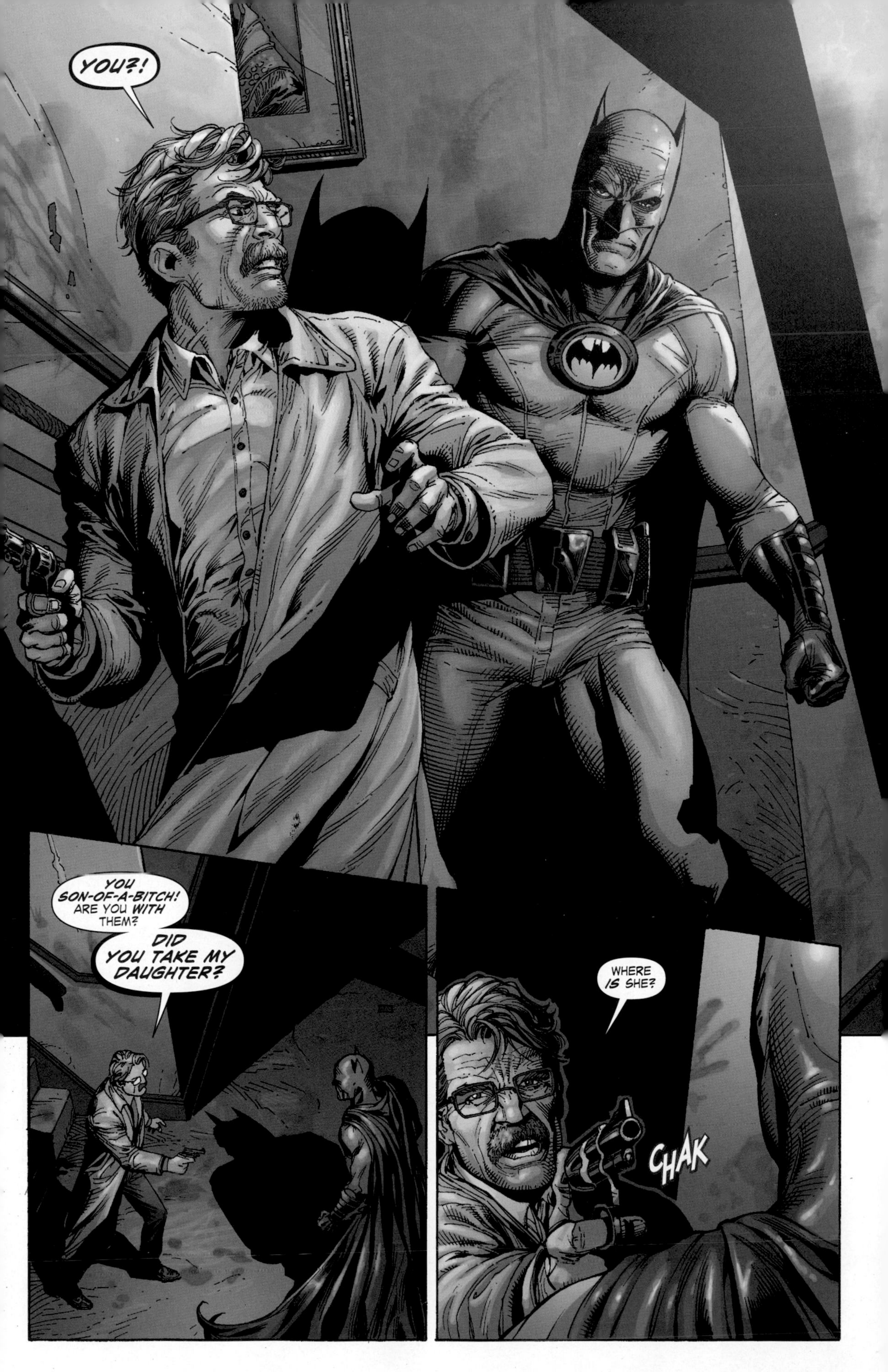
YOU?!
YOU SON-OF-A-BITCH! ARE YOU WITH THEM?
DID YOU TAKE MY DAUGHTER?
WHERE IS SHE?
CHAK

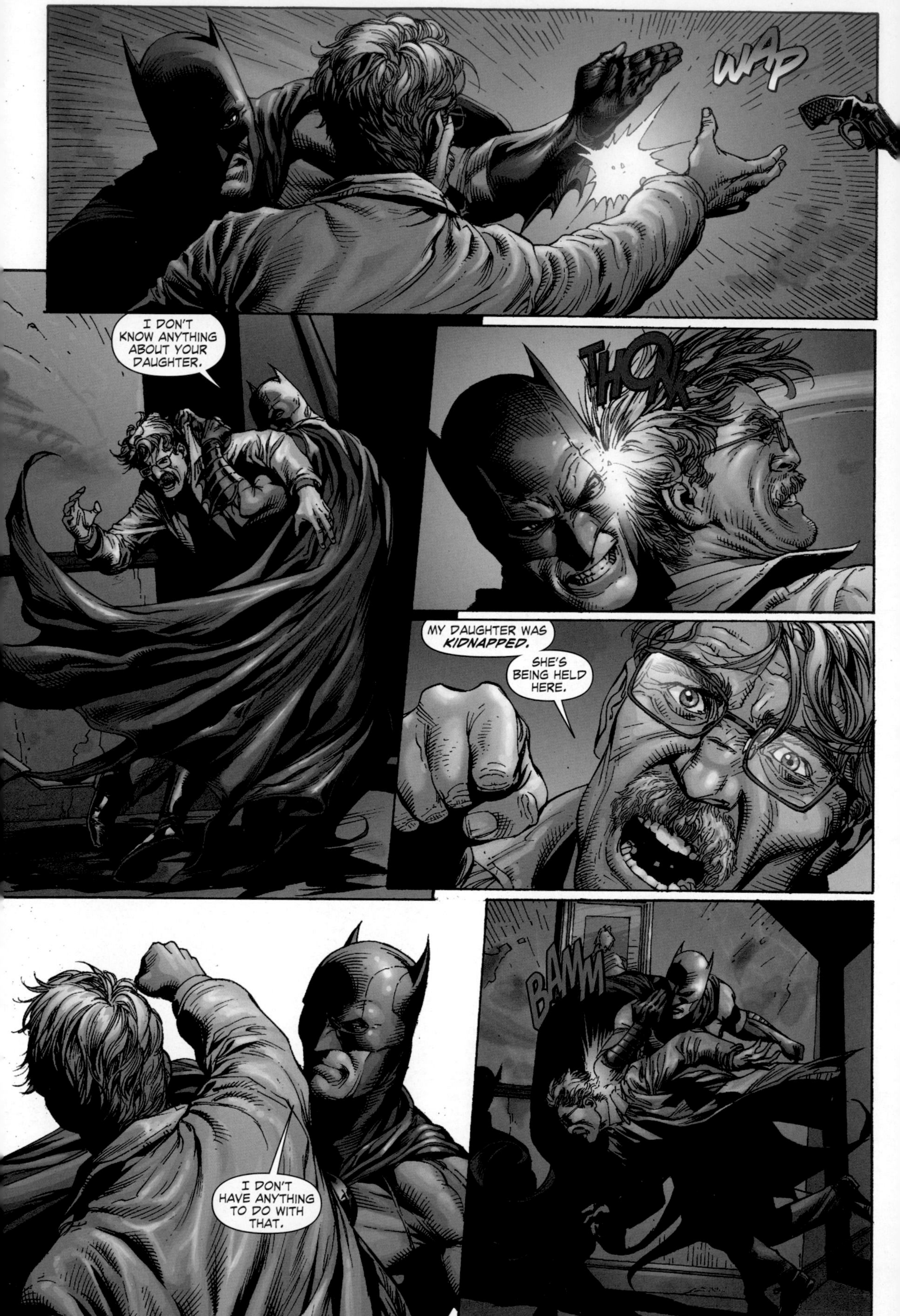
WAP
I DON'T KNOW ANYTHING ABOUT YOUR DAUGHTER.
THOK
MY DAUGHTER WAS *KIDNAPPED.*
SHE'S BEING HELD HERE.
I DON'T HAVE ANYTHING TO DO WITH THAT.
BAMM

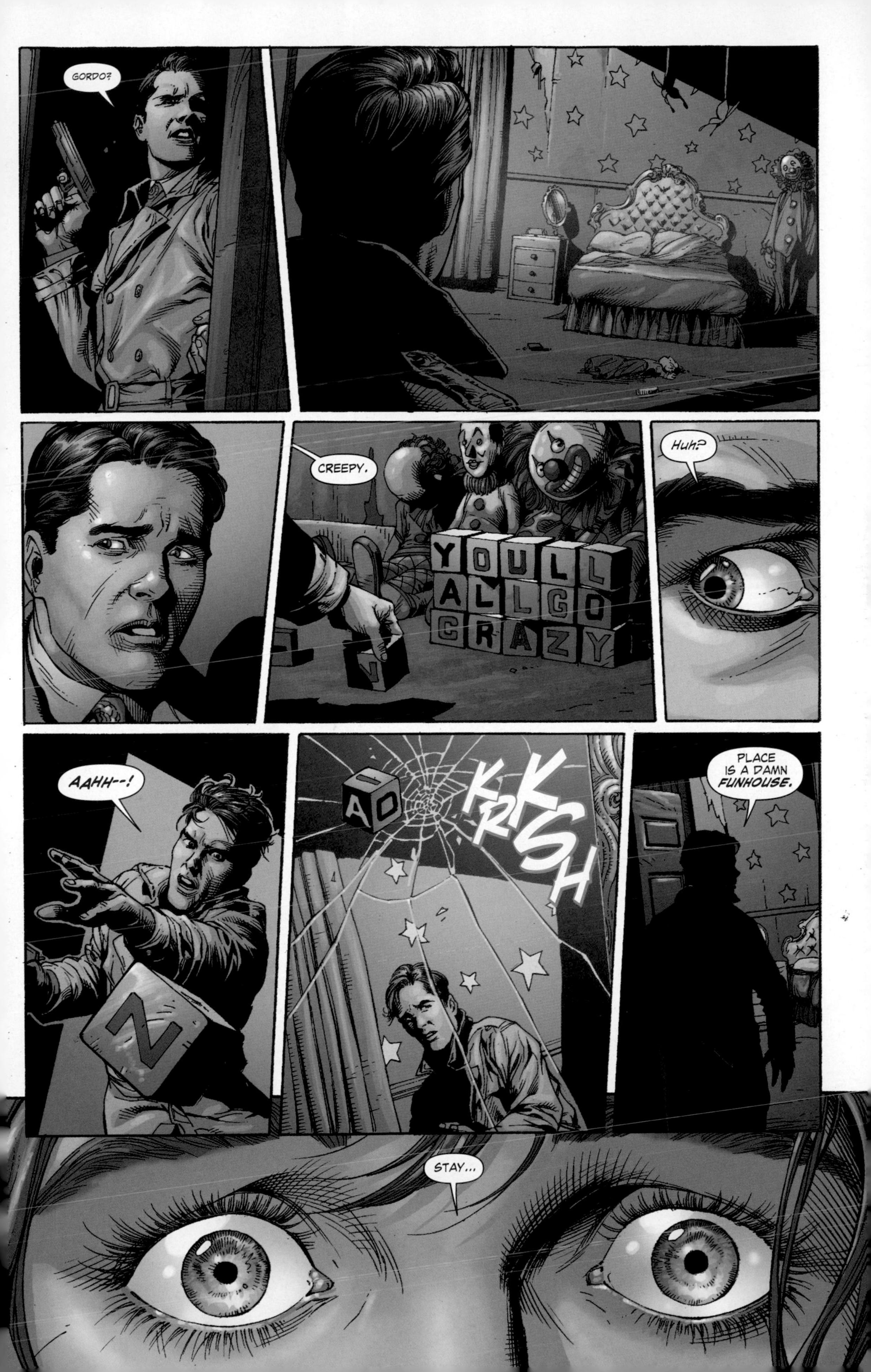
GORDO?
CREEPY.
YOULL ALLGO CRAZY
Huh?
AAHH--!
KRKSH
PLACE IS A DAMN FUNHOUSE.
STAY...

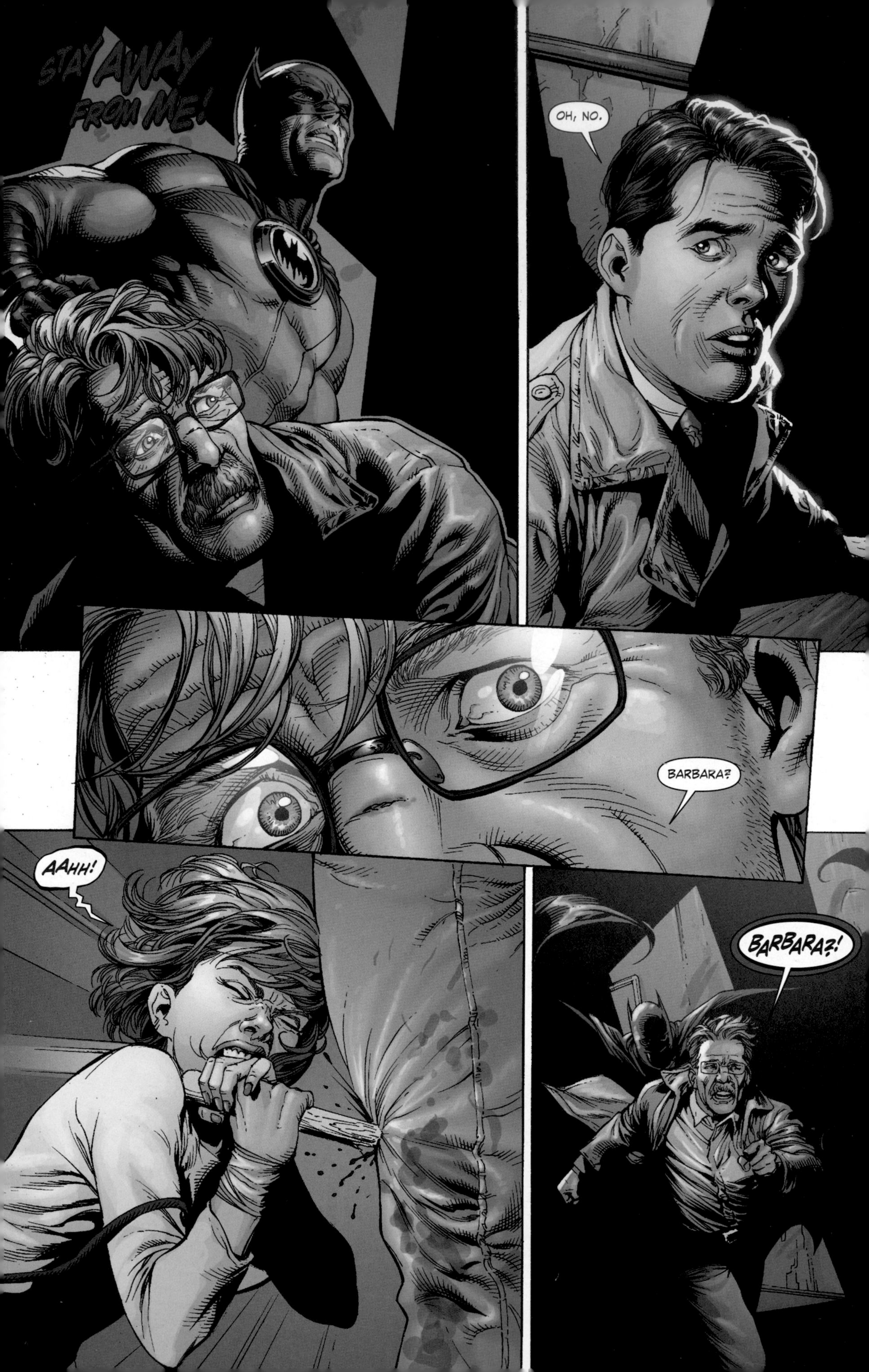
STAY AWAY FROM ME!
OH, NO.
BARBARA?
AAHH!
BARBARA?!

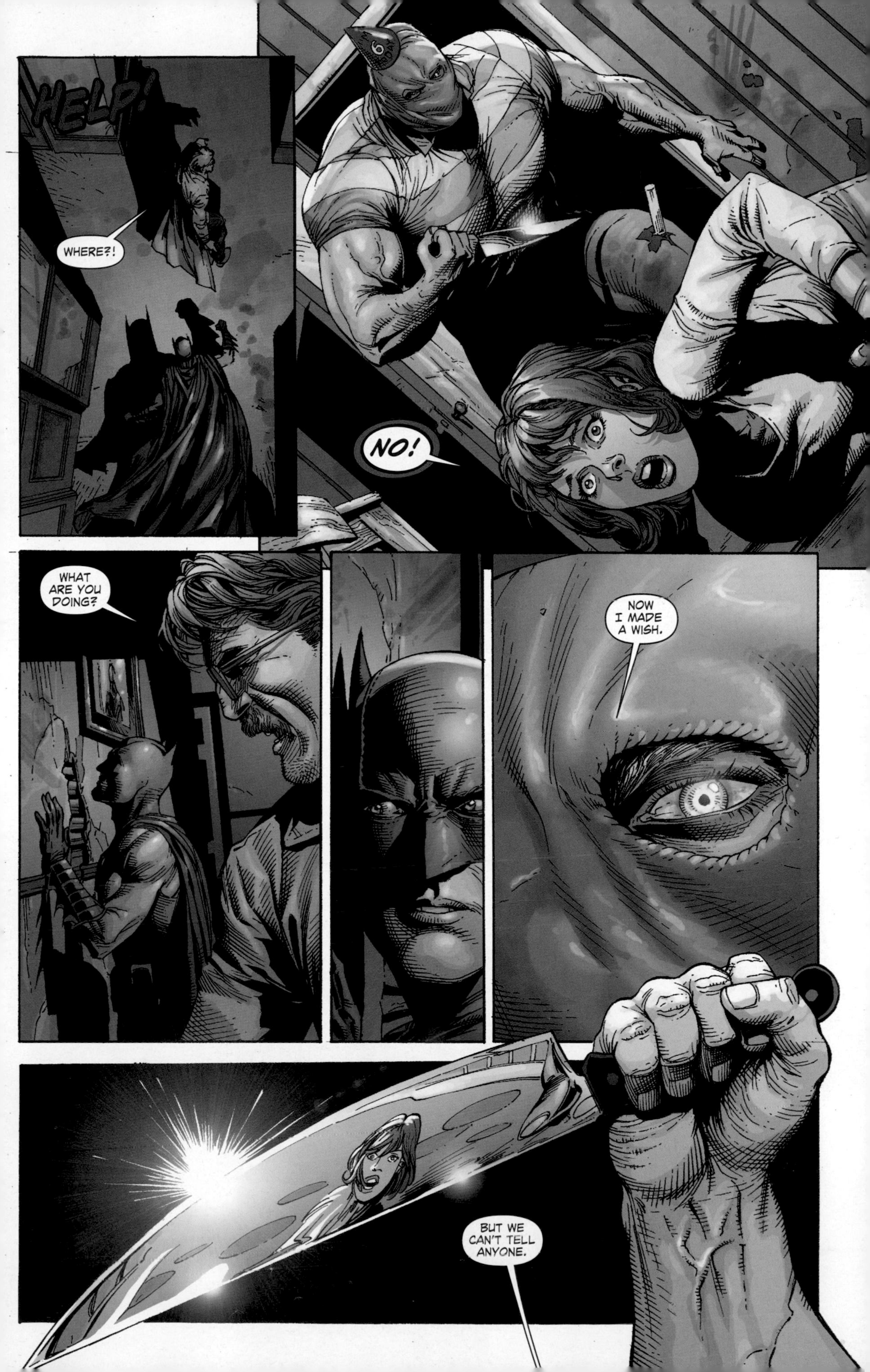
HELP!
WHERE?!
NO!
WHAT ARE YOU DOING?
NOW I MADE A WISH.
BUT WE CAN'T TELL ANYONE.

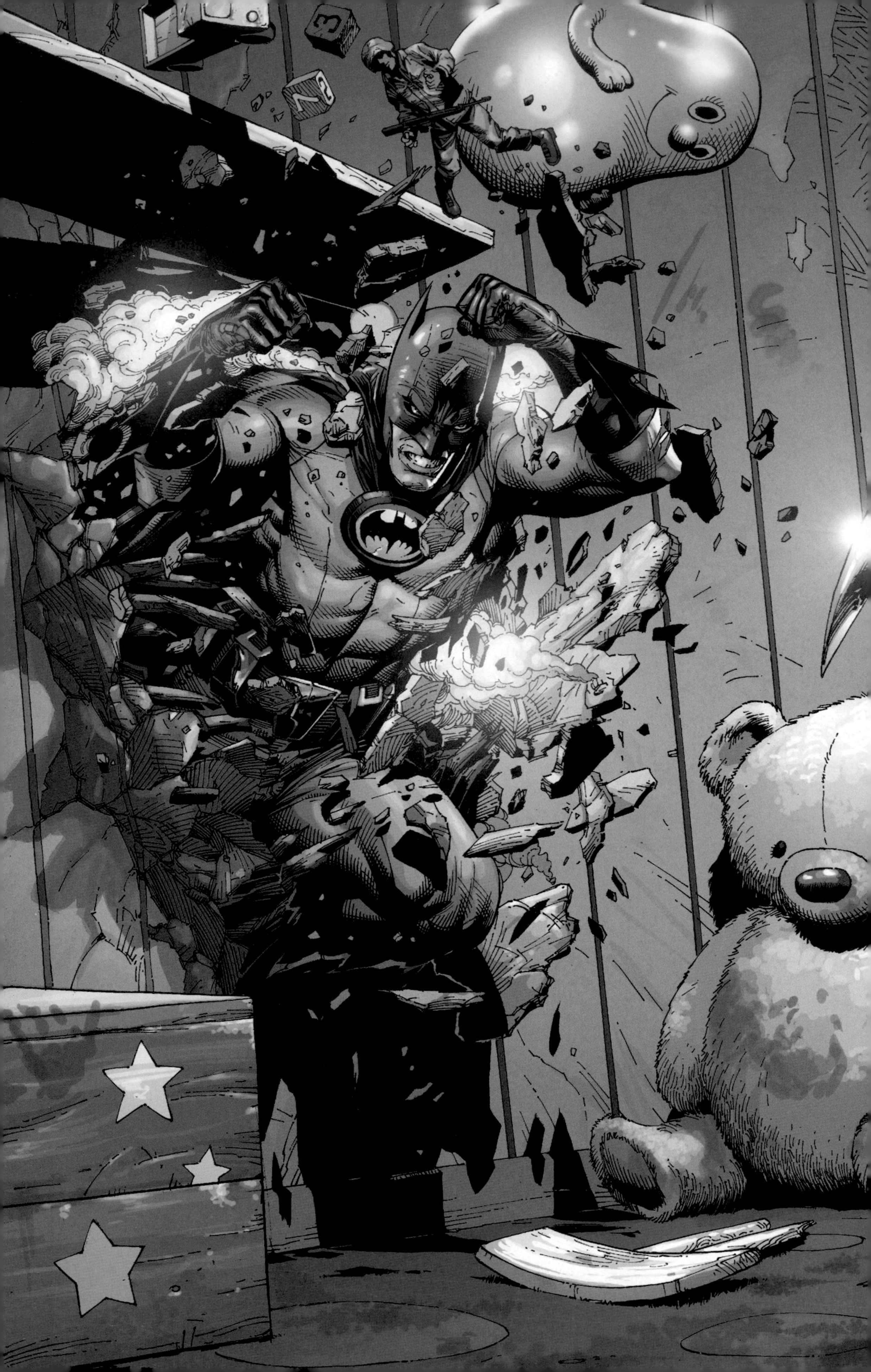

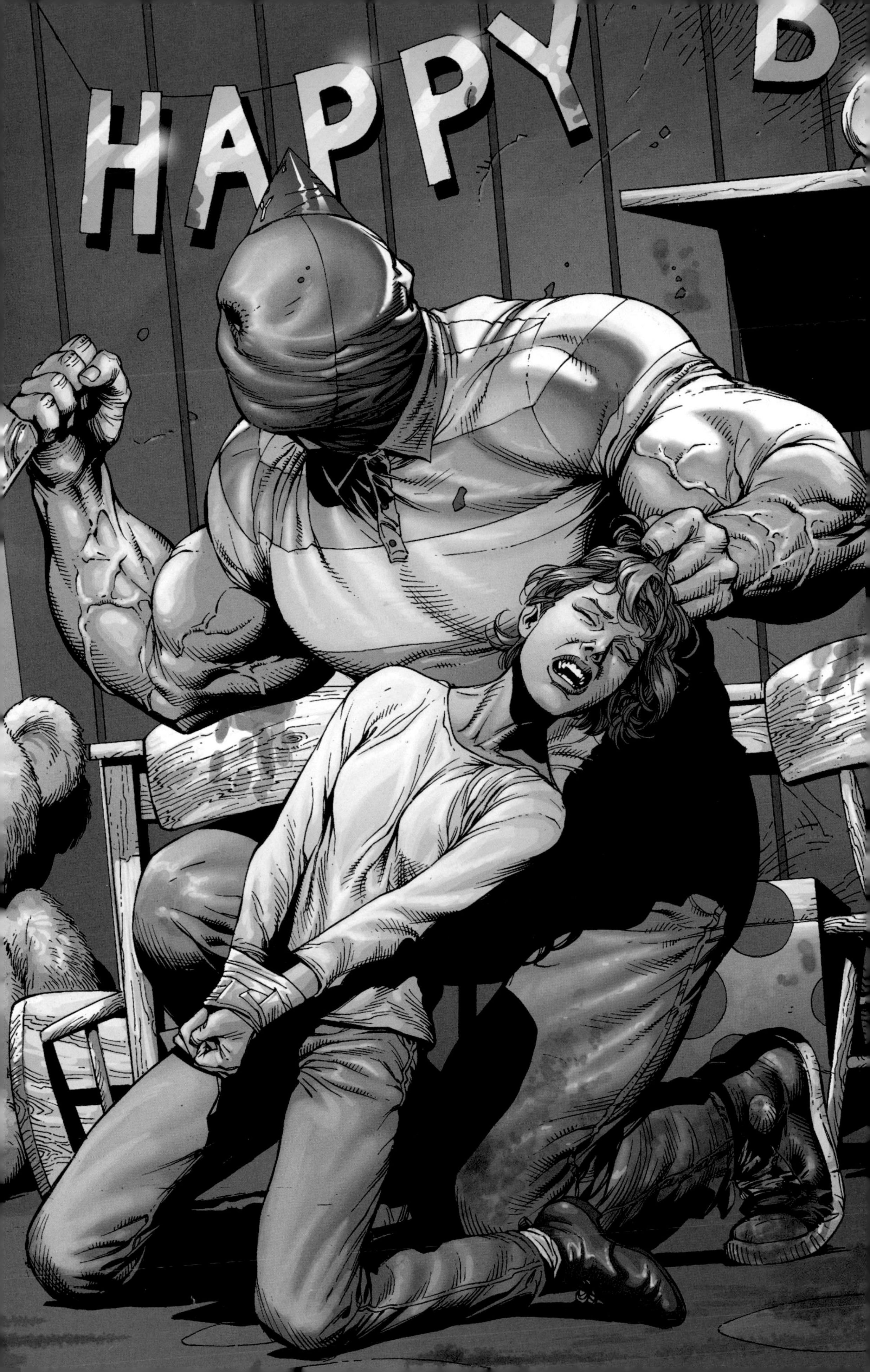
HAPPY

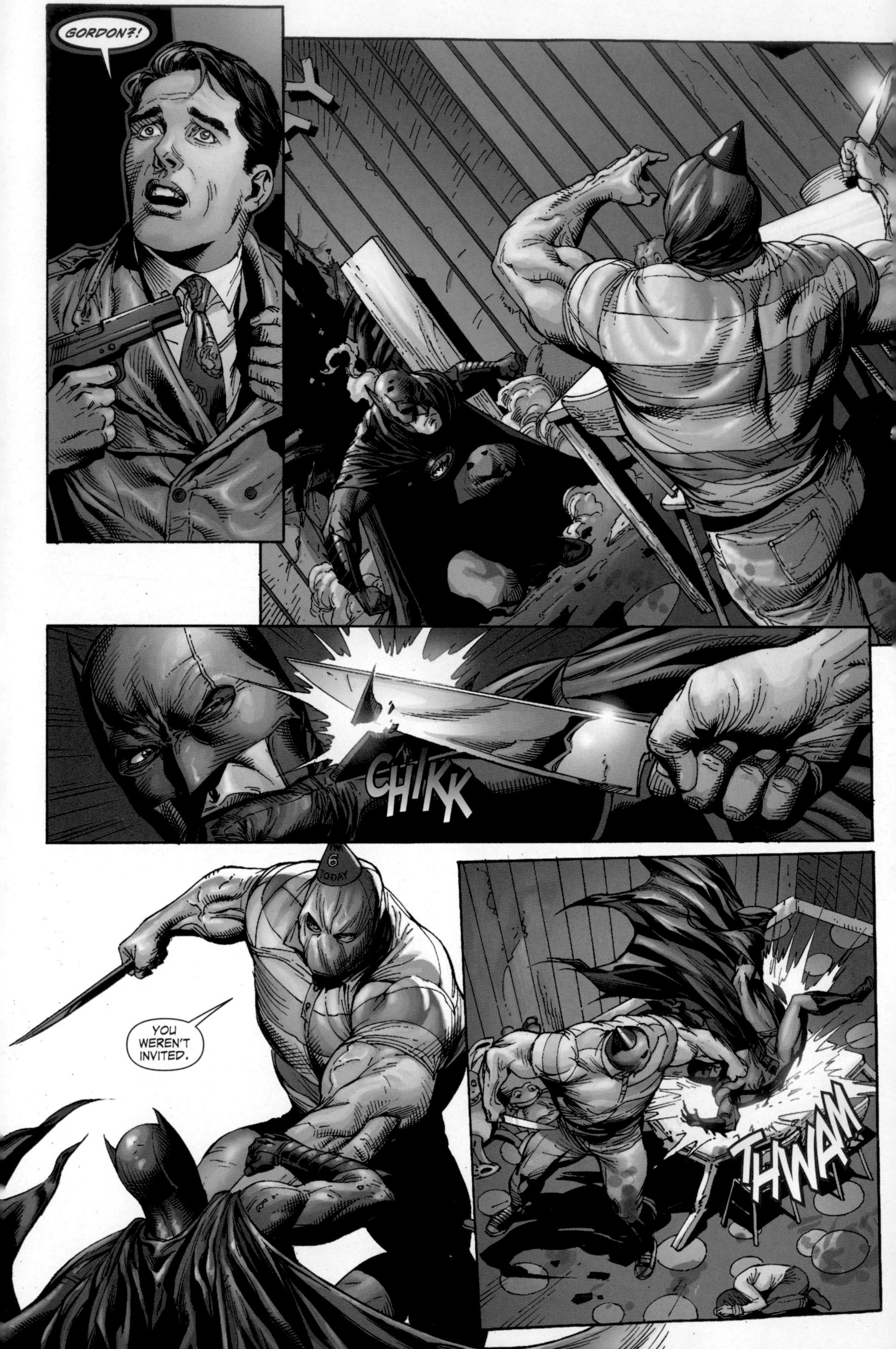
GORDON?!
CHIKK
6 TODAY
YOU WEREN'T INVITED.
THWAM

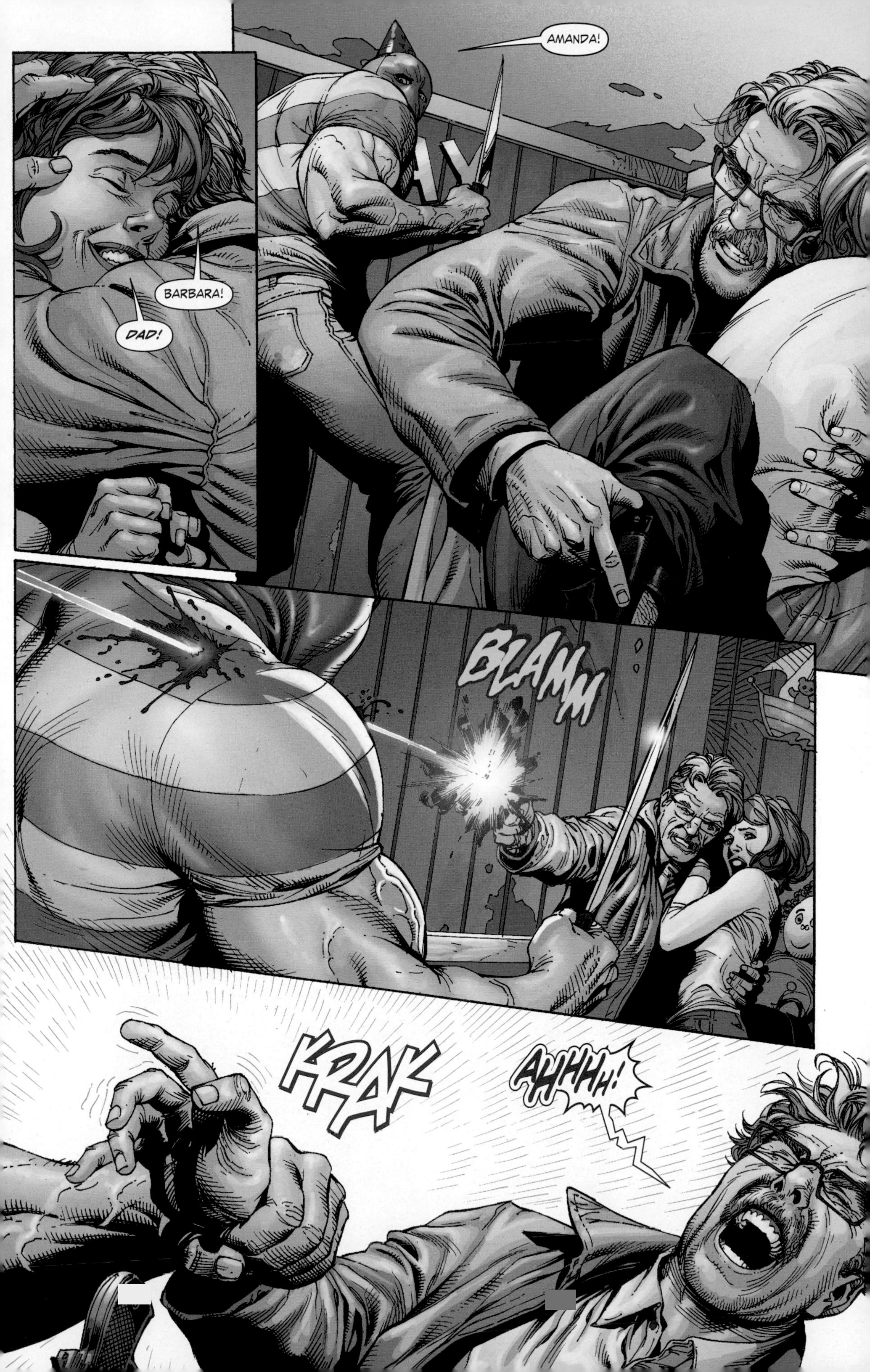
AMANDA!
BARBARA!
DAD!
BLAMM
KRAK
AHHHH!

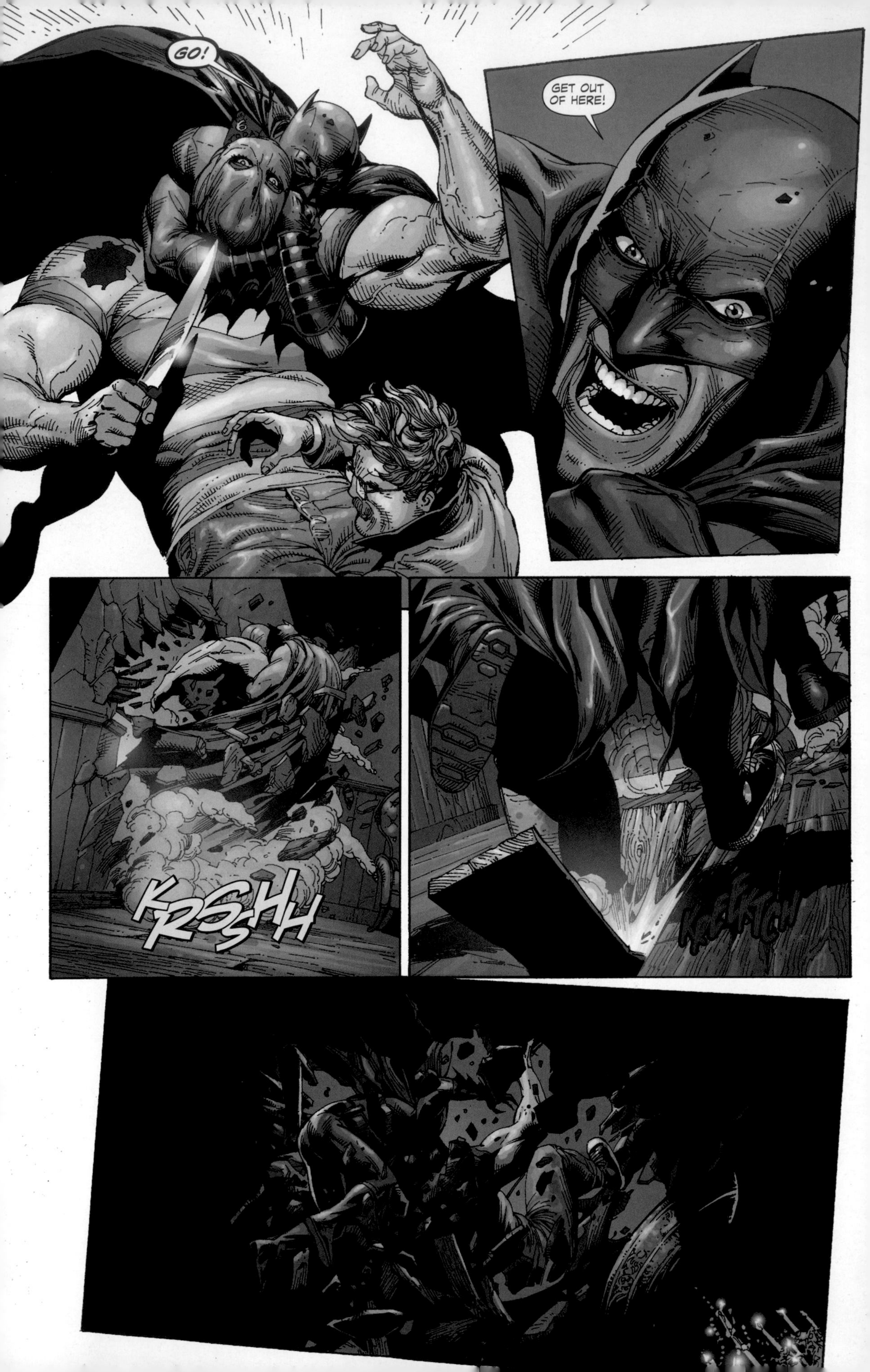
GO!
GET OUT OF HERE!
KRSSHH

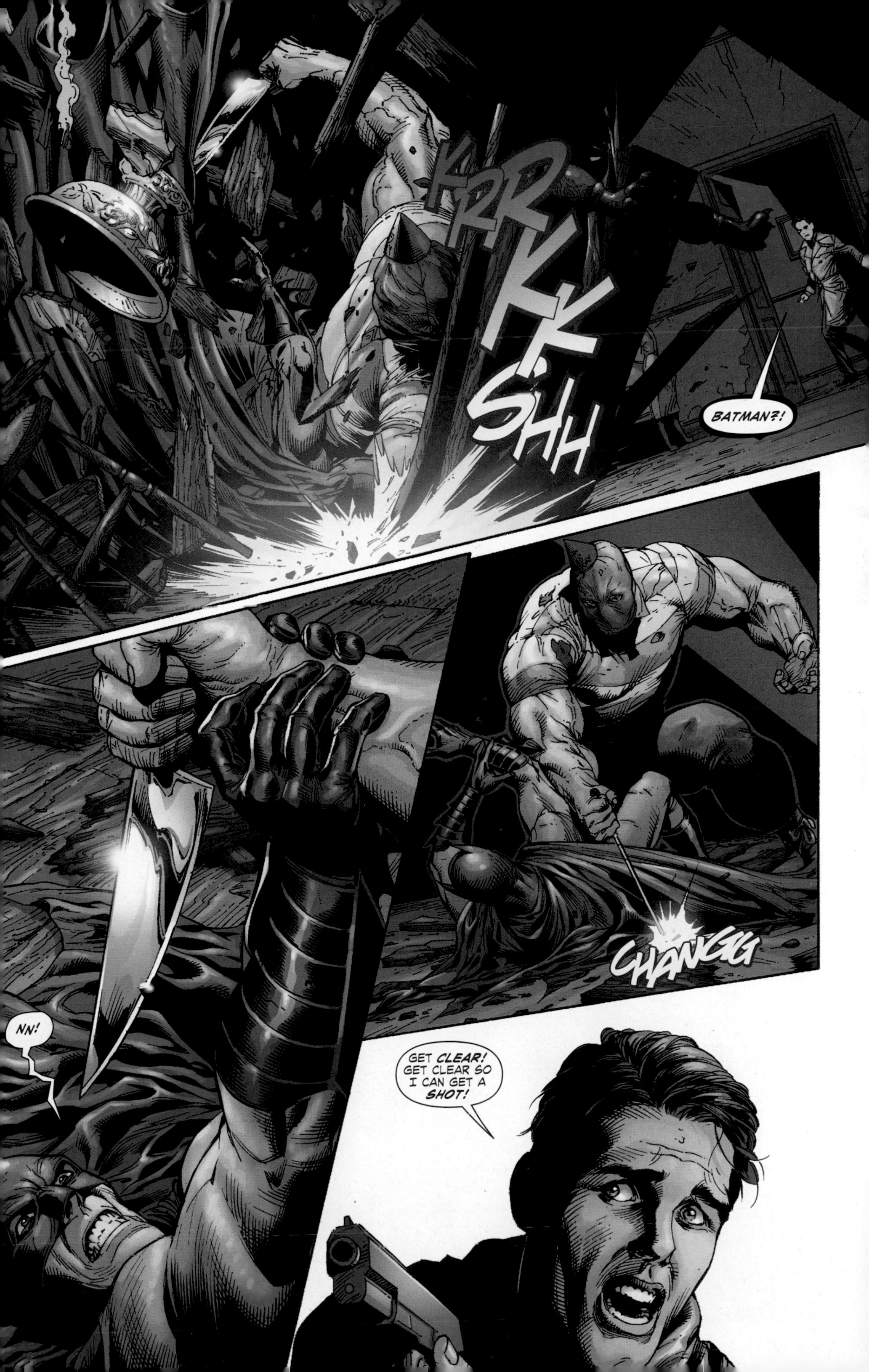
KRRKK SHH
BATMAN?!
CHANGG
NN!
GET CLEAR! GET CLEAR SO I CAN GET A SHOT!

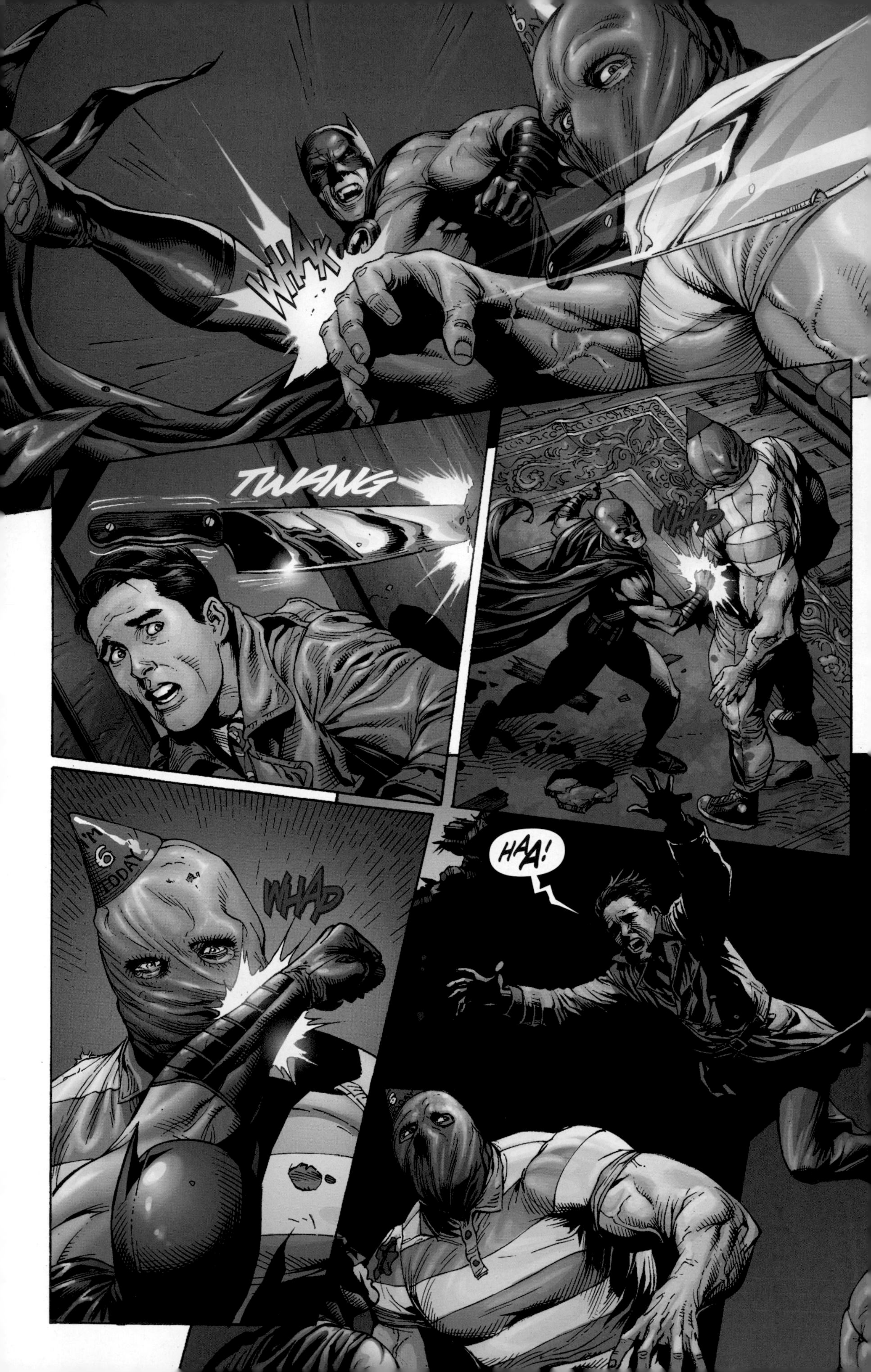
WHAK
TWANG
WHAP
I'M 6 TODAY
WHAP
HAA!

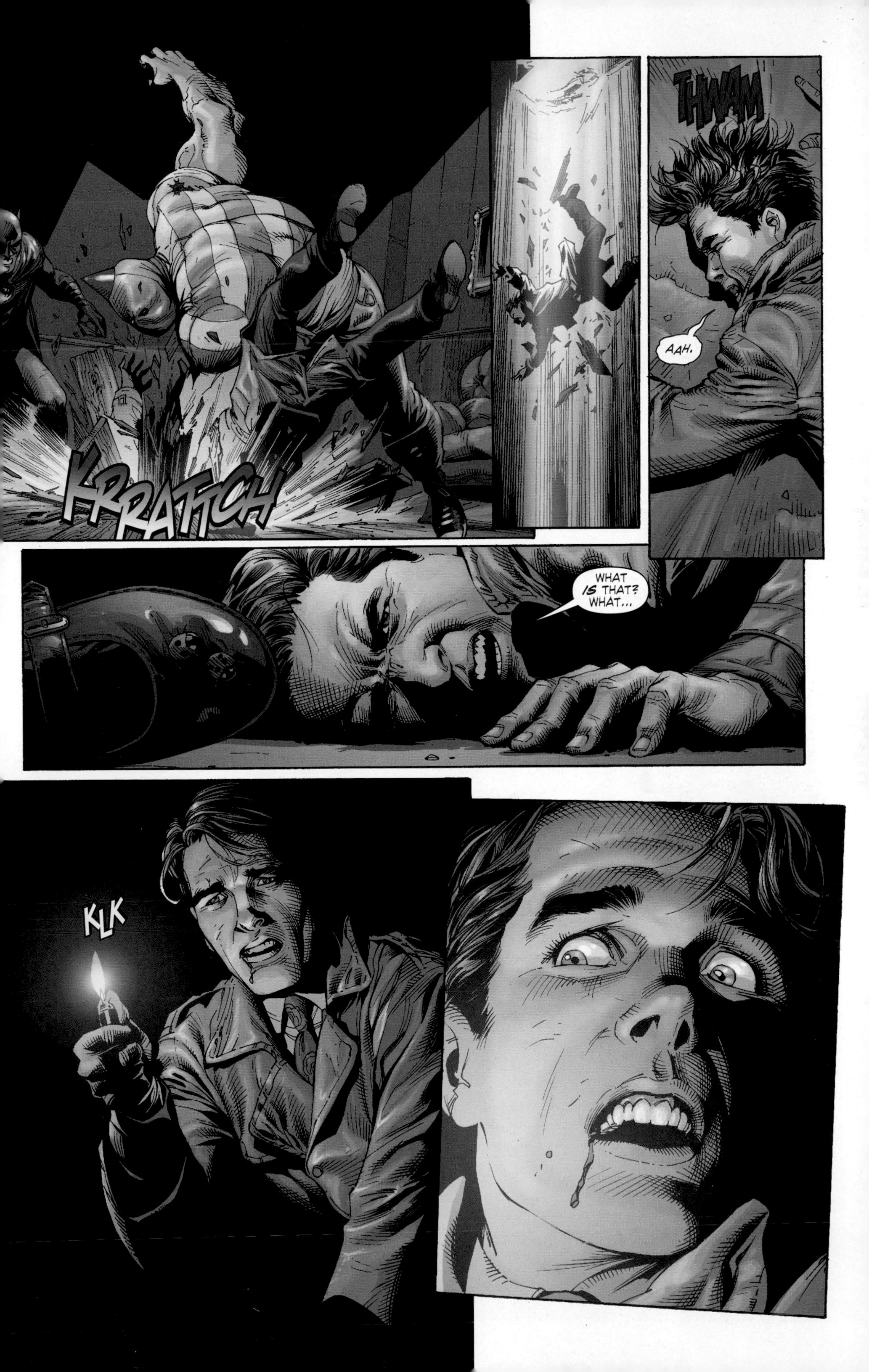
KRRATTCH
THWAM
AAH.
WHAT IS THAT? WHAT...
KLK

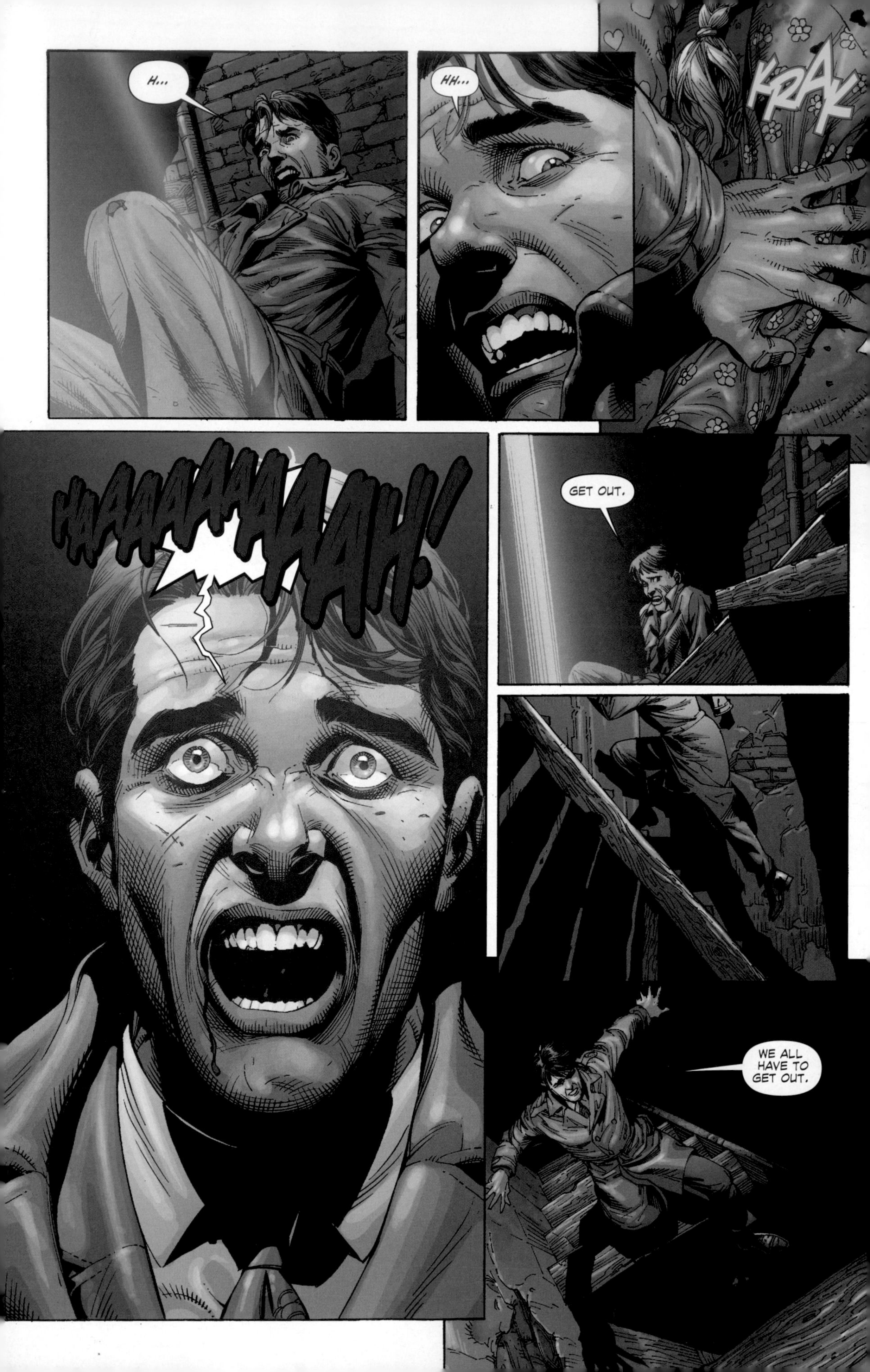
H...
HH...
KRAK
HAAAAAAAAAAH!
GET OUT.
WE ALL HAVE TO GET OUT.

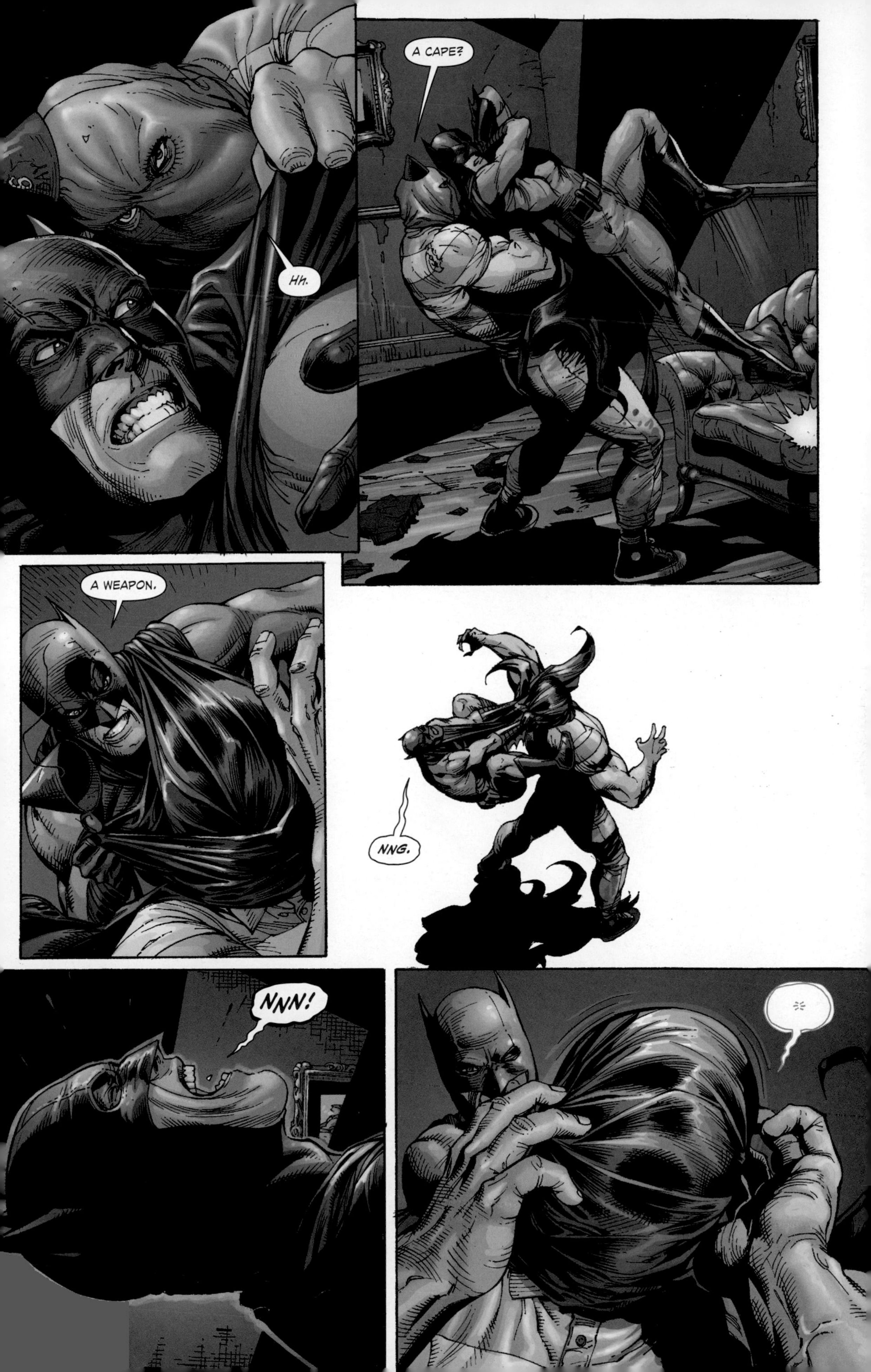
Hh.
A CAPE?
A WEAPON.
NNG.
NNN!

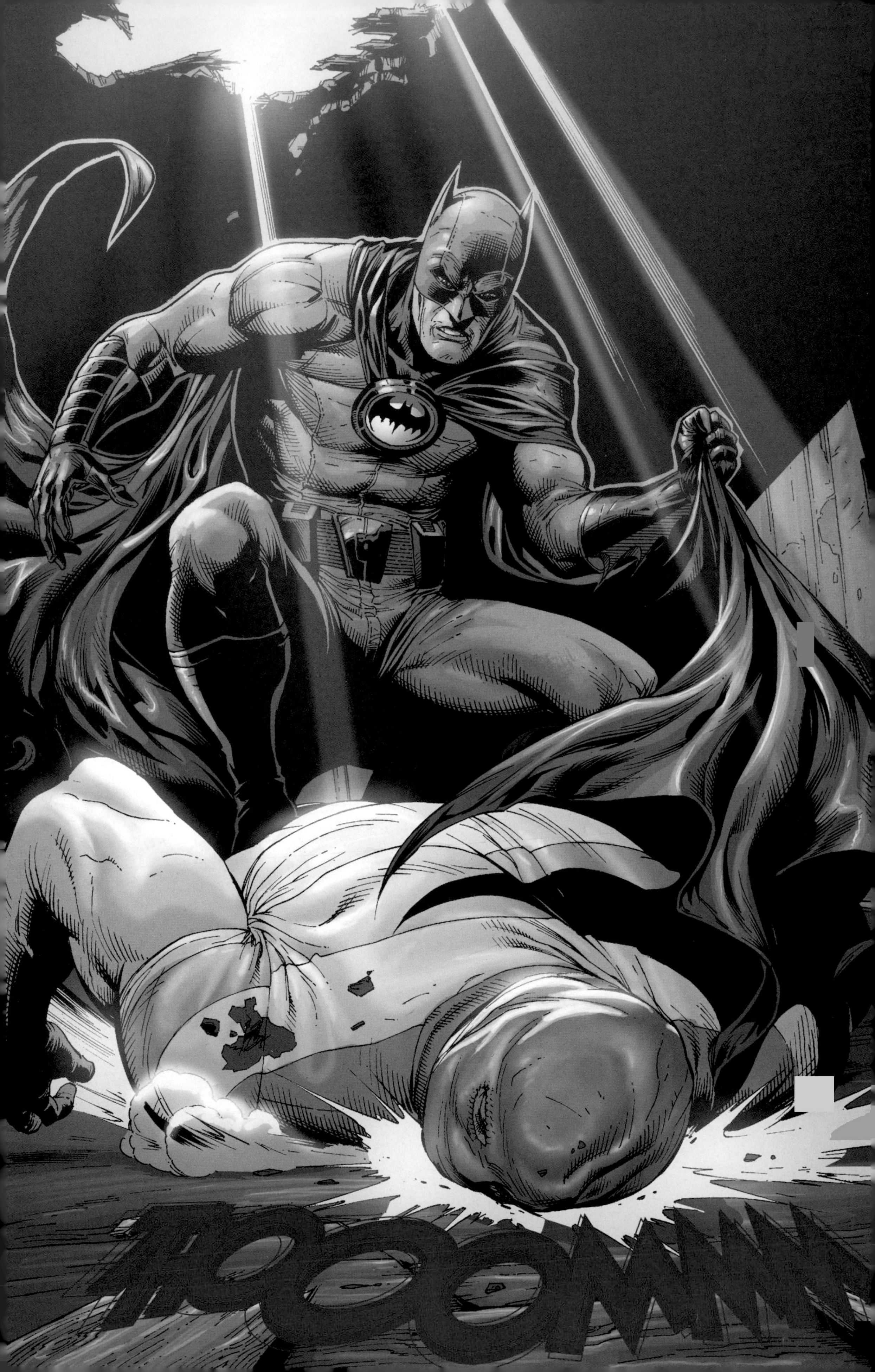

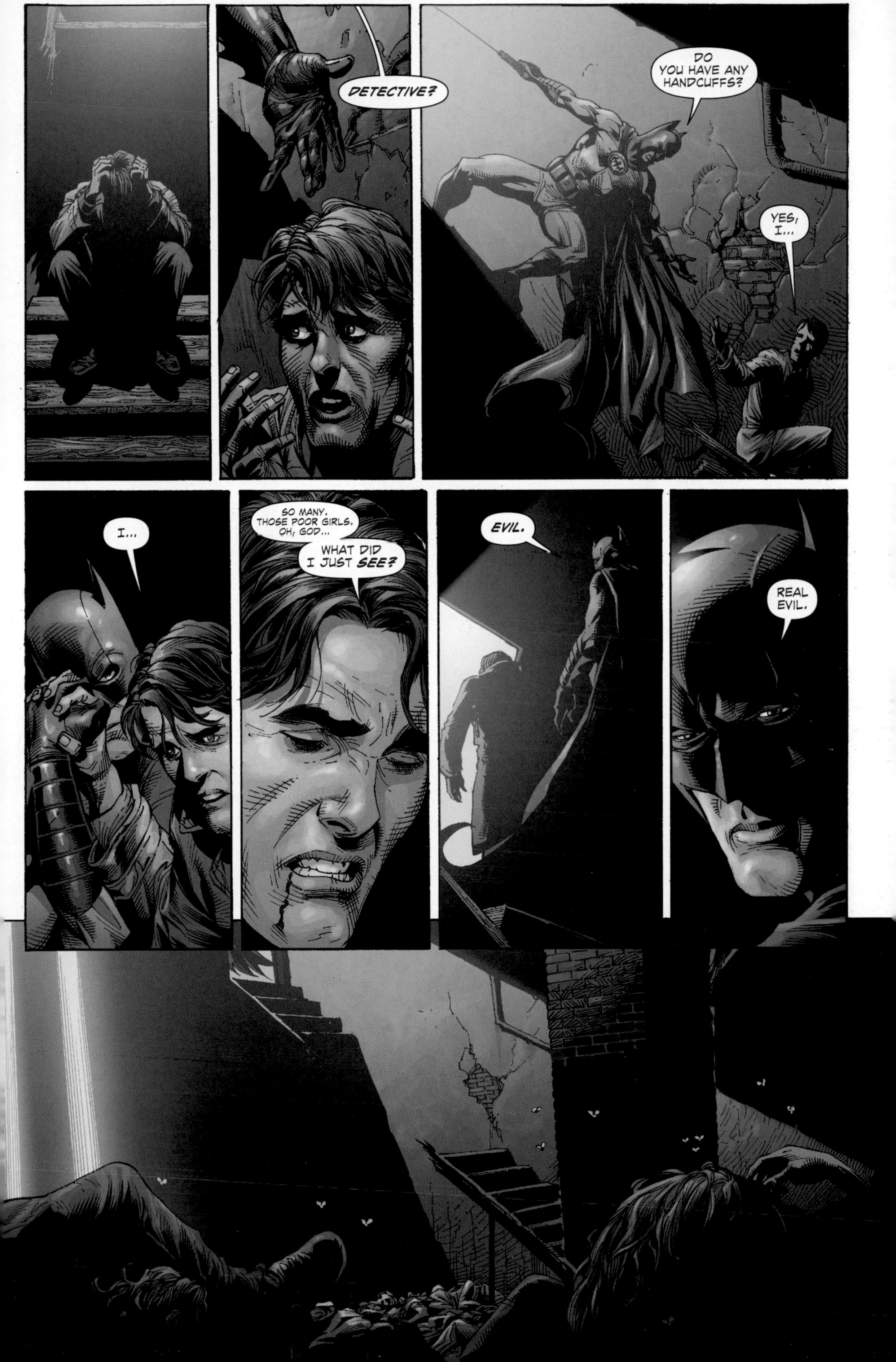
DETECTIVE?
DO YOU HAVE ANY HANDCUFFS?
YES, I...
I...
SO MANY. THOSE POOR GIRLS. OH, GOD...
WHAT DID I JUST SEE?
EVIL.
REAL EVIL.

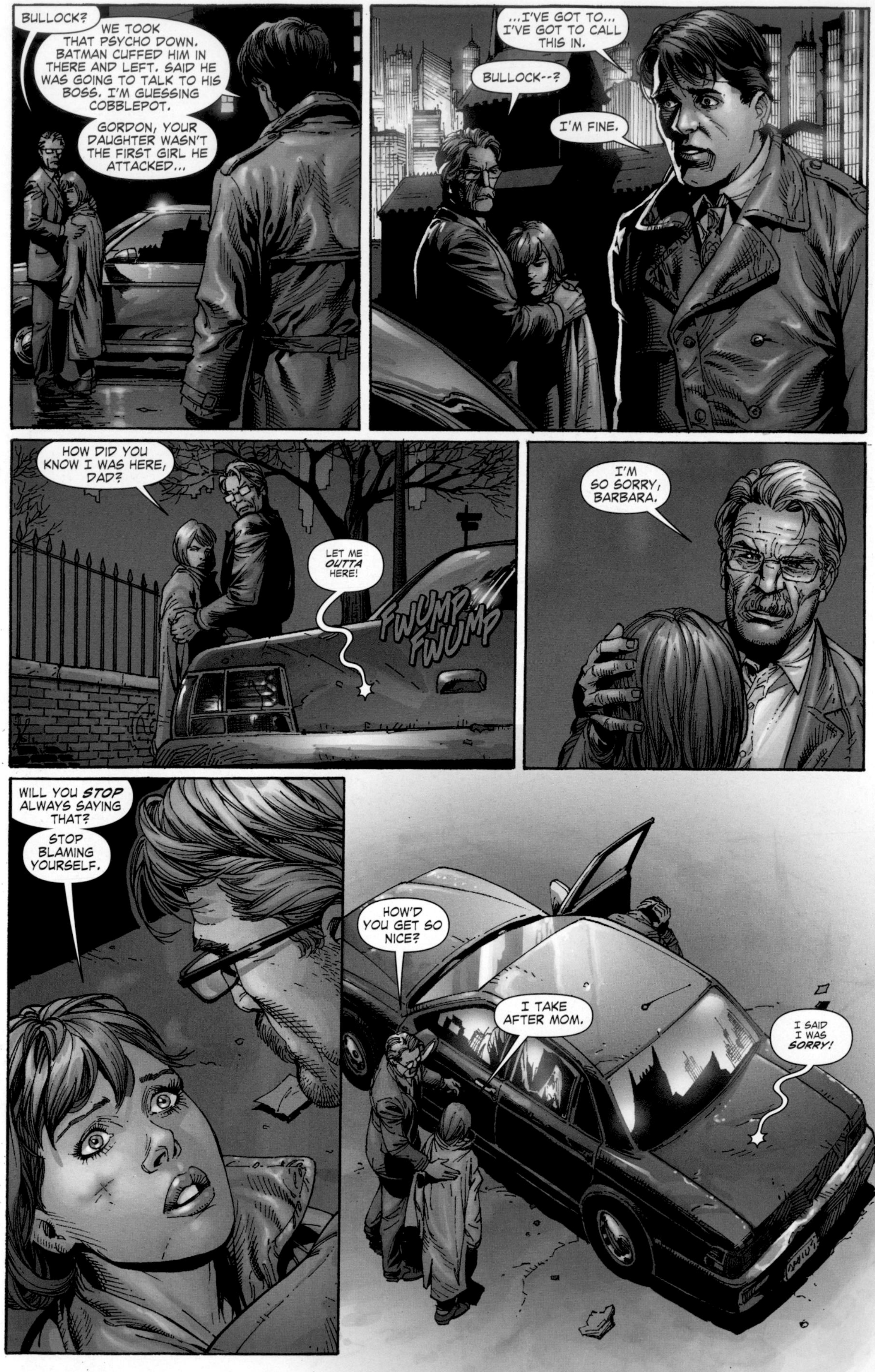
BULLOCK?
WE TOOK THAT PSYCHO DOWN. BATMAN CUFFED HIM IN THERE AND LEFT. SAID HE WAS GOING TO TALK TO HIS BOSS. I'M GUESSING COBBLEPOT.
GORDON, YOUR DAUGHTER WASN'T THE FIRST GIRL HE ATTACKED...
...I'VE GOT TO... I'VE GOT TO CALL THIS IN.
BULLOCK--?
I'M FINE.
HOW DID YOU KNOW I WAS HERE, DAD?
LET ME OUTTA HERE!
FWUMP FWUMP
I'M SO SORRY, BARBARA.
WILL YOU STOP ALWAYS SAYING THAT?
STOP BLAMING YOURSELF.
HOW'D YOU GET SO NICE?
I TAKE AFTER MOM.
I SAID I WAS SORRY!

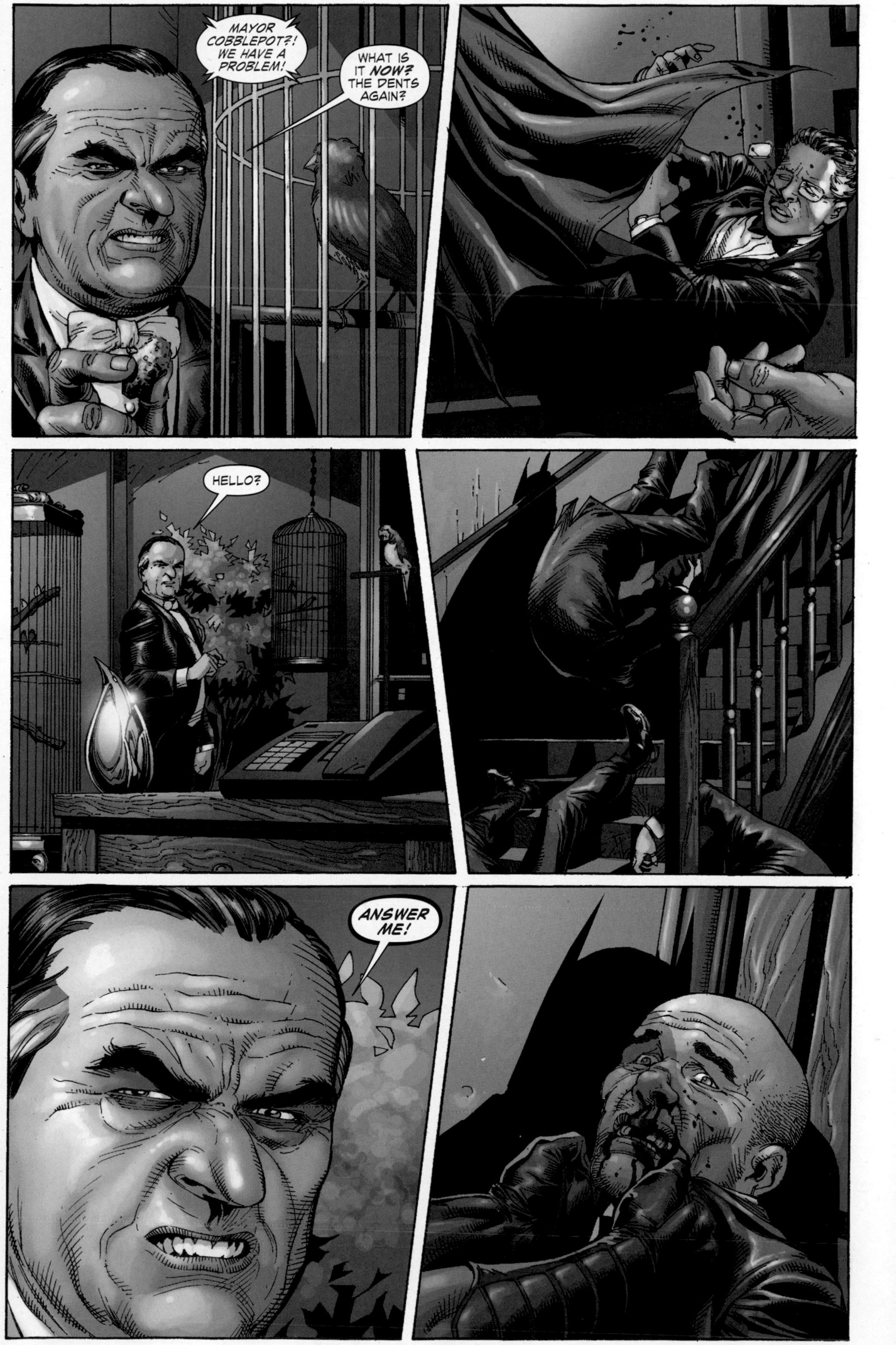
MAYOR COBBLEPOT?! WE HAVE A PROBLEM!
WHAT IS IT NOW? THE DENTS AGAIN?
HELLO?
ANSWER ME!

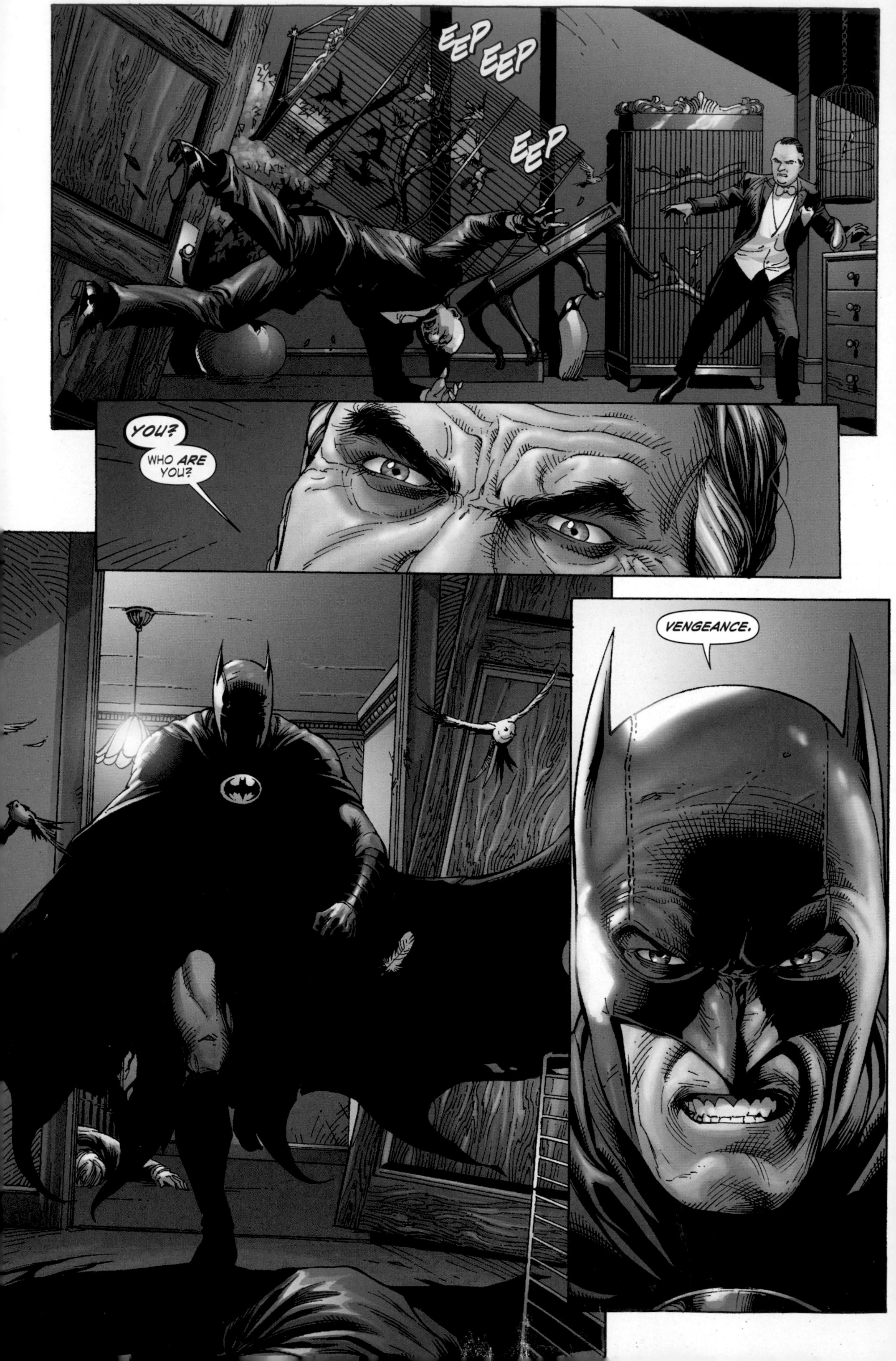
EEP EEP
EEP
YOU?
WHO ARE YOU?
VENGEANCE.

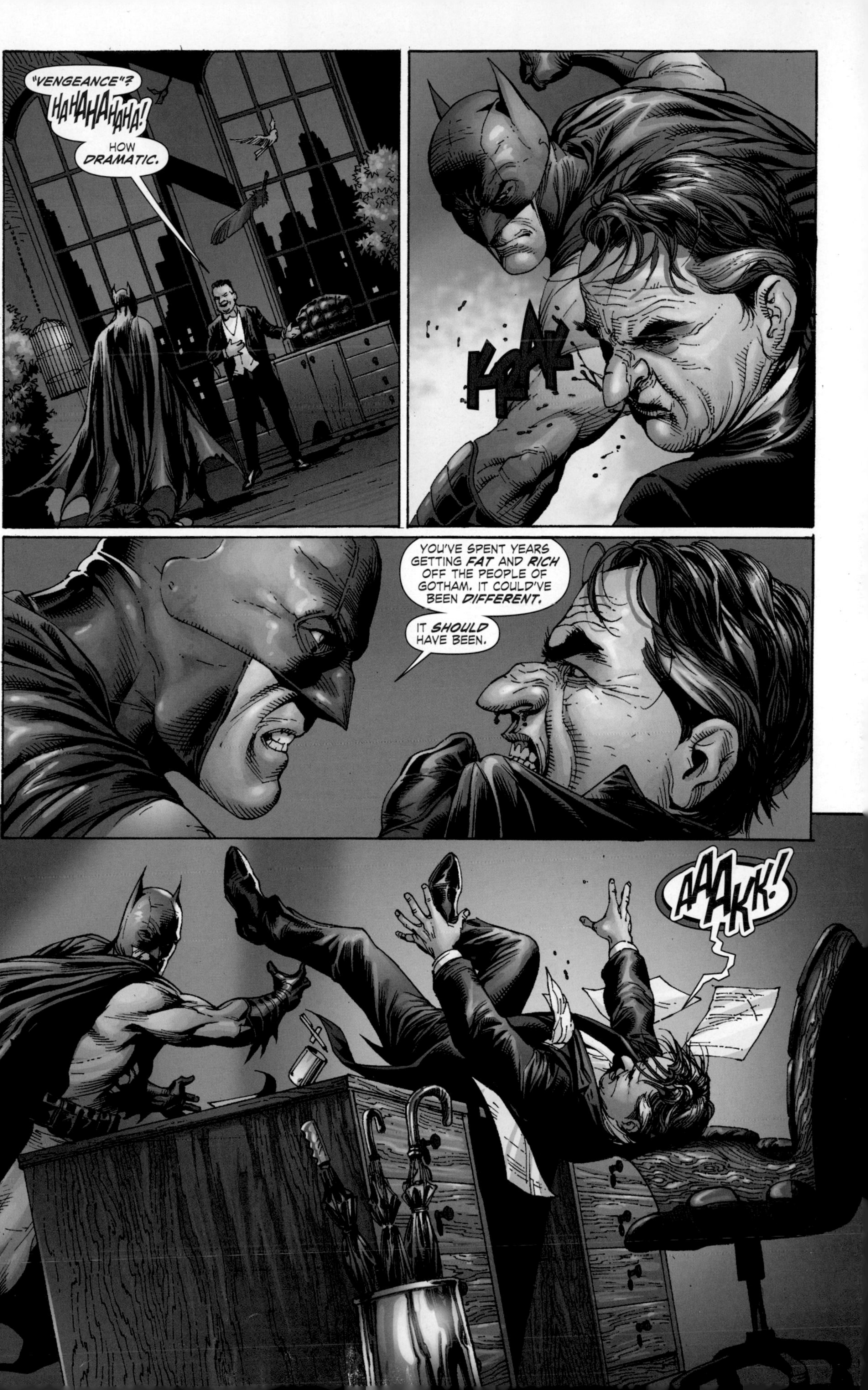
"VENGEANCE"? HAHAHAHAHA! HOW DRAMATIC.
KRAK
YOU'VE SPENT YEARS GETTING FAT AND RICH OFF THE PEOPLE OF GOTHAM. IT COULD'VE BEEN DIFFERENT.
IT SHOULD HAVE BEEN.
AAAKK!

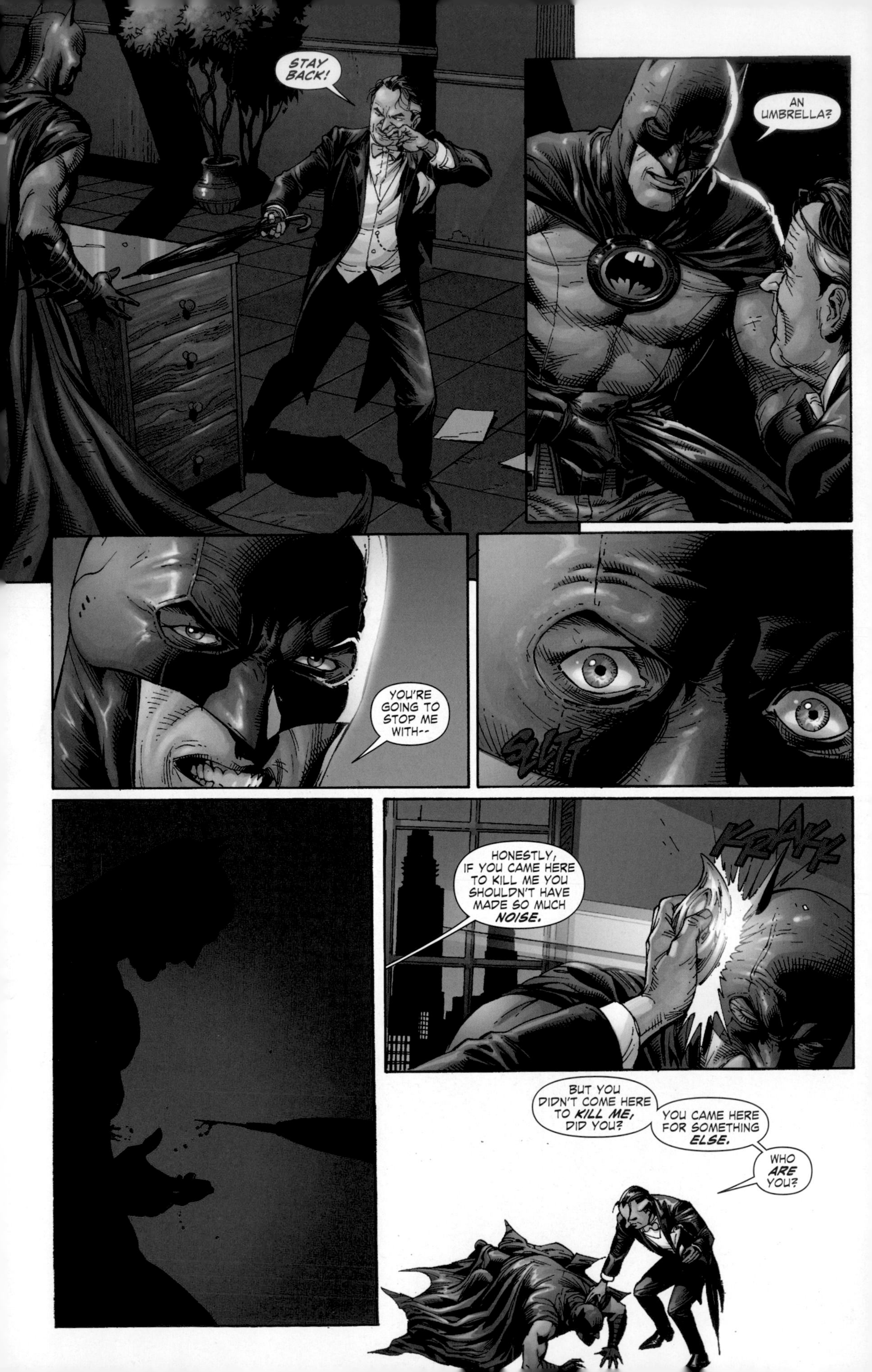
STAY BACK!
AN UMBRELLA?
YOU'RE GOING TO STOP ME WITH--
SLITT
HONESTLY, IF YOU CAME HERE TO KILL ME YOU SHOULDN'T HAVE MADE SO MUCH NOISE.
KRAKK
BUT YOU DIDN'T COME HERE TO KILL ME, DID YOU?
YOU CAME HERE FOR SOMETHING ELSE.
WHO ARE YOU?

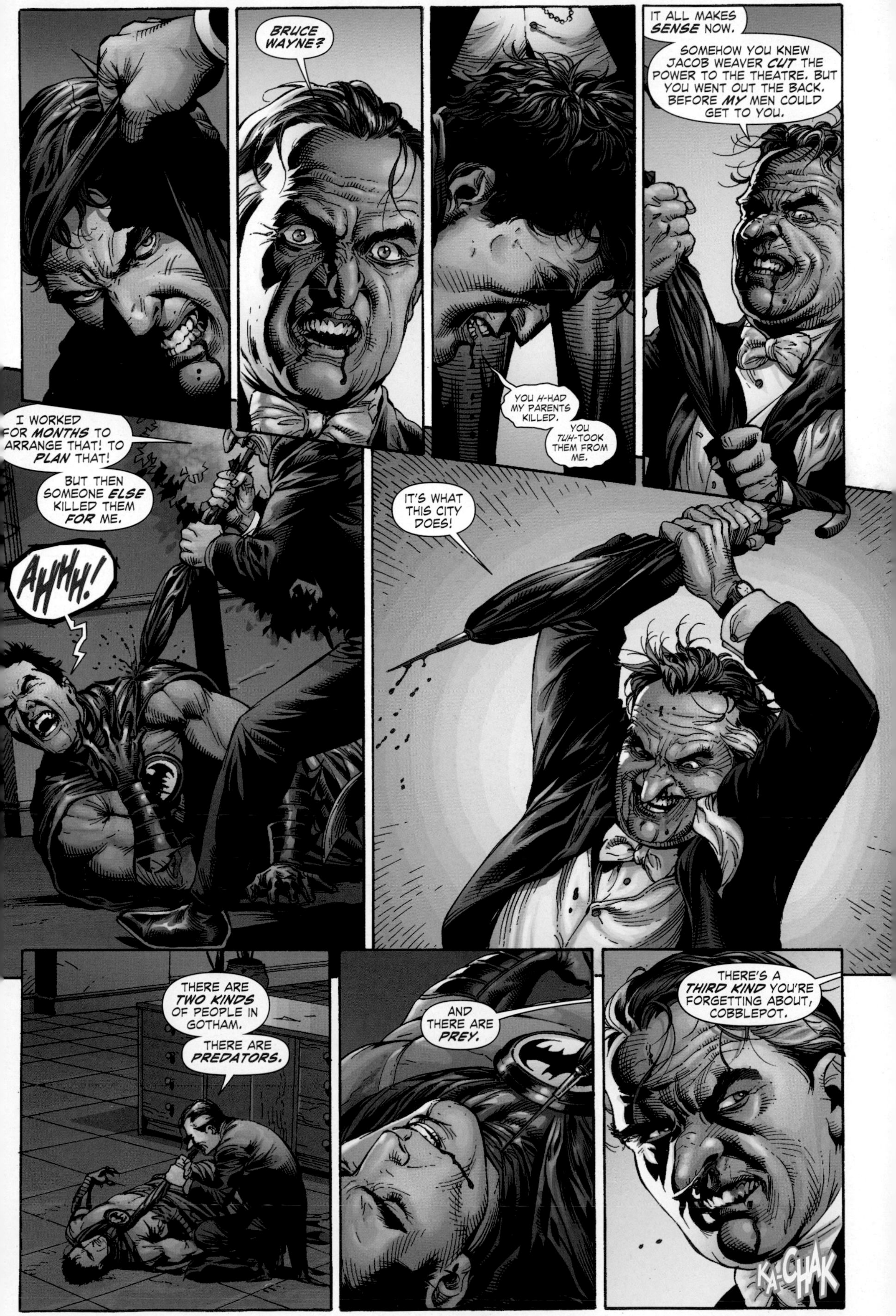
BRUCE WAYNE?
IT ALL MAKES SENSE NOW.
SOMEHOW YOU KNEW JACOB WEAVER CUT THE POWER TO THE THEATRE. BUT YOU WENT OUT THE BACK. BEFORE MY MEN COULD GET TO YOU.
YOU H-HAD MY PARENTS KILLED.
YOU TUH-TOOK THEM FROM ME.
I WORKED FOR MONTHS TO ARRANGE THAT! TO PLAN THAT!
BUT THEN SOMEONE ELSE KILLED THEM FOR ME.
AHHH!
IT'S WHAT THIS CITY DOES!
THERE ARE TWO KINDS OF PEOPLE IN GOTHAM.
THERE ARE PREDATORS.
AND THERE ARE PREY.
THERE'S A THIRD KIND YOU'RE FORGETTING ABOUT, COBBLEPOT.
KA-CHAK

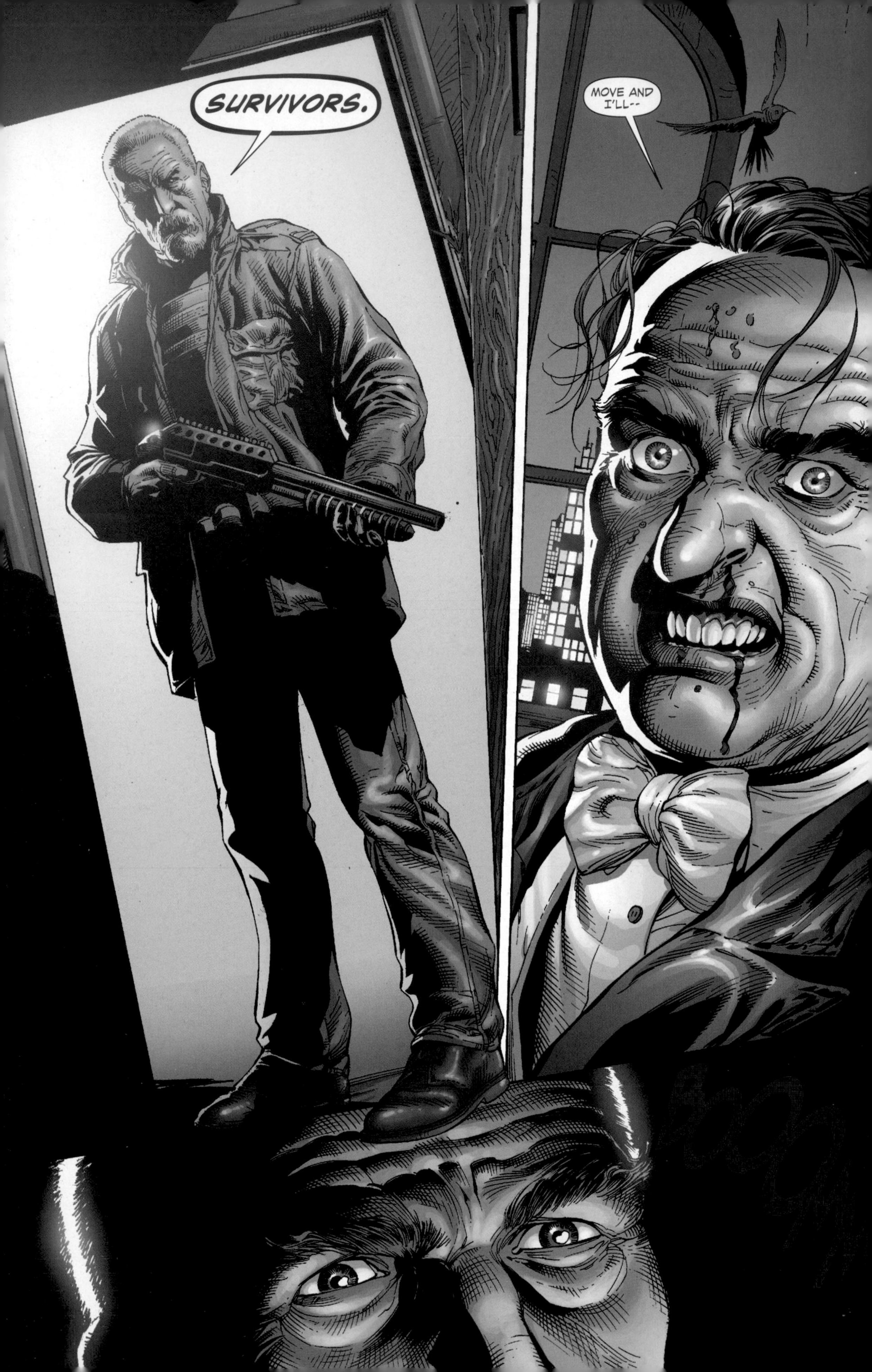
SURVIVORS.
MOVE AND I'LL--

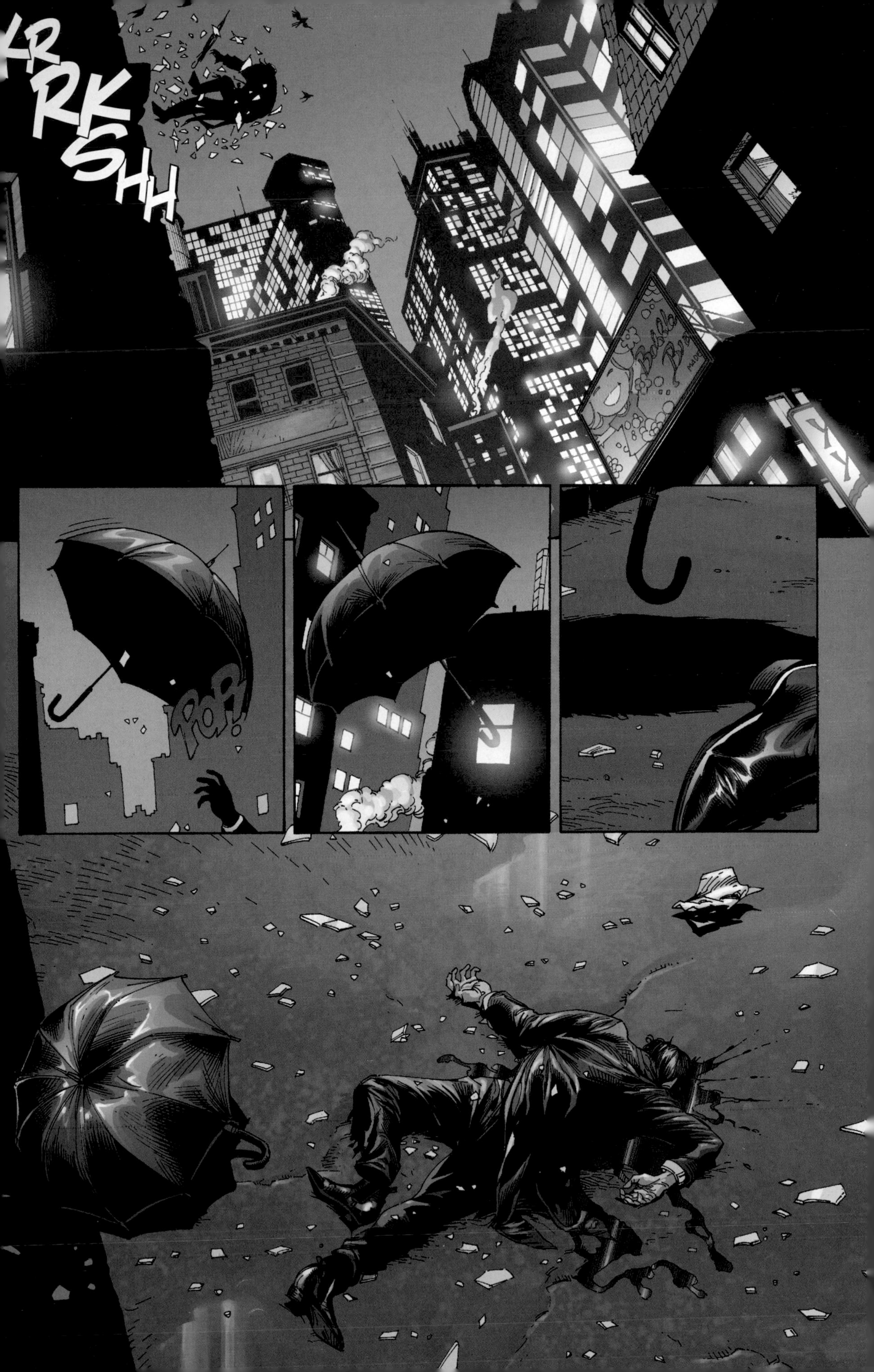
KRRKSHH
POP!

COME ON, BRUCE. COME ON.

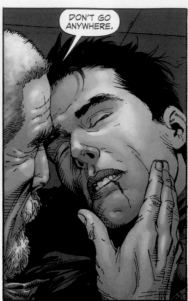

DON'T GO ANYWHERE.

STAY WITH ME.

ALFRED...

LET'S GET YOU HOME.

EEP

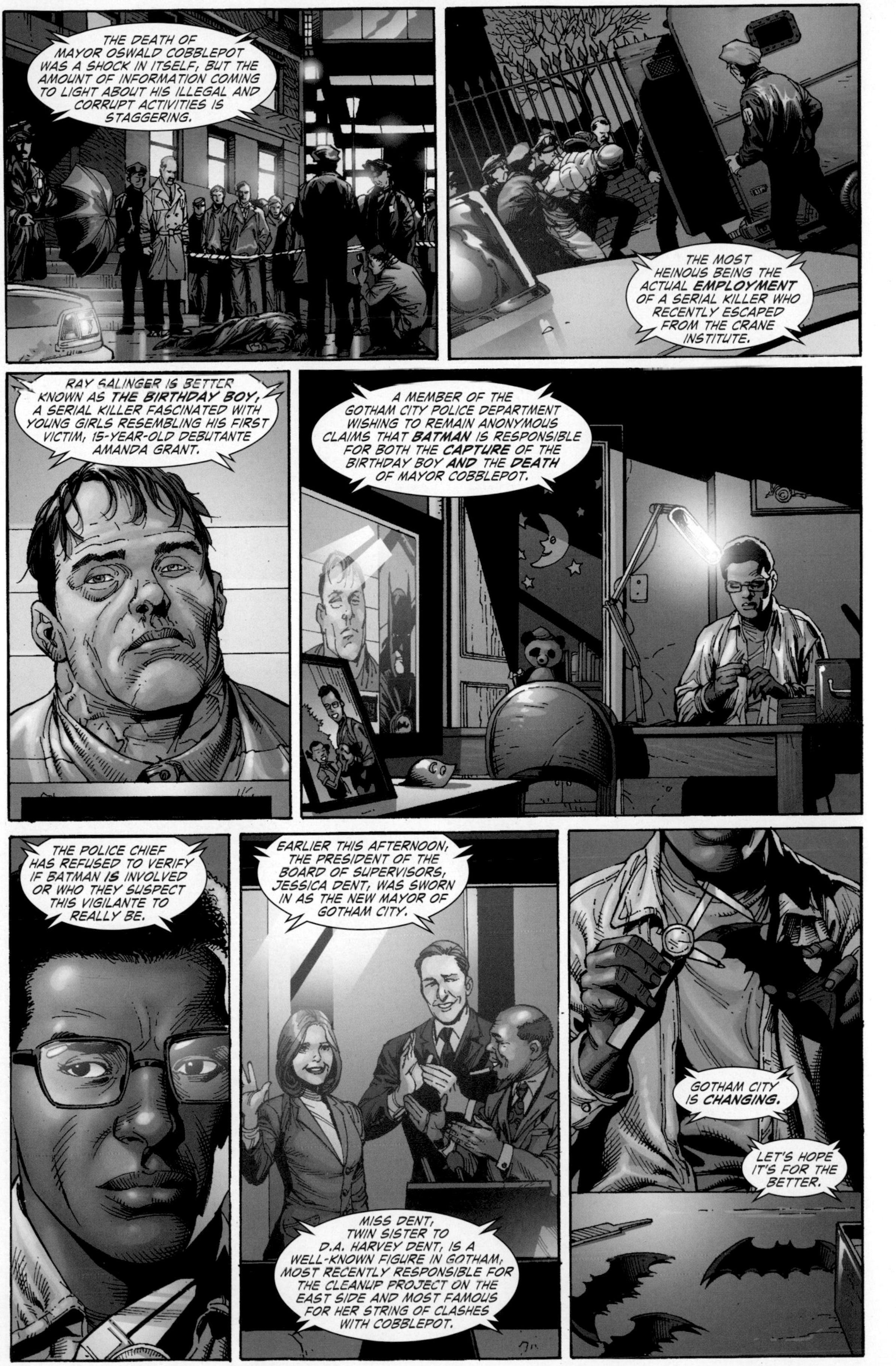
THE DEATH OF MAYOR OSWALD COBBLEPOT WAS A SHOCK IN ITSELF, BUT THE AMOUNT OF INFORMATION COMING TO LIGHT ABOUT HIS ILLEGAL AND CORRUPT ACTIVITIES IS STAGGERING.
THE MOST HEINOUS BEING THE ACTUAL **EMPLOYMENT** OF A SERIAL KILLER WHO RECENTLY ESCAPED FROM THE CRANE INSTITUTE.
RAY SALINGER IS BETTER KNOWN AS **THE BIRTHDAY BOY,** A SERIAL KILLER FASCINATED WITH YOUNG GIRLS RESEMBLING HIS FIRST VICTIM, 15-YEAR-OLD DEBUTANTE AMANDA GRANT.
A MEMBER OF THE GOTHAM CITY POLICE DEPARTMENT WISHING TO REMAIN ANONYMOUS CLAIMS THAT **BATMAN** IS RESPONSIBLE FOR BOTH THE **CAPTURE** OF THE BIRTHDAY BOY **AND** THE **DEATH** OF MAYOR COBBLEPOT.
THE POLICE CHIEF HAS REFUSED TO VERIFY IF BATMAN **IS** INVOLVED OR WHO THEY SUSPECT THIS VIGILANTE TO REALLY BE.
EARLIER THIS AFTERNOON, THE PRESIDENT OF THE BOARD OF SUPERVISORS, JESSICA DENT, WAS SWORN IN AS THE NEW MAYOR OF GOTHAM CITY.
MISS DENT, TWIN SISTER TO D.A. HARVEY DENT, IS A WELL-KNOWN FIGURE IN GOTHAM, MOST RECENTLY RESPONSIBLE FOR THE CLEANUP PROJECT ON THE EAST SIDE AND MOST FAMOUS FOR HER STRING OF CLASHES WITH COBBLEPOT.
GOTHAM CITY IS **CHANGING.**
LET'S HOPE IT'S FOR THE BETTER.

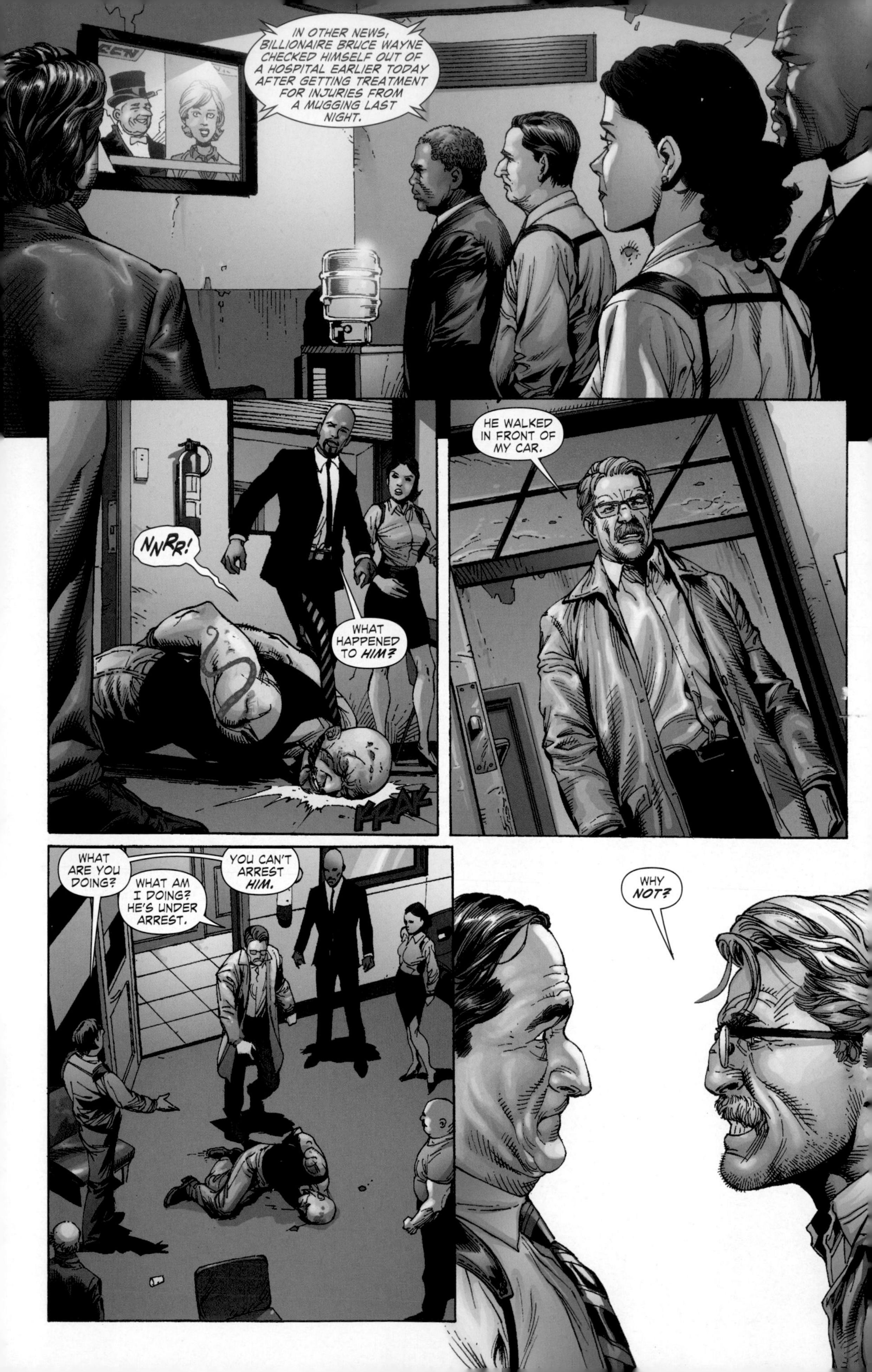
IN OTHER NEWS, BILLIONAIRE BRUCE WAYNE CHECKED HIMSELF OUT OF A HOSPITAL EARLIER TODAY AFTER GETTING TREATMENT FOR INJURIES FROM A MUGGING LAST NIGHT.
NNRR!
WHAT HAPPENED TO HIM?
KRAK
HE WALKED IN FRONT OF MY CAR.
WHAT ARE YOU DOING?
WHAT AM I DOING? HE'S UNDER ARREST.
YOU CAN'T ARREST HIM.
WHY NOT?

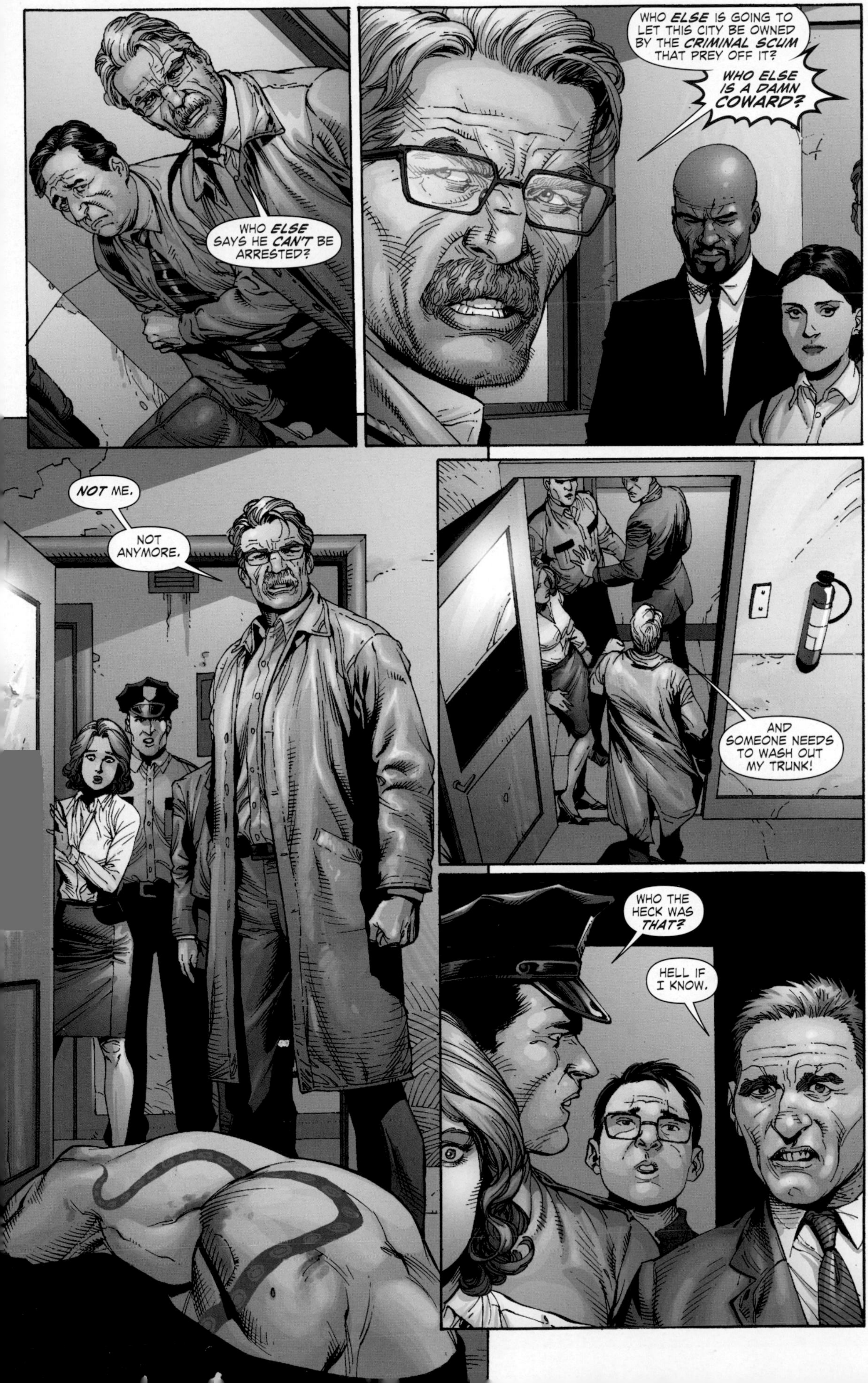
WHO ELSE SAYS HE CAN'T BE ARRESTED?
WHO ELSE IS GOING TO LET THIS CITY BE OWNED BY THE CRIMINAL SCUM THAT PREY OFF IT?
WHO ELSE IS A DAMN COWARD?
NOT ME.
NOT ANYMORE.
AND SOMEONE NEEDS TO WASH OUT MY TRUNK!
WHO THE HECK WAS THAT?
HELL IF I KNOW.

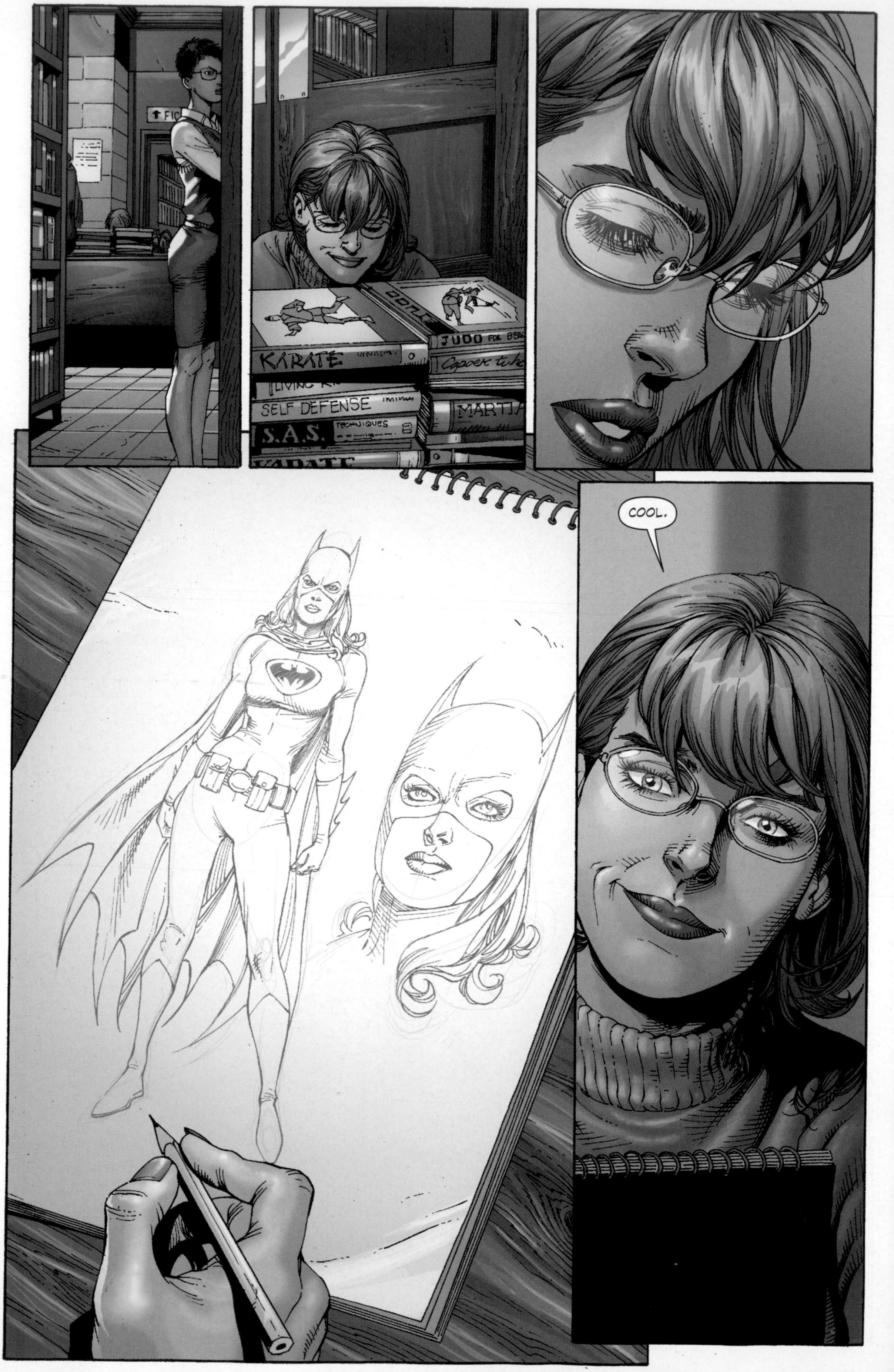
KARATE
JUDO
SELF DEFENSE
S.A.S.
TECHNIQUES
COOL.

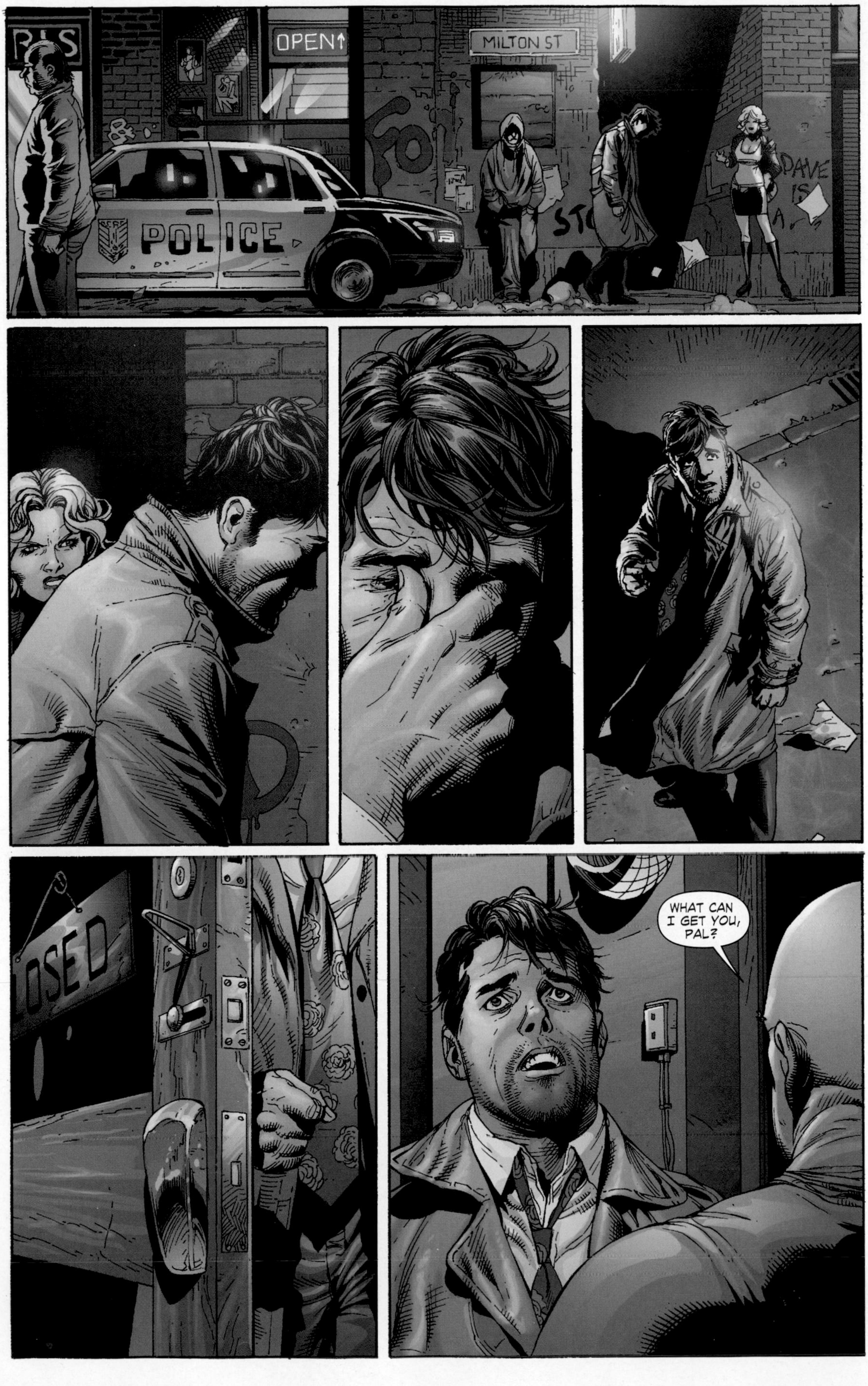
OPEN
MILTON ST
POLICE
WHAT CAN I GET YOU, PAL?

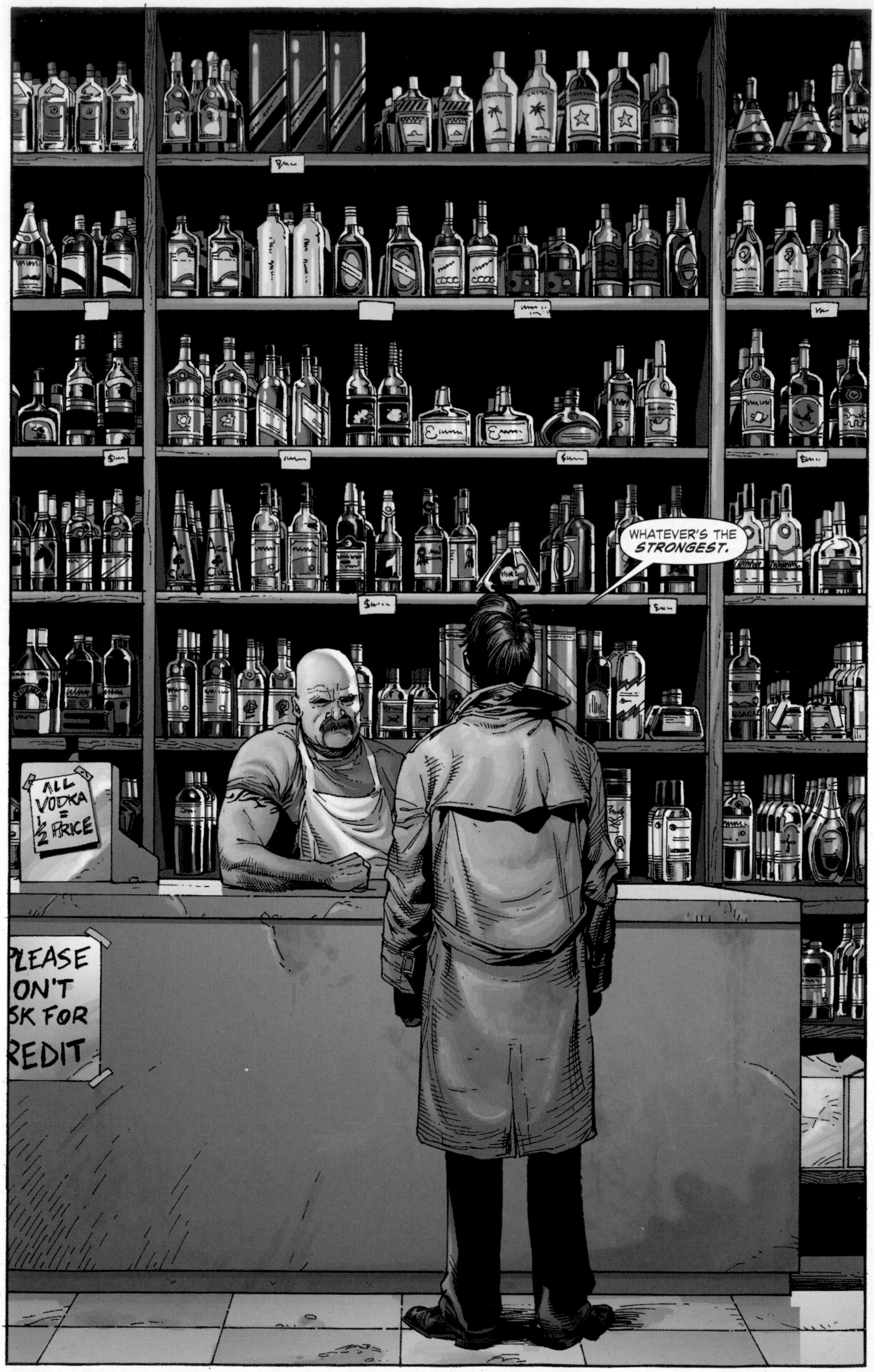
WHATEVER'S THE STRONGEST.
ALL VODKA = 1/2 PRICE
PLEASE
ON'T
SK FOR
REDIT

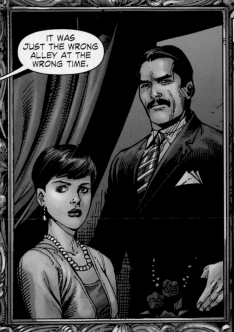

IT WAS JUST THE WRONG ALLEY AT THE WRONG TIME.

THERE *WAS* NO CONSPIRACY, BRUCE. IT WAS A STUPID, RANDOM ROBBERY.

SO NOW YOU CAN PUT AWAY THAT *COSTUME.*

NOW YOU CAN *STOP.*

NO, ALFRED.

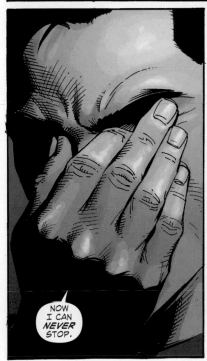

NOW I CAN *NEVER* STOP.

NOW I'LL ALWAYS BE ALONE.

BRUCE...

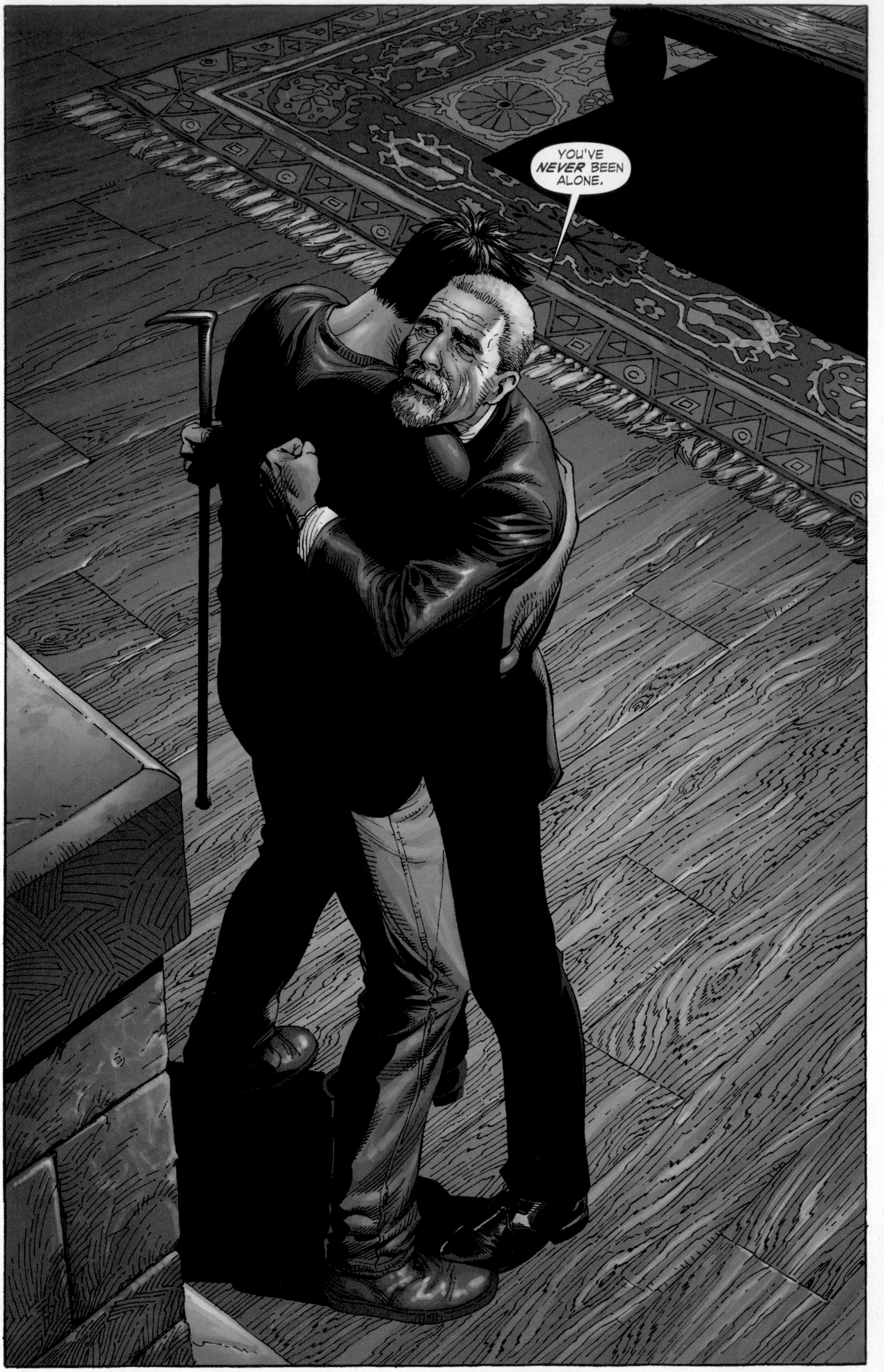
YOU'VE *NEVER* BEEN ALONE.

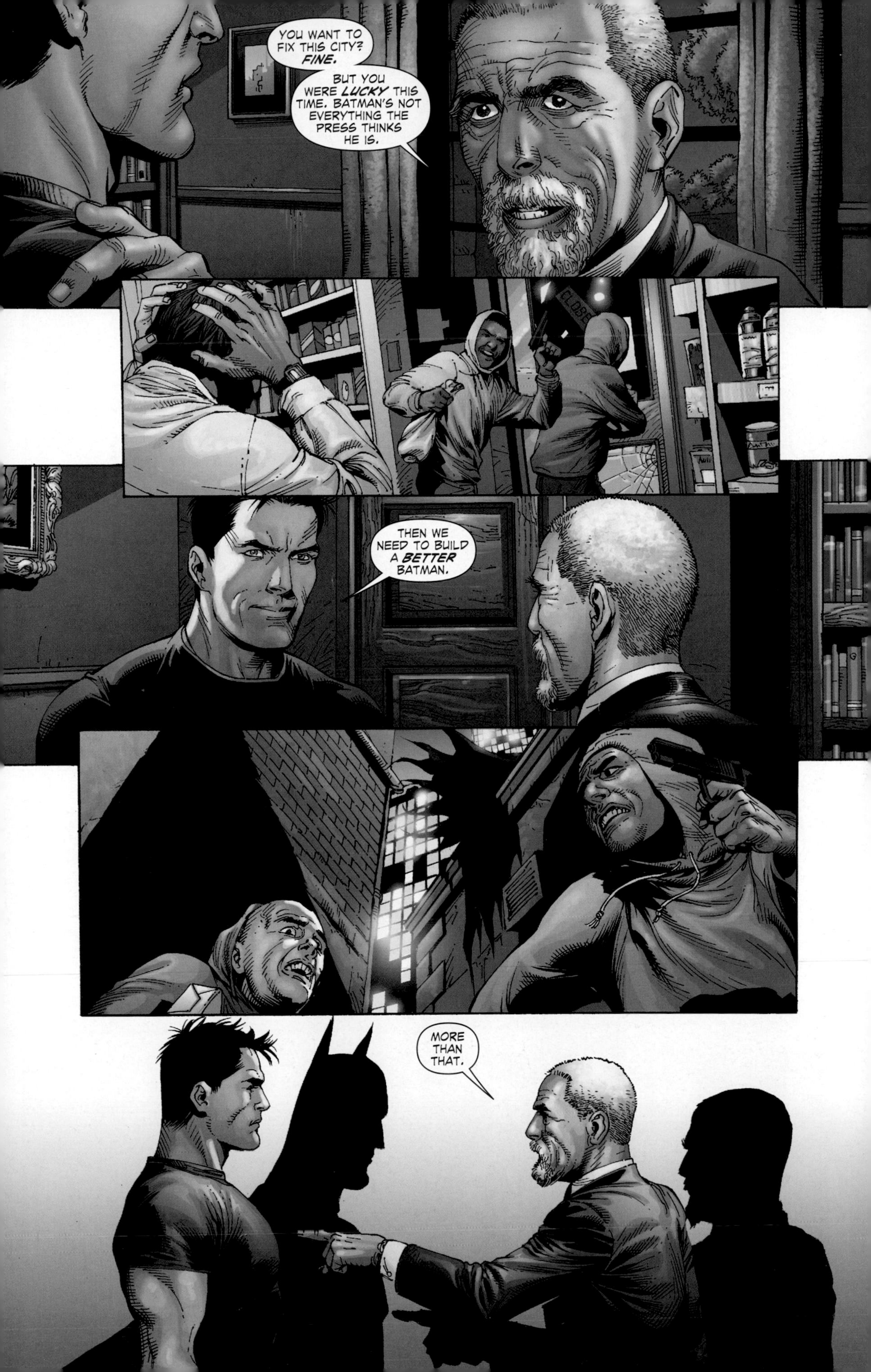
YOU WANT TO FIX THIS CITY? FINE.
BUT YOU WERE LUCKY THIS TIME. BATMAN'S NOT EVERYTHING THE PRESS THINKS HE IS.
THEN WE NEED TO BUILD A BETTER BATMAN.
MORE THAN THAT.

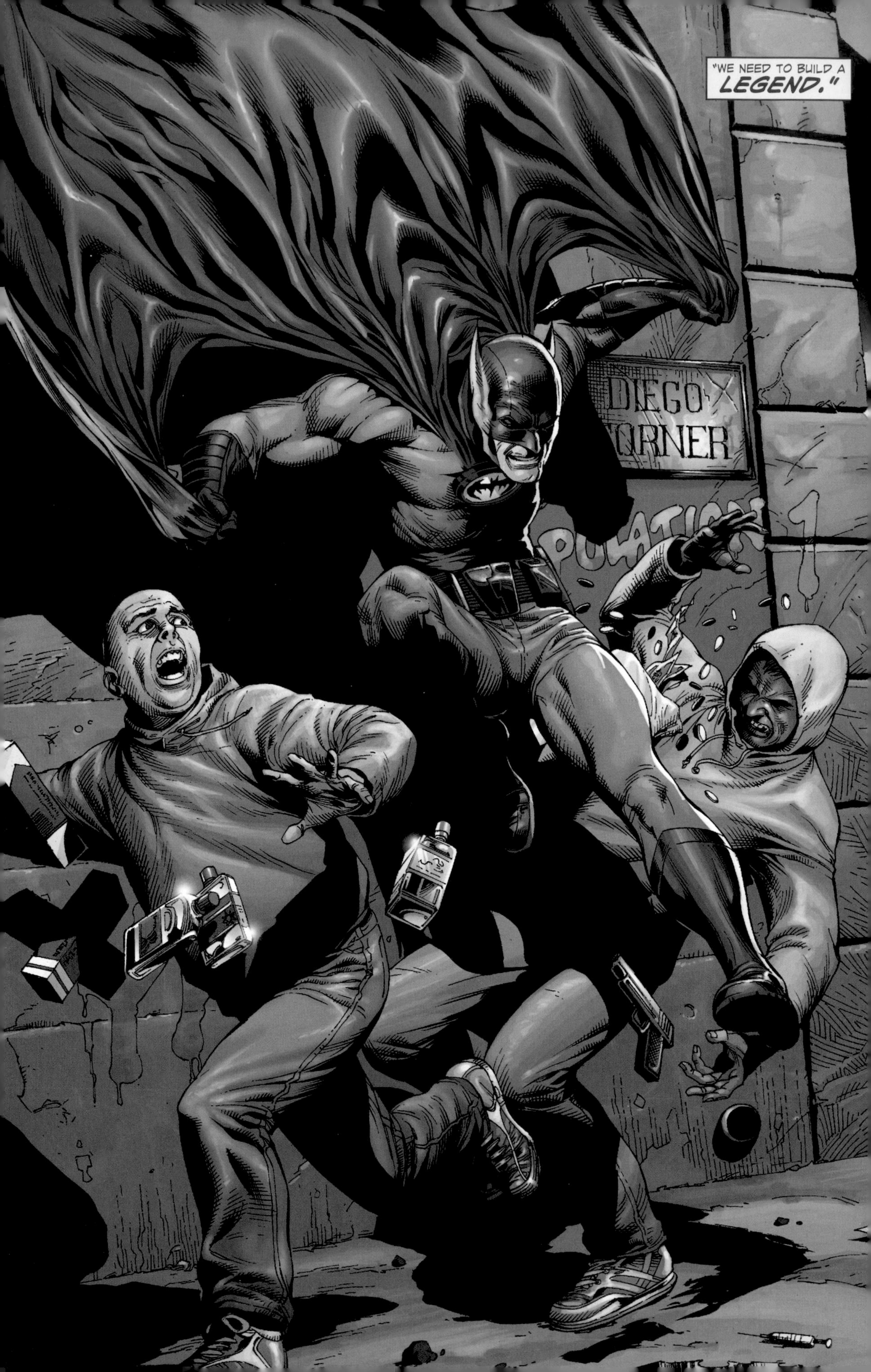
"WE NEED TO BUILD A LEGEND."
DIEGO CORNER
PULATION

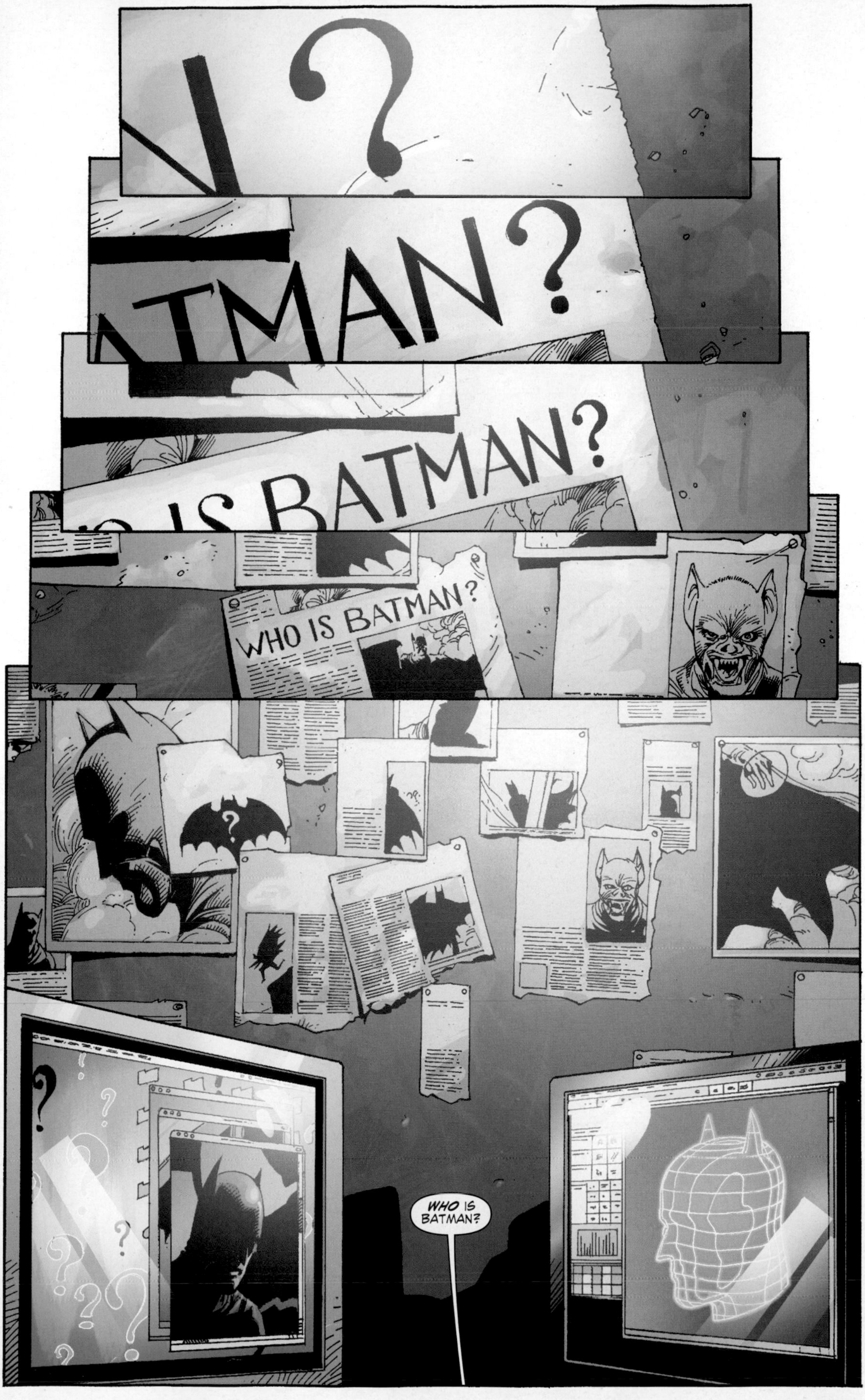
WHO IS BATMAN?
WHO IS BATMAN?

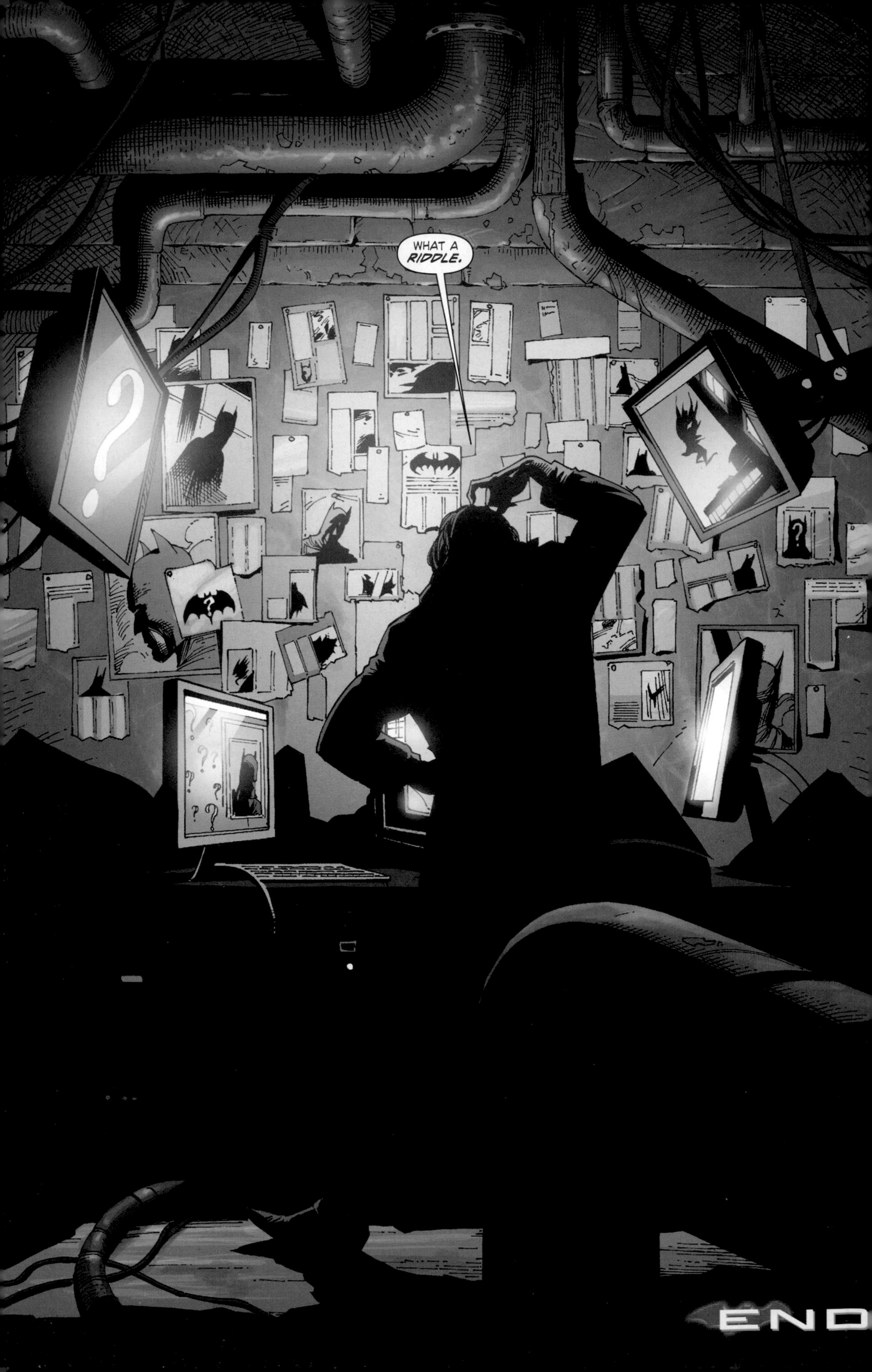
WHAT A *RIDDLE.*
END

GEOFF JOHNS is one of the most prolific and popular contemporary comic book writers. He has written highly acclaimed stories starring Superman, Green Lantern, the Flash, Teen Titans, and Justice Society of America. He is the author of the *New York Times* best-selling graphic novels GREEN LANTERN: RAGE OF THE RED LANTERNS, GREEN LANTERN: SINESTRO CORPS WAR, JUSTICE SOCIETY OF AMERICA: THY KINGDOM COME, SUPERMAN: BRAINIAC and BLACKEST NIGHT.

Johns was born in Detroit and studied media arts, screenwriting, film production and film theory at Michigan State University. After moving to Los Angeles, he worked as an intern and later an assistant for film director Richard Donner, whose credits include *Superman: The Movie*, *Lethal Weapon 4* and *Conspiracy Theory*.

Johns began his comics career writing STARS AND S.T.R.I.P.E. and creating Stargirl for DC Comics. He received the Wizard Fan Award for Breakout Talent of 2002 and Writer of the Year for 2005, 2006, 2007 and 2008 as well as the CBG Writer of the Year 2003 through 2005 and 2007 and 2008, and CBG Best Comic Book Series for JSA 2001 through 2005.

After acclaimed runs on THE FLASH, TEEN TITANS and the best-selling INFINITE CRISIS miniseries, Johns co-wrote a run on ACTION COMICS with his mentor Donner. In 2006, he co-wrote 52, an ambitious weekly comic book series set in real time, with Grant Morrison, Greg Rucka and Mark Waid. Johns has also written for various other media, including the acclaimed "Legion" episode of SMALLVILLE and the fourth season of ROBOT CHICKEN. He is writing the story of the DC Universe Online massively multiplayer action game from Sony Online Entertainment LLC and recently joined DC Entertainment as its Chief Creative Officer.

Johns currently resides in Los Angeles, California.

GARY FRANK, a native of Bristol, England, began his comics career working on various titles for Marvel UK before entering the American comics scene as the penciller on Marvel's *Incredible Hulk*. Frank then came to DC Comics where he was the original artist on BIRDS OF PREY and pencilled the adventures of SUPERGIRL. He has also worked on WildStorm's GEN 13 as well as his creator-owned series *The Kin*.

DC COMICS™

FROM THE WRITER OF *JUSTICE LEAGUE* & *GREEN LANTERN*

GEOFF JOHNS
SUPERMAN: SECRET ORIGIN
with GARY FRANK

SUPERMAN: LAST SON

with RICHARD DONNER & ADAM KUBERT

SUPERMAN & THE LEGION OF SUPER-HEROES

with GARY FRANK

SUPERMAN: BRAINIAC

with GARY FRANK

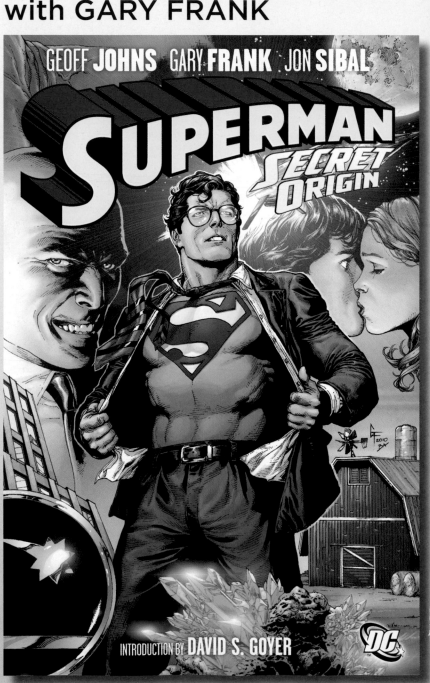

GEOFF **JOHNS** GARY **FRANK** JON **SIBAL**

SUPERMAN
SECRET ORIGIN

INTRODUCTION BY **DAVID S. GOYER**